JOHN MILLINGTON SYNGE

AND THE IRISH THEATRE

"No man at all can be living for ever, and we must be satisfied."—*Riders to the Sea.*

"It should be a sweet thing to have what is best and richest, if it's for a short space only."—*Deirdre of the Sorrows.*

S

SOUTH DUBLIN BOOKSTORE
TO RENEW ANY ITEM TEL: 459 7834

Items should be returned on or before the last date below. Fines,
as displayed in the Library, will be charged on overdue items.

Your cordially

J. M. Synge

From an oil painting by James Paterson, R.S.A. (1913)

JOHN MILLINGTON SYNGE AND THE IRISH THEATRE

BY

MAURICE BOURGEOIS

BENJAMIN BLOM   New York / London

First Published 1913
Reissued 1968
by Benjamin Blom, Inc. Bronx, New York 10452
and 56 Doughty Street London, W.C. 1

Library of Congress Catalog Card Number 65-16228

Printed in U.S.A.

TO

PROFESSOR AND MADAME LOUIS CAZAMIAN

THE PRESENT ESSAY IS RESPECTFULLY INSCRIBED

AS AN INSUFFICIENT TOKEN OF THE WRITER'S

ATTACHMENT AND GRATITUDE

AUTHOR'S NOTE

I BEG to thank the many kinsmen and friends of the late John M. Synge who have kindly helped me in this attempt at a systematic study of his life and writings in their relation to the Irish Theatre at large. With no sinister piratical intention, I have freely tapped all available sources, and placed on record such facts as can be verified, such views as may safely be endorsed. I have thus been enabled to offer a biographical and sociological, rather than a purely literary, interpretation of Synge's life-work. Some of my specific obligations are mentioned in the text or in the footnotes ; but, as individual recognition would be somewhat lengthy, and in certain cases against the wishes of my informants, a collective acknowledgment of my indebtedness must here suffice. Moreover, a prefatory display of famous names might possibly raise expectations which I am afraid this book does not fulfil.

M. B.

Ireland, 1913.

CHRONOLOGICAL STATEMENT

THE present monograph, which was originally written in English, was begun if not before, at least simultaneously with, Mr. W. B. Yeats's *Synge and the Ireland of his Time*, issued by the Cuala Press on July 26, 1911. It was sent in (May 28, 1912) and received with the "mention très honorable" (June 22, 1912) as a thesis in fulfilment of the requirements for the "Diplôme d'Études Supérieures," Paris University. Mr. P. P. Howe's *J. M. Synge: A Critical Study* (London: Martin Secker; New York: Mitchell Kennerley), Mr. Francis Bickley's *J. M. Synge and the Irish Dramatic Movement* (London: Constable; Boston and New York: Houghton Mifflin) and Mr. Cornelius Weygandt's *Irish Plays and Playwrights* (same publishers) came out respectively on June 7, September 30, 1912, and February 14, 1913. During my stay at Coole Park in July, 1913, Lady Gregory most kindly allowed me to read the manuscript of her forthcoming book, *Our Irish Theatre: A Chapter of Autobiography*, which Putnams are bringing out in the Autumn.

CONTENTS

CONTENTS

NOTE.—The Collected Edition of Synge's Works (Dublin: Maunsel, 1910, 4 vols.), with which this book is uniform, has been quoted throughout the present essay.

ILLUSTRATIONS

xiii

ILLUSTRATIONS

LATE ADDITIONS

ANGLIA (Halle a. S. : Max Niemayer) : June 2, 1913 (xxxvii. 2), pp. 129–45 : "J. M. Synge and the Irish Literary Movement," by James A. Roy (St. Andrews). [Review of Library Edition of Synge's Works and of P. P. Howe's *The Repertory Theatre* and *J. M. Synge : A Critical Study.*]

NORTH AMERICAN REVIEW (N.Y.) : August, 1913, pp. 218–26 : "England's New Dramatists," by P. P. Howe.

Mr. Howe is publishing through Mr. Martin Secker of London a book entitled *Dramatic Portraits*, but it will not contain a chapter on Synge.

Ireland's Hope : A Call to Service (Irish Inter-Collegiate Christian Union : Student Christian Movement, 93 Chancery Lane, London, W.C., 1913). See p. 144 ("Some Irish Movements," by Miss E. Margaret Cunningham).

GIRL'S REALM (London) : September, 1913, pp. 813–6 : "The Irish Players," by Robb Lawson.

"Birmingham, George A." [Rev. James Owen Hannay] : *The Lighter Side of Irish Life* (London & Edinburgh : T. N. Foulis, 1911). See pp. 62–4 : remarks on the drama in Ireland.

IRISH ROSARY (Dublin) : August, 1913 : "Irish Literature," by Shane Leslie (Synge : see p. 581).

REVUE DE PARIS : September 1, 1913, pp. 191–205 : "Le théâtre irlandais," by Ernest A. Boyd.

JOHN MILLINGTON SYNGE
AND THE IRISH THEATRE

CHAPTER I

EARLY LIFE : FORMATIVE INFLUENCES

And so when all my little work is done
They'll say I came in Eighteen-seventy-one. . .
Poems : On An Anniversary (ii. 216).

It was on April 16 of the fatal year when
Ireland was watching with the keenest interest
the conclusion of the Franco-Prussian war [1] that
Edmund John Millington Synge was born at
Newtown Little, near Rathfarnham, a suburban
village three and three-quarter miles south of
Dublin. He was the youngest child in a family
of eight, three of whom (John William, Kathleen and Basil) had died when very young.
One sister, three brothers, and several nephews
survive him.

Of his parents little need be said. His father
was the late John Hatch Synge, barrister-at-law,
a modest, thoughtful man who preferred the
quiet of home life to any outside amusement.

---

[1] Cf. L. Paul-Dubois, *Contemporary Ireland*, Part I, chap.
iii, § v.

I

JOHN MILLINGTON SYNGE

He was a younger son of a large family, born (1824) and reared at the family seat, Glanmore Castle, Co. Wicklow, and provided for in life by being sent to the Bar (1847), a profession for which he was not particularly well suited, but by which, with the help of some private means derived from landed property in Co. Galway, he managed to live quite comfortably.[1] Those of the Synges who took a profession usually went into holy orders in the Church of Ireland, and their education and culture were clearly of the type to be found in people long connected with the Church. Synge's mother, Kathleen Traill (who first met John Hatch Synge at about the age of sixteen, and married him on January 18, 1856, before she was twenty), also came of an ecclesiastical family. She was the daughter of the Rev. Robert Traill (b. 1793), D.D., M.R.I.A., whose excellent translation of Flavius Josephus largely superseded that of William Whiston,[2] and who died (1847) in the parish of West Schull, Co. Cork, of which he was rector, from fever contracted during his attempts to help the poor in the great potato famine. The life of Synge's parents was the happiest possible, and they brought up their children in that strict form of Protestantism to which they themselves belonged. Neither of

---

[1] Information kindly supplied by Mr. E. M. Stephens, Synge's nephew.

[2] Cf. *Athenæum* (1851), 850; S. Austin Allibone's *Critical Dictionary of English Literature*, iii. 2444, 2878; Knight's *Eng. Cyc. Biogr.*, iii. (1856), 657, etc.

them cared much for society, but both were polite and kind to those with whom they came in contact, and hated anything artificial, ostentatious or vulgar.

The Synges themselves are a large and well-known County Wicklow[1] family. Yet they are not of pure Irish origin. They are said to be descended from the Millingtons of Millington Hall, Cheshire (near Knutsford, now a farmhouse), who afterwards settled at Bridgnorth, Salop. The surname Synge was originally a kind of nickname or by-name: according to tradition, John Millington, a " canon "[2] or precentor of the Chapel Royal, sang so sweetly that King Henry VIII[3] bade him take the name of Sing or Synge.[4] The whole story—which shews

[1] Cf. in *The People of the Glens* (iv. 39) what the old man who knew all families from Baltinglass to the sea told Synge about his forefathers.

[2] Lodge's *Peerage, Baronetage, Knightage and Companionage of the British Empire* (1912), p. 1830; *D.N.B.* lv. 281, art. " Synge, Edward."

[3] *Not* Queen Elizabeth, as stated by Anthony Wood and Walter Harris (*The Whole Works of Sir James Ware, Revised and Improved*, Dublin, 1739-64, i. 570), Bp. Richard Mant (*History of the Church of Ireland*, London, 1840, ii. 311), and the Rev. James Wills (*Lives of Illustrious and Distinguished Irishmen*, Dublin, 1842, iv. 456). Bridgnorth Castle (subsequently destroyed by Cromwell : only part of the tower is left and is about as crooked as the leaning tower at Pisa) was a royal residence, and Henry VIII most certainly went there.

[4] " By a singular irony, at the present day," writes Mr. Arthur Synge Owen (Synge's Oxford cousin) in an unpublished essay, " there are a very large number of the family who are tone-deaf and incapable of making the most familiar air recognizable by their vocal efforts."

3

that the puzzling name is not to be pronounced
either *à la française* or like the verb "to singe" [1]—
may be an invention which the man's will or
some other document would expose ; yet a
picture of a stained-glass window formerly in
Bowden Church, now among the Harleian manuscripts (No. 2151, Cheshire Monuments), representing a kneeling abbot with the legend "Orate
pro bono statu Roberti Mellenton," [2] the date
being 1382, and the coat of arms *the same* as that
of the Synge or Sing family, goes some little
way to confirm the legend. It will be observed
that Synge's full name was identically that of his
progenitor. Curiously enough, there are two
namesakes of J. M. Synge now alive : one is
Mr. John Millington Sing, who has been Warden
of St. Edward's School, Oxford, since 1904 ; [3]
the other, Mr. John Millington Synge, the
second son of the Rev. Francis P. Synge, Vicar
of Kington St. Michael, Chippenham, Wiltshire.

This remote English origin of the Synge

[1] The pronunciation "sing" is moreover shewn to be the
correct one by a satire on Bp. Edward Synge's Sermon on
Toleration, entitled "An excellent new song to an old tune"
(1727), now in the British Museum, and beginning : "I synge
[*sic*] of a sermon, a sermon of worth." Cf. also the rhymes in
Synge's poem, *The Curse* (ii. 227) : "Lord, this judgment quickly
bring,—And I'm your servant, J. M. Synge." Synge first introduced himself to Mr. R. I. Best as "Synge—*not* singe " [the
French word].

[2] Robert Mellenton (*i.e.* Millington : the difference in
spelling is *quite* immaterial) was abbot of a priory at Birkenhead.

[3] I am indebted for information to Mr. J. M. Sing and his
brother, Mr. Alexander Millington Sing, also to Rev. F. P.
Synge.

Cœlestia canimus

A GENEALOGICAL CHART
OF THE SYNGE FAMILY SHEWING
J. M. SYNGE'S PARENTAGE AND
LINEAL ANCESTRY

[Compiled from Lodge's *Peerage, Baronetage, Knightage
and Companionage of the British Empire* (Kelly's Directories,
Ltd., 1912, pp. 1830–1), Burke and Debrett's *Irish Pedigrees*,
Morgan's *Kith and Kin*, and other works of reference ; also
from private sources.[1]]

---

[1] I have much pleasure in thanking Miss M. B. Synge, Colonel Synge-Hutchinson,
Mr. John Millington Sing and Mr. Alexander Millington Sing for their kindness in
checking this tree.

Milling of Cheshire   ? Millington of Bridgnorth, Shropshire?

JOHN MILLINGTON =
"corrupit dictus Synge de Brugenorth in com. Salop . . . .
cognominatus Synge quia canonicus fuit."

1st son · 2nd son · 3rd son

Thomas Millington = dau. of Adams of Clerton

denominatus Synge or Sing of Bridgnorth Co. Salop
Treasurer to the Corporation of Bridgnorth in the 29th
year of King Henry VIII 1538

William

Hugo

Dorothy = **George** Sing or Synge = Annie or Anne
dau. of Whitbrook · Alderman of Bridgnorth · dau. of Hugh or Roger
or Hugh Millington · and Bailiff in 1564, 1571, · Catestrey or Catistree
(1st wife) · 1581, 1594, 1601 (d.) · of Catestree or Catistree
· · in the Co. of Salop
· · (2nd wife)

William · George · Anna · Barbara · Margery · Elizabeth · Joha..na · | · Margeria · Francisca · Johanna · **Richard** = Alicia
· · · · · · · · · · · d. 1631 · dau. of
· · · · · · · · · · · · Roger Rowley
· · · · · · · · · · · · of Rowley
· · · · · · · · · · · · in the Co. of Salop

Joseph · Benjamin · Thomas · Richard · John · Samuel · **Edward**¹ * † ‡ = Barbara Catherine O'Dogherty · Joshua · Anna
· · · · · · d. 1678 · of Innishowen
George * · · · · · M.A., D.D., T.C.D. · or Barbara Latham
1594–1653 · · · · · Bp. of Ardfert 1661 · (probably the former)
b. and d. in Bridgnorth · · · Bp. of Limerick 1661
M.A. Balliol Oxon. 1616 · · · Bp. of Cork, Cloyne
Bp. of Cloyne 1638 · · · & Ross 1663
Bp. of Cork, Cloyne & Ross
Nominated Abp. of Tuam 1647

Samuel · **Edward** * § = Jane dau. of Rev. · Joane or Barbara · Annie · Margaret · Helena · Mary
· 1659–1741¹ · Nicholas Proud
· M.A., T.C.D.
· Bp. of Raphoe 1714
· Abp. of Tuam 1716
· published sermons

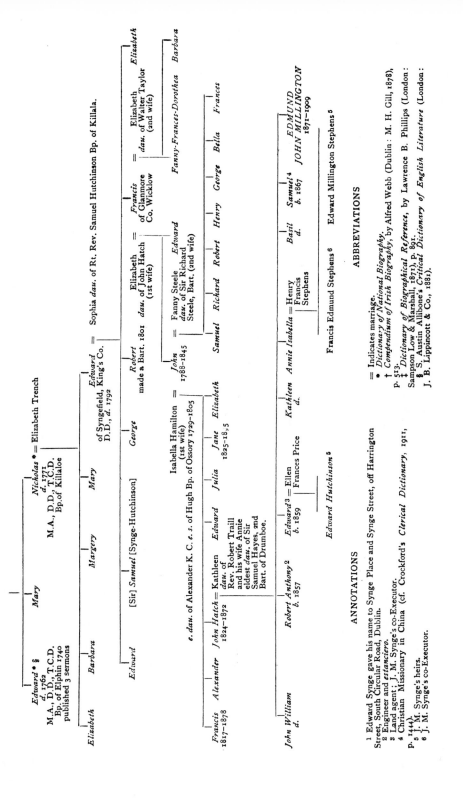

ANNOTATIONS

1 Edward Synge gave his name to Synge Place and Synge Street, off Harrington Street, South Circular Road, Dublin.
2 Engineer and *estanciero*.
3 Land agent; J. M. Synge's co-Executor.
4 Christian Missionary in China (cf. Crockford's *Clerical Dictionary*, 1911, p. 1444).
5 J. M. Synge's heirs.
6 J. M. Synge's co-Executor.

ABBREVIATIONS

= Indicates marriage.
* *Dictionary of National Biography.*
† *Compendium of Irish Biography*, by Alfred Webb (Dublin : M. H. Gill, 1878), p. 513.
‡ *Dictionary of Biographical Reference*, by Lawrence B. Phillips (London : Sampson Low & Marshall, 1871), p. 891.
§ S. Austin Allibone's *Critical Dictionary of English Literature* (London : J. B. Lippincott & Co., 1881).

family is a fact not unworthy of brief consideration. While it can hardly account for the favourable attitude of English opinion towards Synge, it explains the hostility of certain Irish critics who infer a sort of *a priori* un-Irishness in his work from the fact that his family belonged to Anglo-Ireland—to the so-called " Englishry "— and who trace Synge's one-sided and somewhat unsympathetic view of Ireland to the circumstance that his forefathers were members of the English colony, of the Protestant landlord class.[1] Nothing is more venturesome, more difficult to substantiate by quoting specific facts than this eternal speculation on the congenital influence of the racial factor in the making of a writer's genius. At all events, atavism, in Synge's case, would serve as an extenuating, not an aggravating, circumstance. Supposing Synge has actually been unfair to Ireland because of his being a distant scion of a " Sassenach " family, then he cannot be held personally responsible for his unfairness. But this attractive study in heredity must, we think, be discarded at the outset as sheer fallacy.[2] Synge *was* born in Ireland ; of course he was no true-born Irishman, for the constant intermarriage of races, which has taken place in Ireland more than anywhere else, has made the aboriginal

---

[1] In *A Landlord's Garden in County Wicklow* (iv. 51) Synge speaks of the tragedy of his own class in Ireland.

[2] This applies not only to Synge himself, but to most of the other " Irish " dramatists, whom the same critics have found fault with on the same score.

Gael in all his purity a veritable myth ; nay, despite the apparent paradox, Synge's English extraction proves him to be peculiarly Irish : indeed, it is to be remembered that, owing to Ireland's unsurpassable capacity for assimilating foreign elements, the English inhabitants of Ireland (the so-called " Pale," " Garrison," " Oligarchy," or " Ascendancy ") have often become, psychologically and otherwise, more Irish than the Irish themselves—*Hibernis ipsis Hiberniores*—have, in fact, supplied National Ireland with most of its heroes and prophets. If Synge's episcopal ancestors were opposed to Irish aspirations, his parents were sincere patriots[1] ; and, if Irish means anti-English, then Synge was intensely Irish, for he always loathed, or at least ignored, England and the English in general— apart from the Synges.

Synge's father dying on April 13, 1872, when Synge was quite a small child, cannot be said to have affected his upbringing in any way. Synge's mother found herself in somewhat reduced circumstances, and came to live at Orwell Park, Rathgar (about a mile nearer Dublin), which was his home until 1890.[2] He received a somewhat desultory education, at which in

---

[1] His great-grandfather, Francis Synge, sat in the last independent Parliament of Ireland, and voted against the Act or Union with England.

[2] We know practically nothing of Synge's early childhood. He himself vaguely refers to his infancy in the preface to *The Playboy of the Western World* (ii. 1) when, speaking of the language of the play, he says : " I have used one or two words only that I have not . . . spoken in my own nursery before I could read the newspapers."

after life he would sneer with a violent, sardonic scorn—attending classes at private schools in Dublin [1] and then in Bray, a seaside resort south-east of the city. But his health being always very delicate, he was obliged to leave school when about fourteen years of age to read at home with a private tutor till he entered college (1885-8).

An examination of Synge's early days really does help to establish what may be termed the spiritual continuity of his life. His juvenile activities were exercised in three main directions which he never entirely forsook in after years. We have reason to believe that the influence of home never greatly told on him; indeed, as a lad, Synge was strangely reserved and even unboyish to a certain extent: he shunned rather than desired companionship; he would hardly take part in the games of his age, and much preferred open-air exercise and solitary rambles in his beloved Dublin mountains to indoor life. In later years he went a-wandering in strange places, ever and always a sad and lonely man. It was by solitude that he asserted his personality in the gentle,

---

[1] He alludes to his schooldays in Dublin in his article "Good Pictures in Dublin: the Municipal Art Gallery" (*Manchester Guardian*, Jan. 24, 1908, p. 12): "Perhaps none but Dublin men who have lived abroad can quite realize the strange thrill it gave me to turn in from Harcourt Street—where I passed to school long ago—and to find myself among Monets and Manets and Renoirs, things I connect so directly with the life of Paris." (Synge, we shall see, was always very fond of pictures; he actually attempted painting, and for many years was a member of the United Arts Club, Dublin.)

7

unromantic manner that always was his; and from the very start he was and remained himself and nothing but himself.

Natural history was undoubtedly what attracted him most. From a boy he joined the Dublin Naturalists' Field Club, acquiring a very fair knowledge of botany and mineralogy, and he is said to have "delighted in taking long walks through the country, generally alone, and studying the habits and ways of every living thing."[1] He had made a large collection of moths and beetles, and in one of his unpublished writings, which Mr. Yeats read, he mentions having fed the family squirrel. His knowledge of ornithology was especially remarkable. "He knew the note and plumage of every bird, and when and where they were to be found."[2] He had a number of uncanny tricks of speaking to animals and calling them to him. He once carried a bullfinch on his bicycle to amuse his nephews, and talked to kittens, making them purr. Judging from his description of himself in his charming poem, *In Glencullen*,[3] he must have practised bird's-nesting:

> Thrush, linnet, stare and wren,
> Brown lark beside the sun,
> Take thought of kestril, sparrow-hawk,
> Birdlime and roving gun.

---

[1] From a letter by Mrs. Stephens, Synge's sister, quoted by Mr. John Masefield in his memoir of J. M. Synge in the *Dictionary of National Biography*.
[2] *Ibid.*   [3] ii. 220.

potent influence on his endowments as a stylist
and playwright.[1]

Lastly, he had a natural capacity for languages. He could speak Irish, and his knowledge of the Gaelic idiom was to be of great
assistance to him in his long excursions through
the West of Ireland. He also picked up, but
never entirely mastered, several modern Continental languages during his years at Trinity
College, Dublin, which he had entered as a
pensioner on June 18, 1888, his college tutor
being Dr. Anthony Traill (now Provost), who
was the first cousin of his mother. Synge
did not go in for Honours during his course
at Trinity, but passed his Little Go in the
Michaelmas Term of 1890 (Third Class), ob-
taining prizes in Irish and Hebrew in Trinity
Term, 1892, and his B.A. degree examination
(Second Class) in the Michaelmas Term of the
same year. The degree was conferred on him
in December, 1892, and his name went off the
college books six months later (June 3, 1893).[2]

---

[1] It is noteworthy that several recent Irish plays have for
their subject the mighty sway exercised by the fiddle over
its masters. For instance, it is the theme of " Rutherford
Mayne "'s *The Turn of the Road* (Ulster Literary Theatre,
December, 1906), and of Mr. Pádraic Colum's *The Fiddler's
House* (Cluitcheoirí na n-Éireann (The Theatre of Ireland),
March 21, 1907, also of E. K. Worthington's unpublished
one-act play, *The Burden* (Cork Dramatic Society, May 11,
1910). Synge, unlike these writers, was influenced by music
much more in point of language and dramatic technique than
of subject-matter.

[2] Although Synge's University career was fairly successful,

JOHN MILLINGTON SYNGE

Some critics have pointed out that the almost Biblical grandeur and simplicity of Synge's own style may be traced to his acquaintance with the beauties of Hebrew literature. Yet let it be here remarked that, as regards Synge's speaking knowledge of languages, he always was seriously handicapped, even in the use of the mother-tongue, by his guttural and somewhat jerky utterance.

Synge's early life was accordingly character-ized by extreme versatility of interest and consequent indecision of purpose. Many a weary year was spent before he could find an adequate outlet for expression and discover the field in which he was to achieve especial dis-tinction. He had to travel extensively over Europe in hopes of thereby enlarging his general culture and developing the possibilities which he perceived lay dormant within him. This roving, adventurous life was further con-ditioned by Synge's natural tendencies: for he always had something of the " scholar gypsy " temperament, and the irresistible *Wanderlust*, the nostalgia for the Nowhere or the Anywhere that had possessed men like George Borrow[1]

he always spoke ill of Trinity, which he disliked from a Nationalist standpoint; yet he always frequented the Library, where he studied " le vieil irlandais."

[1] An interesting parallel might be established between Borrow and Synge: both had a wandering youth and travelled widely on the Continent; both were highly gifted linguists; and Borrow's interest in gypsies was not unlike Synge's par-tiality to tramps and tinkers. Synge was an ardent Borrovian.

and Lafcadio Hearn,[1] was in his blood. Nor was it only an individual motive which induced him to leave Ireland.[2] In so doing Synge was also following the tradition of literary absenteeism which has set in with most of the modern Irish writers—Oscar Wilde, Mr. G. B. Shaw, Mr. George Moore, Mr. W. B. Yeats. In fact, Turgenjef's oft-repeated dictum that " Russia can do without any one of us, but none of us can do without Russia " is, it appears, wholly inapplicable to Ireland. The general belief is that an Irishman *cannot* prosper at home ; to succeed he *must* go abroad. Hence, the very same instinct which causes the Irish landlord

---

He had a great admiration for Rarey, the American horse-trainer who could talk to horses, because he was so much like the well-known characters in Borrow's novels.

[1] Synge prided himself on being related to Hearn in a way which he never otherwise explained. There was no blood relationship between them at all : Charles Hearn (Lafcadio's father) was the brother of Mrs. Stephens, the mother-in-law of Synge's sister, Miss Annie Isabella Synge (Mrs. H. F. Stephens). Synge greatly admired Hearn's " fiery prose style," and praised immensely—immoderately, even—the passage in " Of Moon-desire " (*Exotics and Retrospectives*, pp. 177–83) beginning : " The wish to become is reasonable . . ." and ending : " The burning of billions of suns, the whirling of trillions of worlds."

[2] Before leaving Ireland Synge had an unfortunate and mysterious love-affair, which, it appears, somewhat darkened his outlook on life. Cf. *Under Ether* (iv. 253, 258) : " I felt I was talking of a lady I had known years before, and sudden terror seized me that I should spread forth all the secrets of my life." " When they left me I looked vaguely through some books that were brought to me, and here became aware of my own collapse, for all allusions to sadness or affairs of the heart sent up a dew into my eyes."

13

to reside in London, which incites the Irish peasant to leave the " ould sod " for good at the earliest opportunity and emigrate to that Land of Heart's Desire yclept U.S.A., sends most Irishmen of note out of their native country, and is, in particular, responsible for the well-nigh general exodus of Irish artists and men of letters. The difference in Synge's case was that, whereas others seek fame abroad, and, as a rule, do find it, Synge had still to become famous when he returned home.

J. M. SYNGE IN DARGLE GLEN
From a snapshot by Pan Karel Musek (July, 1906)

J. M. SYNGE WITH POINTER DOG "BEN"
From a photograph by Mr. E. M. Stephens (*circa* 1897

CHAPTER II

CONTINENTAL WANDER-YEARS

LET it be observed at the outset that Synge seldom told his family and friends of his experiences abroad,[1] and that it is only from scattered allusions in his non-dramatic writings —especially *The Aran Islands*—and from personal and private sources that we are able to derive some outline of his peregrinations on the Continent, which are here recorded for the first time.

Being, as we have just seen, a musician of no mean order not only in theory but in practice— he had attempted original composition—Synge first intended to train himself for the musical profession, which led to his going to Germany, where he spent thirteen months in all. He first stayed in Darmstadt and Coblentz, where he pursued his violin studies, and then (in the spring of 1894) at Würzburg on the Main.[2] In the latter city he perfected his technical

---

[1] "He had wandered a lot about Europe. He was silent about all that. I never heard him mention his early life . . ." (John Masefield, "John M. Synge," *Contemporary Review*, April, 1911). "Synge had travelled a great deal in Italy . . . and in Germany and in France, but he only occasionally spoke to me about these places" (Jack B. Yeats, "With Synge in Connemara," *ap.* W. B. Yeats, *Synge and the Ireland of his Time*, p. 42).

[2] He mentions Würzburg in *The Aran Islands* (iii. 31). Passing references to Germany and the Germans will be found iii. 21, 57, 170, 179, 180, 244 and iv. 238.

knowledge of harmony. He often went to the cathedral to hear the Kapellmeister, and it was in the cloister that he saw the tomb of Walther von der Vogelweide.[1] The mere fact that Synge was able to read the lyrics of the great mediæval Minnesinger in the Middle High German text and that he translated one of them into the Anglo-Irish dialect[2] seems to indicate that he had a thorough and even scholarly knowledge of the German tongue. Yet, owing to his, at that period, characteristic lack of perseverance, or to some other cause,[3] Synge more and more began to realize that he would never become an efficient professional musician ; and in the same year, 1894, either in Ireland during the Summer, or at Coblentz in the Autumn, he finally abandoned his project.

Before leaving Germany he visited Munich

[1] Walther von der Vogelweide, according to a legend which probably is but a poetic development of his name (Walter of the Birds' Pasture, an estate in Tyrol), is said to have ordered in his will that the birds frequenting the galleries of the Würzburg Cloister should be fed on his tomb. The story has been made the subject of a "song" by Longfellow (ed. Tauchnitz, Leipzig, 1856, i. 257), on which see R. Sprenger, "Longfellow's *Walther von der Vogelweide*," in *Zeitschrift für den deutschen Unterricht*, vii. 1893.

[2] *Translations from Villon and Others* (ii. 250).

[3] Synge once told his nephew, Mr. E. H. Synge, that it was impossible for him to go near the Germans in composing and that he was too nervous to perform in public. On the other hand, Dr. Michel Elmassian, who knew Synge in Paris, states most authoritatively that Synge gave up music because he had been unsuccessful at a competition in original composition, where he had failed to develop a given theme.

and Berlin, and there became acquainted with the works of Heine, and with modern German and Austrian drama. He saw or read some Viennese character farces—the well-known " Possen " or " Staberliades "—and witnessed the production of a few plays by the so-called " static realists "—Jacques-Jules David, Holz and Schlaf. The peasant theatre of Ludwig Anzengruber, with its rural dialect, quaint imagery and loosely-knit intrigues, must have especially appealed to him; and it is extremely likely that Synge gained much of his fine sense of constructive technique from the earlier Gerhardt Hauptmann. However, the ever-subtle and underhand workings of international influence and the lack of more precise data make incontrovertible statements on this point a total impossibility.[1]

---

[1] Later in life (July, 1906) Synge became acquainted with the national movement of Bohemia through his friend Pan Karel Mušek, stage-manager of the Royal Bohemian National Theatre, Prague. We can state with certainty that Synge never visited Poland or Russia, in spite of the allusions in *The Aran Islands* (iii. 170, 179, 244), and of the poem *Winter with Little Money in a Great City* (ii. 226), in which he refers to " These Jews and Russian Poles "—texts on which Mr. Edmund Gosse's surmise (" The Playwright of the Western Wild," in *Morning Post*, Jan. 26, 1911) that Synge " betrays an acquaintance . . . perhaps with Warsaw " seems to be based. Nor is the line in *Beg-Innish* (ii. 213) : " Four strings I've brought from *Spain* and France " to be taken literally : France and Spain always go together in the Irish mind, especially the mind of the Irish-speaking people, as the lands of heroism and luxury ; this either dates only from the flight of the Wild Geese, or is older in view of the legends of Clan Mileadh

JOHN MILLINGTON SYNGE

We do not know what route Synge followed on his way back. He was the guest of some ladies living on the banks of the Rhine, and is said to have led a free, unconventional life in those days, listening to stories in the Harz and the Bavarian woods, making friends with servants and poor people, and more than once sleeping out under a hedge or in a farm or a hay-loft.

However unproductive this short stay in Germany had been in the way of positive results, Synge had nevertheless read both well and widely ; he had begun to take a keen interest in folklore, and it was by a natural psychological evolution that he decided to go to France [1] in order to qualify himself for literary criticism. It was then his intention, native Irishman though he was, to become for the benefit of English and Irish readers an interpreter of French art and thought, from the French standpoint, and, as far as he could, in the French language. This scheme had for its natural counterpart the no less ambitious project of popularizing English and Irish literature in

coming from Spain ; and although Synge refers to the Spanish drama in the preface to *The Tinker's Wedding* (i. 135), to Cervantes in *On An Anniversary* (ii. 216) and in *A Landlord's Garden in County Wicklow* (iv. 53), he never went to Spain.

[1] A paper by the present writer on " J. M. Synge's Life in France and his Relations to French Literature " was read before the National Literary Society, Dublin, Jan. 22, 1912, and fully reported in the Dublin papers (notably the *Freeman's Journal*) of Jan. 23, 1912, also in the *Irish Book-Lover*, March, 1912, pp. 132–3. The writer also lectured on " Synge and France " at the Irish Literary Society, London, on April 12, 1913.

France and elsewhere on the Continent. How Synge was to carry out this vague and interesting plan we shall soon examine; suffice it here to point out how highly characteristic it was of the man with his multifarious interests.

It is possible, though exceedingly difficult, to fix the exact dates of Synge's successive visits to Paris. He appears to have settled there (as a student) for the first time from January till June, 1895. Comparatively little is known of this first residence. While at Trinity he had, as we have seen, acquired a fairly good knowledge of French, and was in a position to make himself understood, though he spoke and read it with some difficulty.[1] Yet he was already conversant with French authors and newspapers,[2] and it was, in

---

[1] For a short specimen of Synge's spoken French, cf. *The People of the Glens* (iv. 41). M. Anatole le Braz, the great Breton folklorist and romance-writer, whom M. Henry Lebeau introduced to Synge in Dublin in April, 1905, writes in the unpublished diary of his tour : " Il [Synge] baragouine un peu le français, ayant vécu quelques mois à Paris où il a même assisté, me raconte-t-il, à la causerie que je fis, un soir, à l'Union Chrétienne des Jeunes Gens fondée par le pasteur Jean Monnier. Est-ce parce qu'il craint de s'exprimer insuffisamment qu'il a ce perpétuel tremblement des lèvres ? Ou n'est-ce pas plutôt un effet de cette nervosité exaspérée, si caractéristique de cette race où le 'celtisme,' de quelque façon qu'on l'entende, dans les choses comme dans les gens, est, en quelque sorte, élevé à sa suprême puissance, à son dernier coefficient ? " Synge had a marked tendency to interlard his English with French words, generally slang terms or colloquial phrases such as " Ce sont des blagues " and " Ce sont des balançoires," of which he was very fond.

[2] He used to wade through the *Journal* in the days of Fernand Xau, its founder, and thought M. Paul Adam's articles

fact, the fascination of French literature that had lured him to Paris. All this amounts to saying that he did not feel a stranger there. The more so as he found fellow-countrymen.

It may be of interest to take a glimpse of Parisian Ireland in Synge's day. Leaving aside the students of the Irish College, the Irish colony was not very large—not more than about fifty in all. But they were all extremely representative. To name but a few, there were Pádraic MacManus, brother of Seumas, the well-known Ulster novelist ; John O'Leary, the veteran patriot ; Dr. Arthur Lynch, now M.P., then the Paris correspondent of the London *Daily Mail* ;[1] Count Margerin de Crémont,[2] President

---

difficult to understand. Dr. Arthur Lynch, to whom we refer further down, was a personal friend of M. Paul Adam, also of M. Jean Lorrain, M. Hugues le Roux and M. Georges d'Esparbès, who dedicated his *Briseurs de Fer* to him.

[1] Dr. Lynch was Colonel of the Irish Brigade No. II on the Boer side during the South African War (see his articl⌐ "En Campagne avec les Boers," par Arthur Lynch, Colone. de la brigade irlandaise au Transvaal, in the *Revue de Paris*, Oct. 1, 1900). Synge has immortalized him in the first act of the *Playboy*, in which Philly says : "Maybe he went fighting for the Boers, *the like of the man beyond, was judged to be hanged, quartered and drawn.* Were you off east, young fellow, fighting bloody wars for Kruger and the freedom of the Boers?" (The italics are ours.) The allusion has nothing to do with the play : Synge simply brought it in in memory of his friendship with Dr. Lynch. Dr. Lynch referred to his acquaintance with Synge in his speech on the theatre in the House of Commons, April, 1913.

[2] Cf. an article on Count Margerin de Crémont (descended from the Margerins, the ancient kings of Leinster), by Miss O'Delany in the *Irish Daily Independent and Nation* (Dublin), February 17, 1904, p. 6.

of the Société de Saint Patrice ; Mr. and Mrs. Stephen MacKenna, both of them extreme Nationalists ; Madame Rowley, a political agitator, now dead ; Miss M. Barry O'Delany ; and above all, Mr. William Butler Yeats (only on flying visits) and Miss (now Madame) Maud Gonne.[1] A painter and unprofessional actress [2] of singular beauty and talent, and a protagonist of the Nationalist and agrarian agitation in Ireland, this heroic lady—whom it was then common to speak of as " the Celtic Druidess " or " the Irish Joan of Arc," and whom Mr. W. B. Yeats once heralded as " the new Speranza " [3]—had founded a Paris branch of the Young Ireland Society known as *L'Association Irlandaise*. Its avowed objects were to promote the independence of Ireland, to strengthen the bonds of sympathy between France and Ireland, to provide a centre of intercourse for persons of Irish nationality residing in Paris, to foster national opinions among them, to form a library of French and Irish books upon Irish subjects ;

---

[1] Formerly Mrs. Gonne-McBride. I am indebted to Madame Gonne, Mr. W. B. Yeats, Mr. and Mrs. Stephen MacKenna, Dr. Arthur Lynch, Miss O'Delany, Count de Crémont and others, for information on this part of Synge's life. On the whole period, see Mr. Chris Healy's amusing but somewhat untrustworthy *Confessions of a Journalist* (London : Chatto and Windus, 1904).

[2] It was Miss Gonne who first acted as Mr. Yeats's *Kathleen ni Houlihan* (see *infra*, chap. v. p. 125) : " Miss Gonne played very finely," wrote Mr. Yeats, " and her great height made Cathleen seem a divine being fallen into our mortal infirmity."

[3] The title of an article by Mr. Yeats in *United Ireland*, Jan. 16, 1892, p. 5.

lastly, to keep the French enthusiasts informed of the true state of the Irish problem in its political as well as intellectual [1] bearings. Miss Gonne edited a paper entitled *L'Irlande Libre* with Irish and French contributors ; she made collections on behalf of the Irish Political Prisoners' Amnesty Association—whose then Secretary was a Mr. Sheridan in London—in order to enable families of prisoners to visit them. Audiences of over a thousand at her public lectures were not infrequent,[2] and she had once been celebrated by the French poet Clovis Hugues.[3] Synge found this curious Franco-Irish organization in full swing, and joined it,[4] although not, as has been sometimes believed, in the capacity of Honorary Secretary : his Nationalist convictions—at least politically speaking— were not practical enough at the time to enable him to assume such duties. But he was a constant attendant at the meetings of the Society and was indefatigable in his efforts to find suitable rooms for its headquarters and those of its organ.

---

[1] The society had indeed a cultural aim : " I have founded societies with this aim " (*viz.* " to make possible a literature that, finding its subject-matter all ready in men's minds, would be, not as ours is, an interest for scholars, but the possession of a people "), "and was indeed founding one in Paris when I first met with J. M. Synge " (W. B. Yeats, *op. cit.*, p. 10). The Paris Young Ireland Branch does not at present enjoy even a nominal existence.

[2] Cf. *United Ireland*, May 27, 1893, p. 2.

[3] Cf. *United Ireland*, Jan. 30, 1892.

[4] He was presented for membership by his friend Mr. (afterwards Dr.) Crée, now deceased.

These were the days of the war between
Greece and Turkey, and once the *Association
Irlandaise* sent a message to the King of Greece
expressing its sympathy with the Cretan people
in their struggle for liberty, while a band of
Irish volunteers, who were members of the
London Young Ireland Branch, actually started
for Crete. At another meeting the Society
adjourned early in order that the members might
assist at a demonstration of students and *rapins*
in favour of Greece. Synge went to the Latin
Quarter from the rooms of the Society (at 6
Rue des Martyrs), accompanied by Dr. and Mrs.
Lynch, Madame Rowley, Miss Maud Gonne,
and one or two other friends. After having
paced the *Boul' Mich'* and actively *conspué les
Turcs*, the party had refreshments at the terrace
of the Café d'Harcourt ; but the police, who had
been massed in force in the Rue Champollion,
suddenly emerged and charged in a solid phalanx,
obliging Synge and his friends to take refuge
inside the café through the doors and windows,
which had been left open, it being Summer.
Synge did not escape in time and was severely
bruised on the head. He turned deathly pale,
but said nothing, and his friends were under
the impression that he had shewn the white
feather. Only months afterwards did they become aware that what they had mistaken for
cowardice was an almost superhuman self-control
and a reticent stoicism in bearing pain.

At a later meeting Synge, who had just come

back from Ireland, gave a vivid and pathetic description of the misery he had witnessed there. His eyes flashed with anger when the conversation turned upon the brutality of the police in Ireland ; and it was on the same day that he told someone how he had been on the point of letting loose a mad bull or cow that was in a field close to where an eviction was taking place. The only thing that prevented him from doing so was fear lest women and children should be injured. Mingled with his manly indignation against the police there was a boyish delight in the thought of the havoc the wild animal would have wrought if let loose upon them.

For the next few years Synge spent part of the year (at least five months, generally in the winter-time) in France, and part in Ireland, either in Aran for a couple of months, or in Dublin and Wicklow with his mother and relatives — who had removed in 1890 to 31 Crosthwaite Park, Kingstown, which was his home until shortly before his death.[1] However, from February to May, 1896, he stayed in Italy—mostly at Florence, and also at Rome with a Count—long enough to learn the language and to achieve his unsurpassable renderings of Petrarch and Leopardi into the Anglo-Irish dialect.[2] He read Dante, and told

---

[1] In 1908 he lived for 12s. 6d. a week at 47 York Road, Rathmines, in order to be nearer the Abbey Theatre.
[2] *Translations*, ii. 231–42, 251.

a friend that Cary's translation did not convey the " curious eager charm " of the original. Throughout his book on the Aran Islands and in one of his Wicklow sketches [1] he incidentally refers to Italy and the Italian people, and betrays an acquaintance with out-of-the-way Italian writers. [2] Possibly he knew something of Gabriele d'Annunzio's school, the *morbidezza* of which must have strangely appealed to him. We know that he saw the Pope [3]—whom some of the peasant characters in his yet-to-be-born plays were to treat with such racy irreverence —not, it appears, in a private interview, but simply in some ceremony at the Vatican, while His Holiness was being carried in state in the *sede gestatoria*. But, as in Germany, Synge's main interest was in Art and in the life of the people. He admired the crowds in Rome, and was a lover of wine-shops. It was at this time that he formed the project of translating the *Little Flowers* (not the *Companions*) of St. Francis of Assisi into English, but gave up the idea on hearing that a very readable translation had just been issued by Messrs. Dent in their " Everyman's Library."

He had paid two flying visits to Paris both before and after going to Italy (January and June, 1896), and came back in October, 1896, staying till May of the following year. It was a

---

[1] *The Aran Islands* (iii. 6, 136, 244) ; *On the Road* (iv. 25).
[2] *On the Road* (iii. 30–1).
[3] Leo XIII (iii. 57 ; iv. 25).

little after this sojourn that he met (in September,
1897, or thereabouts) his friend Richard Irvine
Best, now Librarian in the National Library of
Ireland and Honorary Secretary of the School
of Irish Learning.[1] Synge had then just
undergone an operation for the removal of a
glandular swelling in his neck ; and though the
operation had been successful, he looked extremely delicate. He used to take long walks
every day,[2] and fancied that everybody in the
streets turned back to look at him, which made
him extremely nervous. He was afraid that
the glandule would come again, till at last a
doctor treated it with arsenic, which brought it
down for ever. But his health was apt to give
way, and in Paris he had some very serious break-
downs. Friends were obliged to come and nurse
him through frequent attacks of influenza, bringing up to him daily the syphons of soda-water
with which he combated *la grippe*. A little later
one of his intimates noticed that he wore a

---

[1] My thanks are due to Mr. Best for his memories of Synge
at this period.

[2] Either in the Luxembourg Gardens, where he watched
the children playing near the Fontaine Médicis (cf. *In West
Kerry*, iv. 94 : "An old photograph of myself that had been
taken many years ago in the Luxembourg Gardens"), or down
to the fortifications, Montrouge way, to study the *rôdeurs de
barrière* (in whom his interest had been awakened by the
reading of Jules Bois' *Satanisme et Magie*, a work describing
how they tell people's fortunes, etc.), or along the embankment,
where he bought back numbers of the *Mercure de France*.
On Sundays he visited friends in Clamart, and went to Ville
d'Avray through the woods with them. On the whole Synge
lived almost exclusively on the Rive Gauche.

wig, which in the heat of an argument had got displaced. Synge told him of his ill-health and removed the hirsute adornment. Through some nervous malady his hair had all come off, but was growing again in patches. This was a trouble to him, so he had a wig made. He was soon able to dispense with it altogether, and at the time of his death had a good shaggy head of hair—hardly to be distinguished from the wig itself.—The reader will not consider as wholly irrelevant these biographical details of a somewhat intimate and possibly unpleasant nature, when he fully realizes how much the pathological factor had to do with the harsh and pessimistic imagination usually associated with Synge's name.

Under Ether, which now figures in vol. iv. of Synge's Collected Works, is the vivid account of his experiences during the operation. Like Maupassant's *Le Horla*, it reveals in the writer acute introspective powers, and is distinctly reminiscent of Henley's serial poem, *In Hospital*,[1] in which he has embodied his impressions of the Old Edinburgh Infirmary in the years 1873–5. While in Paris Synge wrote many other sketches, among which a number of impressionistic essays in French and English, and a playlet or rather dramatic short story about a violinist, which was sickly and not very

---

[1] *Poems*, 9th impression (London : D. Nutt, 1906), pp. 3–45.

good.[1] He kept all these unpublished MSS. in his trunk, and occasionally produced them in the presence of his bosom friends. It is fitting that we should here say something of Synge's early experiments in literary composition—most of which are now in the hands of his Executors. They are few and, as a rule, unimportant, except to the curious student of his later work. When a lad Synge had written a great mass of quite worthless poetry, far too self-revelatory ever to be published, and a few chaotic plays in a crabbed style, which are now in the possession of his sister. His only published contribution to literature at the time was a sonnet entitled *Glen Cullen*, which had appeared in *Kottabos* (a Dublin University magazine) for 1893.[2]

His method of work at this and other periods of his life are interesting and well known. He used to work between ten and twelve in the morning, and would then refuse to see his friends. He had a small portable typewriter [3] on which

---

[1] "A morbid thing about a mad fiddler in Paris which I hate" (Synge in a letter, May 4, 1908, printed by Mr. W. B. Yeats in the preface to *Synge and the Ireland of his Time*).

[2] Page 103 (quoted on p. 232 of the present essay). Oscar Wilde—or, to call him by his full Irish name, Oscar Fingal O'Flahertie Wills Wilde—and his brothers also contributed to *Kottabos* (cf. W: P. Ryan, *The Irish Literary Revival: its history, pioneers, and possibilities*, 1894, p. 120).

[3] "I do not know the make" (John Masefield, *Contemporary Review*, April, 1911). It was a "Blick" (Blickensderfer), which he had bought for eight pounds in Dublin. He was proud of it and fond of taking it to pieces, and caused a friend to buy one, telling him to oil it well, because otherwise he would "spoil the thing he had spent MONEY for."

28

he composed directly—a practice, it seems, most unusual with men of letters. He would first make quite a rough draft of the things he wrote —articles, essays, poems or plays as the case might be—and then re-type an indefinite number of complete versions, distinguishing them with letters and running half through the alphabet before he had the result to his liking. Later in life he retained the same habit. At the time of his long visit to his cousin, the late Mr. Edward Millington Synge, the engraver,[1] at Wintersells Farm,[2] Byfleet, Surrey, in December, 1906, the *Playboy* had reached the letter K ; and he once told Mr. George Moore that he had re-written the third act no less than thirteen times. This custom of endless re-casting has survived him in the Irish school. Mr. Yeats republishes the collected edition of his writings in a revised and, according to certain critics, less satisfactory, form ; while it is a common complaint in Dublin that the younger Irish dramatists spend most of their time in re-casting bad plays, instead of writing new ones which might be better. In Synge, who, it seems, originated the tradition, it bears witness to a curious mental process. Unlike most playwrights, Synge seldom made erasures

---

[1] Who had a studio in the Boulevard Montparnasse while Synge was in Paris.

[2] The Brooklands motor track was then being built round the house, and Synge, on seeing the use that was being made of the land, said that he could well understand how people became Socialists and Anarchists.

and textual emendations. Thought—and especially dramatic thought—came to him as an unanalyzable whole, like the flux of life itself, which drama is meant to depict. His successive intuitions were more or less distinct; and if the earlier drafts have not been destroyed, one could have an exceedingly interesting "critical edition" of his works. However, when the final version was arrived at, Synge stuck to it, and would never alter a word in his plays after the first performance.

Of course he was then very far from having attained any clear and definite idea as to his aims and intentions in Art. Yet, although still rudimentary and comparatively unproductive, his literary talent was already conscious of itself. However, he always asked his friends to revise his writings for him, for he spelt badly [1] and had no punctuation whatever; he listened to their suggestions with a gentle and touching humility, but rarely took their advice, alleging that, if he did, the work would not be quite his own.

His personal income being rather insufficient —forty pounds in all,[2] a good portion of which

---

[1] His spelling had been spoilt by reading Elizabethan literature; but the defect was also hereditary. He spelt "cradel"; and if one spelt the words to him, he would go as far as to mistake "crime" for "cat" and "devolution" for "demonstration."

[2] "'Forty pounds a year and a new suit when I am too shabby,' he used with a laugh to put down as his income" (Lady Gregory, "Synge," *English Review*, March, 1913).

was expended in travelling—he had to take to professional journalism, writing appreciations of Maeterlinck and Anatole le Braz for the *Dublin Daily Express* of 1898–9 [1]—then edited by Mr. T. P. Gill, now Secretary of the Department of Agriculture and Technical Instruction for Ireland—and articles on French literature,[2] which were almost invariably declined by Mr. W. K. Magee ["John Eglinton"] and the late Mr. Fred. Ryan, the joint Editors of the short-lived periodical *Dana*. In fact— leaving aside the case of *Dana*, whose literary standard was decidedly high—Synge was too much of a writer to be a good journalist. Or rather he was an unjournalistic journalist. He loathed journalese with all its welter of spurious neologisms, and the hideous lingo of professional book-reviewing was Greek to him. Moreover, he was so slow and painstaking that he could not turn out an article within a given time. He would labour for months at a sentence because it happened to have the same balance or the same ending as another. He was overscrupulous about the choice of his adjectives. He chiselled and polished his prose so punctiliously that his contributions arrived too late and were sent back to him, whilst other articles,

---

[1] He also wrote for the same paper a report of a Socialist meeting at which Sébastien Faure spoke. He once went to hear Jaurès, but was not moved at all. He did not follow him well, yet carried away the impression that he had the "great popular gift."

[2] Notably articles on Anatole France and Jules Lemaître.

JOHN MILLINGTON SYNGE

much inferior to his in literary value, were
accepted. Synge, like so many French writers
of that period, like Walter Pater, whom he read
assiduously at the time—a liking which he seems
to have utterly relinquished afterwards—was a
literary martyr. He himself referred, in characteristic phrases, to his " slaving " and to his
" agony and bloody sweat "; he violently abused
the compositors who misprinted him, and wrote
in a letter to a friend of one Editor who had
rejected his " copy ": " That ass has just returned
my MS. May God blight him ! "

Needless to add, his literary earnings were
practically nil. He had to do as best he could
with his small annuity, which his mother,
although she was not very well off, always supplemented most willingly when his funds ran
low, in order to prevent his having to do without the necessaries of life. " My family have
to subsidize me " was one of his familiar sayings.
Occasionally he got cheques of one guinea for
stray instalments of his " stuff," and then would
stand one of his friends a dinner. At one time
he gave lessons in English, but the work was
uncongenial to him and only incidental. Yet,
on the whole, he underwent no hardship. A
legend has arisen which represents him as suffer-
ing the pangs of poverty, sleeping in ditches,
and, like Goldsmith, his fellow-countryman,
earning a livelihood by playing his fiddle to
peasants. This he was never obliged to do ; or,
if he did, it was out of mere æsthetic interest.

32

However unbusinesslike [1] his temperament, there was not the slightest touch of Bohemianism about him ; on the contrary, he was very matter-of-fact and precise, wanting everything to go straight and be carried out to the letter. Of course he had to lead a simple life so as to prolong his time abroad, but that was choice, not necessity ; there was no actual " roughing it."

What was, then, this purely voluntary method of life ? Synge was always very plainly dressed, wearing a celluloid collar and heavy boots, and generally muffled up in a white neckerchief and a long black cape, while his broad-brimmed slouch hat made him look like a Czech or *Méridional* student. These garments he wore solely for convenience' sake : he said he had come to Paris " to be quiet and wear dirty clothes if he liked "; and although he found some picturesqueness in the *bérets* or sombreros, velveteen coats, brigands' cloaks, fancy-dress costumes and streaming hair of the green-faced decadents, he strongly disliked their feminine affectation, and was opposed to the usual outside advertisements of the professional *littérateur*. He lighted his own fire [2] and cooked his breakfast—two eggs, which he boiled in a paper-bag long before paper-bag cookery had any official existence. When he could not afford Duval or Polidor for lunch, he would buy York ham

---

[1] We do not say " unpractical," for he was most practical. A friend of his writes : " He might have shod a horse : there never was a manlier man walking this earth."

[2] Cf. *The Aran Islands* (iii. 122, 159).

or *veau piqué* at a *charcuterie* in the Rue Vavin. He went but rarely to *tavernes à prix fixe*, which he found utterly repugnant, and often warned his friends against the practice of shilling meals. He drank thin tea in bowls and smoked *caporal*, rolling his own cigarettes and always using a cigarette-holder. In the evening, but never later than ten, he would discuss the whole universe with friends over a glass of hot punch—for, though he had but little conversational powers, he was an excellent debater ; or (when he could afford to permit himself luxuries) he went fairly frequently to concerts,[1] cafés and theatres.

Synge, in the course of his Continental wanderings, had begun to forget Irish Gaelic,[2] and he was particularly anxious not to lose it altogether. He partly kept up his knowledge of it by attending courses at the Collège de France, where the late Prof. H. d'Arbois de Jubainville gave an hour's lecture each week on Celtic philology. It was Miss Maud Gonne who first introduced Synge to these lectures, and subsequently to the lecturer himself ;[3] Synge in his

---

[1] He went a great deal to the Concerts Rouge, which are still in existence. Once he visited Bullier, and did not see much in it. Another time he heard Jehan Rictus give forth his melancholy recitative at some cabaret, and was much impressed by the general atmosphere.

[2] W. B. Yeats, Introduction to *The Well of the Saints* (London : A. H. Bullen, 1905) ; reprinted as "Mr. Synge and his Plays" in Mr. Yeats's *Collected Works*, viii. 173–82.

[3] "Prof. d'Arbois asked me if I could find him a secretary who knew modern Irish. . . . I thought of Synge and introduced him to d'Arbois, with whom I think he worked for some

turn took his friend R. I. Best to the Collège de France ;[1] and in a French article which he published several years later, Synge paid homage to the scholarship of Prof. d'Arbois.[2] " He often lectures to myself only," he used to say. There is an amusing anecdote in connection with this episode of Synge's life which we may be permitted to relate. Prof. d'Arbois made it a point of knowing whether there were any Irish students in the audience attending his lectures. One day it was whispered to him that there was *un Irlandais dans la salle.* The *Irlandais* was J. M. Synge. D'Arbois asked him about the pronunciation of certain words in Gaelic. Synge pronounced them in the modern way—which, as is well known, widely differs from the spelling —whereupon d'Arbois pronounced the same words phonetically, with the remark : " This is how *I* pronounce them—this is how they *are*—

---

time " (Madame Gonne in a letter to the writer). Synge became very intimate with d'Arbois and his family. Among Synge's fellow-students was a somewhat narrow-minded German Catholic priest who, Synge said, " voudrait faire tenir toute la vérité dans le fourneau de sa pipe."

[1] Mr. Best later translated into English Prof. d'Arbois de Jubainville's *Irish Mythological Cycle* (Dublin : O'Donoghue & Co., 1904) ; reviewed by Synge in the *Speaker* for April 2 of the same year.

[2] " La Vieille Littérature Irlandaise, par J. M. Synge, Dublin," in *L'Européen*, March 15, 1902 : " C'est à M. d'Arbois de Jubainville que revient l'honneur d'avoir éclairé par de longs travaux toute cette mythologie irlandaise, et ses *Cours de la littérature celtique* sont d'une valeur inestimable pour tous ceux qui voudraient se renseigner sur ce sujet."

this is eleventh-century pronunciation." And for
several lectures Synge acted as amateur assistant
in Irish at the Collège de France.

But his linguistic activities did not confine
themselves to Erse. He had also begun to learn
Breton,[1] and kept up his knowledge of Latin by
reading a few pages of Spinoza's *Ethics* every
day.[2] Moreover, he was a passionate believer in
experimental phonetics. When his friends mis-
pronounced certain sounds, he would correct
them, shouting : " Oo . . . oo . . . oo " for
quite a long time. He attended (as an *auditeur
libre*) M. Paul Passy's course on " Les Sons du
Français " at the Sorbonne, and caused one of
his fellow-countrymen to purchase a copy of the
book. The lecturer often referred to his father's
well-known peace theories, which Synge pooh-
poohed ; but he agreed with the idea put forward by M. Passy that *patois* had a literary as
well as a purely philological value ; and we shall
see that Synge fully availed himself of the suggestion in his use of the Anglo-Irish dialect.

As a rule Synge stayed with poor people for
economy's sake. In Paris he first boarded with
a man cook and his wife, who was a *couturière*.
He once told Mr. John B. Yeats that they had
but one sitting-room, in which the chef did
his cooking and his wife her sewing, with

---

[1] Mr. W.-B. Yeats, in a letter quoted by Lady Gregory,
art. cit. Cf. Synge's article on " A Celtic Theatre " in Brittany in the *Freeman's Journal* (Dublin), March 22, 1900, p. 4.
[2] Cf. *Under Ether* (iv. 249).

another sempstress who helped. When, as sometimes happened, a large order for hats arrived, Synge deserted his philological studies and most willingly applied himself to hat-making and wire-bending.[1] He told Miss Lily Yeats that he also helped the same people to make tooth-powder.

After a year or so he took his lodgings on the top-floor of a fairly good and respectable hotel, well known to English artists and students, which is still standing, called the Hôtel Corneille, in the street of the same name, opposite the Odéon Theatre.[2] The house has a curious history of its own, too lengthy to narrate. Readers of *Trilby*, then just published (1894) by the Anglo-Parisian artist and writer, George du Maurier, will recollect the fact that this was the home of Little Billee in the novel. Irishmen of note, when coming to Paris, were wont to settle at this hotel, and they owed their knowledge of its existence to the recommendation of John O'Leary, the ex-Fenian, whose residence it had long been. Although the terms were almost

[1] Cf. John B. Yeats, "Synge and the Irish," *Harper's Weekly*, Nov. 25, 1911, p. 17.

[2] Cf. "John M. Synge: A Personal Appreciation," by D. J. O'Donoghue, *Irish Independent*, March 26, 1909. Mr. O'Donoghue (now Librarian of University College, Dublin) spent a few weeks in Paris during the summers of 1897–8–9 and also in 1900, the year of the Exhibition, after Mr. Best's departure in July, 1899. He stayed at the Hôtel Corneille in 1899, but did not meet Synge there ; and it was he, not Synge, who introduced Mr. Best to the world of letters, such as it was.

ridiculously moderate—one pound a week—
Synge had a comfortable bedroom and sitting-
room (not a " garret " or " attic," as misinformed
journalists have repeated *ad nauseam*) and lived
en pension there.

As one entered through the dark vestibule, one
noticed some fifteen books on the mantelpiece,
together with photographs of relatives, and a few
reproductions of paintings by Watts and Burne-
Jones, which Synge did not like. The low bed
—rather a kind of sofa or settee—disappeared
under a brown rug. Eggs were boiling on a
spirit-lamp with the shells thrown into the fire-
place. One day a visitor accidentally spat on the
" beautiful carpet "—a plain brown matting—
which covered the tiled floor. Synge said
nothing at the time, but whenever he recounted
the incident to his friends afterwards, his face
grew sallow with rage, and there he was, like
Old Mahon in the *Playboy*, " cursing and damn-
ing and swearing oaths."

We had intentionally deferred mentioning the
circumstance of Synge's residing at this hotel,
as it was to be the scene of the most momentous
event in his early career. There, in March,
1898,[1] through the introduction of a person
whose name has been forgotten, Synge met Mr.

[1] Mr. Yeats, in his introduction to *The Well of the Saints*,
says "Six years ago"—*i.e.*, by implication, 1899. He has now
admitted that this date is wrong, and a comparison of con-
flicting statements made by him and other friends of Synge has
enabled us to settle the date with greater accuracy.

AND THE IRISH THEATRE

William Butler Yeats, one of the principal
initiators of the Irish Literary Renascence. Mr.
Yeats, himself (as he informs us in the Introduction to *The Well of the Saints*) in rather narrow
circumstances, was also a resident on a lower
storey of the house. He had been, as we already
know, an important associate in the Parisian
Young Ireland organization started in the early
'nineties by Miss Maud Gonne, with whom both
he and Synge were very intimate. Mr. Yeats
has related in *Discoveries* [1] how Verlaine had
once told him in those days that he had given
up translating *In Memoriam*, and how he used to
meet in the Latin Quarter the St. Martinists who,
together with William Blake and his system of
" correspondences," are largely responsible for
the mystic view of life taken by the Irish poet.
Mr. Yeats has always been remarkable for his
almost infallible faculty of detecting literary
genius and his unerring divination of the
field in which a mind artistically inclined will
achieve especial distinction. Although Synge
was then utterly unknown in letters, Mr. Yeats
at once realized how little this brooding soul
was attuned to the artificialities of French life
and poetry, and early perceived the rare gifts that
lay hidden in Synge's nature. One critic, not
without reason, waxes lyrical at the discovery :

[1] A volume of Essays (Dun Emer Press, Dundrum, Co.
Dublin, 1907), pp. 12, 24–6 ; or *Collected Works*, viii. 5, 29.
[2] C. E. M[ontague ?] in the *Manchester Guardian*, Feb. 27,
1911.

JOHN MILLINGTON SYNGE

" It will add to Mr. Yeats's fame to have found Synge, and the man who could discover another Shakespeare would be as famous as Christopher Columbus. The search for him might be vastly exhilarating, and even to find a few Marlowes and Ben Jonsons would not be so bad." Mr. Yeats said to Synge : " Give up Paris; you will never create anything by reading Racine, and Arthur Symons will always be a better critic of French literature. Go to the Aran Islands. Live there as if you were one of the people themselves ; express a life that has never found expression."[1] The poet himself had just been staying one day on Aranmore, and this short visit had been sufficient to make him feel the magnetic charm of primitive life on this secluded archipelago of Far-Western Europe " where men must reap with knives because of the stones."[2] Mr. Yeats's advice was at once acted on : in May, 1898, Synge left Paris for Aranmore, and he paid several other visits to the islands both during and after his life in France. What he did and learnt there will be fully dealt with in another chapter. It will be enough to say that he found abundant inspiration for his art in this unexplored field. Indeed, on his successive returns to Paris, Synge wrote a few sketches of his experiences in Aran, which he later published in the *Gael*, an Irish-American magazine ;[3]

---

[1] Introduction to *The Well of the Saints*.   [2] *Ibid.*
[3] April, 1901, p. 109 ("The Last Fortress of the Celt"), signed " Synge, Paris " ; March, 1904, p. 93 (" A Dream of

WILLIAM BUTLER YEATS
From a pen-and-ink sketch by John B. Yeats, R.H.A.

he began the early versions of his two one-act plays, *In the Shadow of the Glen* and *Riders to the Sea*, the subjects of which he had found in Aran ; and last, but not least, composed a beautiful book of impressions which has made the islands known throughout the English-speaking world.

It is therefore difficult to over-estimate the service rendered by Mr. Yeats to letters—to Anglo-Irish letters especially — the day he directed Synge's steps to his native land. But for this memorable meeting it is highly probable that Synge would have remained a literary waif. His Continental wander-years would have left him inarticulate. He would have continued to do hack work, pondering languidly over problems of æsthetic appreciation or literary criticism, which treat life at second- or even third-hand ; his eyes would have remained unobservant of reality itself. Mr. Yeats's untiring encouragement acted as a powerful stimulus to the creative force in Synge.[1] And Synge himself was well aware of the importance of the meeting. In later years he often spoke of it with intense enthusiasm, as having brought the biggest and most beneficial influence in his whole life.

However, Synge did not " give up Paris " for

Inishmaan "), both incorporated in *The Aran Islands*. " The Last Fortress of the Celt " was reprinted in the Boston *Pilot*.

[1] Add to this that Mr. Yeats told Synge about his theory of rhythm and chanted prose (experimented at the production of *The Land of Heart's Desire*, Avenue Theatre, London, 1894, and later with Miss Florence Farr and Mr. Arnold Dolmetsch), which was to have some influence on Synge's own diction.

good. He still came to France now and then.
After his first residence in Aran he published a
folk-tale in the *New Ireland Review*,[1] and in the
same month (November, 1898) betook himself
to Paris, where he remained till May of the
following year.[2] Before his leaving for Aran his
friend R. I. Best had suggested that he should
give up his *maison meublée* (which was now the
Hôtel de Saint-Malo, Rue d'Odessa, near the
Gare Montparnasse) for unfurnished apartments,
pointing out that he would be able to live still
more economically in that fashion. Synge had
agreed to make the experiment on his return,
which he did by removing to the very rooms
(at 90 Rue d'Assas) where his friend had long
been staying with Dr. Michel Elmassian, now
of the Institut Pasteur, an Armenian bacterio-
logist whose complete ignorance of English
obliged Synge to practise his French. Synge
retained the *garçonnière* for several years. His
two friends took up lodgings at 3 Rue Bois-
sonade, in rooms overlooking the beautiful
garden of a convent of nuns. The view of the
convent prompted in Synge the idea of a play on
monastic life, which Mr. Yeats read in MS.,
and which was marked by a strong eroticism.
Before leaving Paris in July, 1899, Mr. Best had
helped Synge (for in these matters he was most
helpless) to procure the necessary furniture—but
not, or if so only as a joke, the Japanese fans and

[1] " A Story from Inishmaan " (*N. I. R.*, Nov. 1898, p. 153).
[2] Synge's last important visit to Paris was paid in Nov. 1899.

parasols and other gaudy ornaments with which Parisian students are wont to deck their rooms.

A legend represents Synge at the time as leading the reckless life of a Parisian rake, continually beset by the thought of sex. This somewhat sweeping statement demands qualification. Certainly Synge was not a Puritan ; he was much amused by the freaks of his fellow-students, and loved the free-and-easy life of the Parisian people, whom he proclaimed the finest in the world. When he sat in cafés he would contrast the dignity and pleasantness of vicious people in France to their sordidness in Anglo-Saxon countries. True, his language was often coarse, at times, I have heard, almost incredibly gross, and he indulged in magnificent swearwords which had something of the Elizabethan or Rabelaisian licentiousness ; but what he liked in them was their raciness, not their vulgarity. If he knew something of the " poets of Montmartre,"[1] he never promenaded his soul on the fallacious slopes of *La Butte*. Personally he had, I believe, a profound contempt, at least a fundamental distaste for the promiscuous sensuality of the roué. A significant anecdote is told of how a friend, visiting the Salon with him when he was already well advanced in years, criticized the naked figure of a woman in one of Henner's pastoral paintings. Synge said he knew nothing

---

[1] Mr. Yeats once wrote to the London *Nation* to correct a statement made in that journal that Synge had been influenced by the poets of Montmartre : " Synge knew nothing of them.'

of such matters, he was not in a position to judge. To some this deprecatory mood may seem merely a pose, or a passing humour; but from all we have been able to glean it expressed much more. It expressed an habitual point of view. Synge always remained as chaste and pure as ever man was; and the charge of immorality often laid at his door by hostile compatriots is, we maintain, unjust and well-nigh incomprehensible.

Neither was he an atheist. He did not believe in dogma, and had but little regard for rites and outward religious observances. The Roman Catholic service as he saw it performed at Saint-Sulpice and Notre-Dame appeared to him far too sentimental, and he frankly despised missionary work of any kind. Possibly his interest in the Church was more æsthetic than truly religious : the architecture, " the weedy old canons and the women praying in dark corners," appealed to him primordially as things of beauty. Yet he had a keen sense of the mystery of life, and was deeply preoccupied with matters spiritual. Without ever being ardently religious, he always stood on the brink of religion. He had dabbled in the occult, studying Buddhism, theosophy and magic [1] to dismiss them very soon, and had also given up the

---

[1] He had read Papus and Jules Bois' *Satanisme et Magie* (cf. *supra*, p. 26, n. 2), also the latter's articles in the *Journal* on occult science in India. Synge disagreed with Edouard Schuré's *Les Grands Initiés devant la Science*, a book shewing the oneness of religion throughout the different creeds.

mystical poetasters of the day because of their
" air of astral frauds." Once, as he was pacing
the Embankment with a friend, he said to him :
" You put something on the fire and it goes out ;
you are like that." That was his way of
rejecting the idea that we could lift the veil of
the world beyond ; but, saying this, he never
meant to deny the existence of the Unknowable.

His acquaintances other than Irish at the time
were fairly numerous. He often called on a
couple of American ladies ; one of them was a
sculptor and had a life-size statue of a boy at the
Salon the year Rodin's Balzac was exhibited.
There was also a Polish lady—" my Pole " as he
used to call her—with whom he paid frequent
visits to the Louvre and the Luxembourg
Gallery. She too was an artist, and he used to
pass on to his other friends the instruction in art
criticism which he received from her. Synge,
who had attempted painting, had an eye for
colour, and he would explain the function played
by the various tints in the harmony of a picture.
He shared Walter Pater's enthusiasm for *La
Joconde*—he mentions Mona Lisa in his poem
Queens [1]—and said the portrait had a " mystical
quality." His knowledge of the filiation of
painters was most accurate, and he also greatly
admired the moderns, such as Monet, Manet,
Renoir, Poitevin, Maxence and J.-B. Duffaud,[2]

[1] ii. 203.
[2] The first three are mentioned in Synge's article in the
Manchester Guardian, Jan. 24, 1908, p. 12 (*supra*, p. 7, n. 1).

and above all, Jean-François Millet, in whose work, he remarked, the artistic possibilities of peasant life—which Synge himself was to express in the dramatic sphere—were fully revealed and utilized.

He sometimes mentioned the names of M. Henry D. Davray, the well-known contributor to the *Mercure de France*, whom he casually met two or three times after 1899, and of M. Augustin Hamon, the critic and translator of Mr. Shaw's plays, who often came to Madame Gonne's house. The latter (whom Synge really never knew) is not to be confused with Count Louis Hamon, the Editor of a New York financial paper which Synge strongly disliked. Synge had a very dear friend in Brittany—a young gentleman named Cugnier. All we know of him is that he was a charming talker, lived with his mother, and eventually became an officer in the navy and went to the Guinée Francaise. When Synge visited him near Quimper [1] about April, 1899, he left his Perry violin in the keeping of a fellow-countryman, telling him how assiduously he practised the instrument at

---

Synge knew M. Duffaud personally, and greatly admired his painting "Les Anglais en Irlande : 1798," exhibited at the Salon in 1901 under No. 701.

[1] See references to the Pardons of Brittany, iii. 100, and iv. 180. Another friend of Synge, (Dr.) C.-A. Picquenard, contributed under the pen-name "C. de Kerambars" [Keranbarz en là Forêt-Fouësnant, Finistère] to the *Bas-Breton* (the "journal de l'arrondissement de Châteaulin," edited by Ch. Le Goff) for October 7, 1899, p. 3, a Breton poem entitled

one time,[1] and how he used to distress his mother sitting in the room underneath by a habit he had contracted of drumming on the table with the fingers of his left hand in order to strengthen the muscles. He used to do this mechanically, as he was reading, and was quite unaware of it.

Synge persuaded his Breton friend to write a French translation of Oscar Wilde's *Intentions*, which he actually helped him with. Whether the translation was published or not we cannot say; but Cugnier at any rate revised the French of Synge's article on " La Vieille Littérature Irlandaise " in *L'Européen*[2] for March 15, 1902. For Synge had not severed his connection with the Press. In December, 1900, he had begun to contribute reviews of Gaelic and French publications to the *Speaker*, a Liberal six-penny weekly now known as the *Nation*, then edited by Mr. R. Barry O'Brien and in which Mr. George Moore was bringing out a novel in serial form at the time. Towards the end of 1902 Synge finally gave up Paris and spent a few months in London[3] on his way

---

" Karit o Brezonek ! " which he dedicated " Do Sheaghain M. Synge—Mac na h-Eireann," with a translation into French verse entitled " Aimez votre langue bretonne ! " and inscribed " A Monsieur J.-M. Synge—Un fils de l'Irlande."

[1] In Paris he had given it up almost entirely. He only played it to friends at night with (as someone who heard him writes) " the wild passion of a gypsy."

[2] This now defunct periodical was cosmopolitan in its character, and had contributors of all nationalities.

[3] Synge never stayed long in London. Later in life he accompanied the Abbey Theatre players on their tours through

home. At first he stayed at a place described by him as a " den of thieves and other Scriptural persons," which he very soon left, paying a week in advance and going down the stairs as timid as a hare. He then boarded with a Mrs. Moore at 4 Handel Street, Bloomsbury, W.C., and there, on a Monday night of January, 1903, made the acquaintance of Mr. John Masefield, a young English author of exceptional talent. Mr. Masefield, who has now written the life of Synge in the *Dictionary of National Biography*,[1] has left us a vivid account of this first interview with him ;[2] and it is to Synge that he refers in his poem *Biography*—[3]

> " And now I miss that friend who used to walk
> Home to my lodgings with me, deep in talk,
> Wearing the last of night out in still streets
> Trodden by us and policemen on their beats
> And cats, but else deserted ; now I miss
> That lively mind and guttural laugh of his
> And that strange way he had of making gleam,
> Like something real, the art we used to dream."

England and Scotland. He once spent a couple of weeks in Devonshire with Mr. and Mrs. Jack B. Yeats, and a longer time in Surrey with his cousin, Mr. Edward M. Synge, but he never saw the typical counties. In the main he disliked living in England.

[1] Second Supplement, vol. iii. pp. 468–71. The present writer has had the honour of contributing a few items to the article, as very kindly acknowledged by Mr. Masefield.

[2] *Contemporary Review*, April, 1911, p. 470 : " John M. Synge."

[3] *English Review*, May, 1912, p. 169 ; also quoted in *Georgian Poetry* (London : The Poetry Bookshop, 1913), p. 122. Our identification has been confirmed by Mr. Masefield himself.

AND THE IRISH THEATRE

Meanwhile Mr. Masefield had introduced Synge to Mr. J. L. Hammond, the new Editor of the *Speaker*,[1] and it is in the columns of the paper[2] that Synge bade an eternal farewell to French life and literature.

---

[1] In April, May and June, 1903, Mr. Masefield was on the *Speaker*, but was working for it all the year.

[2] April 18, 1903 : " Loti and Huysmans."

CHAPTER III

SYNGE AND FRENCH "INFLUENCE": PERSONAL
CHARACTERISTICS

WHAT was Synge's relation to French literature and to Continental literature at large, it
now remains to examine. The initial question
is, In what manner did the French influence
exercise itself on Synge?

Synge cannot well have been directly influenced by the French authors themselves—
though he may have seen some of them,[1] he
never knew them personally—but only by their
books, of which he read a very large number.
His case is in this respect widely different from,
say, that of Oscar Wilde or Mr. W. B. Yeats,
and more especially of Mr. George Moore, who
was the intimate friend of Verlaine, Manet and
Zola, and whose mind and talent are actually
steeped in French culture.[2] Synge, on the

---

[1] "He told me that once, in Paris, he had gone to hear a
brilliant talker, a French poet, now dead. It was like him that
he did not speak to the talker. 'We sat around on chairs and
the great man talked'" (John Masefield, *Contemporary Review*,
art. cit.). Synge also heard Paul Fort, but did not like him.

[2] In 1885 a translation of Zola's *Pot-Bouille* (under the title
Piping Hot) had expressly avowed the direction taken by Mr.
Moore's literary sympathies. Cf. his *Confessions of a Young
Man, Memoirs of my Dead Life*, and his amusing sentence in
Hail and Farewell: *I. Ave* (Tauchnitz, No. 4314, p. 47): "As
far back as the days when I was a Frenchman."

contrary, lived practically as a recluse ; he did not mix in intellectual circles ; instead of serving an actual apprenticeship under certain masters, or directly imbuing himself with the surrounding literary atmosphere, he was content with discussing literature with students at night and subscribing to a circulating library in the Latin Quarter, of which he would devour a book almost daily.

His method of reading was absolutely unique. He would delve into all manner of letterpress and read on for hours at a time whether he understood or not. When he tackled a difficult French book, such as Mallarmé's *Divagations* (which he read again and again), he was fairly sure not to understand at all—first, because of his insufficient French, then and chiefly owing to his own peculiar tenebrosity of mind. Indeed, his intellectual mistiness was so dense that it often made it difficult for him to follow the easy French of the old *Mercures* which he bought along the *quais*, and even a great deal of English poetry. He was never able to remember the plots of Shakespeare's plays ; [1] and

---

[1] Yet he had a most accurate knowledge of the conjectural dates of Shakespeare's plays ; he was interested in the metrical tests, and valued the late Prof. Dowden's *Shakspere : A Critical Study of his Mind and Art* on that score. He said *King Lear* was the only readable play in the world. He was interested in the Sonnets ; Mr. Masefield (*C. R.*, *art. cit.*, p. 474) reports him as asking his friends how they would translate into French the last line in Sonnet CXXX : " As any she belied with false compare."

when Mr. Yeats's *Shadowy Waters* came out, he
refused to borrow the copy which a friend offered
him : he did not want to know what was in it—
he was afraid " to have to understand." At the
end of his life he could not read anything, even
in English. All the same, during his French
period, the sheer strain of reading made books
subtly suggestive to him ; and he would go on
untroubled. At length, by dint of concentration
and brooding, the light of intuition would flash
upon him ; he would gradually emerge from the
perpetual blank fog of his mind, and, by some
laborious process of defoliation, get to the very
gist of the thing—not the objective thing, but
the purely subjective impression it made on him,
and on him alone. Other writers existed for him
only as part of his own being—only in so far as
they reinforced his personal tendencies, or made
clearer the vision wherein he was absorbed. His
self-feeling was most intense ; to quote from Mr.
Yeats's diary,[1] " he had that egotism of the man
of genius which Nietzsche compares to the
egotism of the woman with child."

These general limitations have to be borne in
mind when one comes to examine how Synge's
purely bookish knowledge of French letters
may have affected his talent. What schools of
writers was he familiar with, and how do their
respective influences manifest themselves in his
work ?

He had a great fondness for old French litera-

---

[1] Cf. *English Review*, March, 1913, p. 558.

ture. At one time (Mr. Yeats informs me) he read many mediæval farces, which possibly were a factor in the formation of his own bitter-sweet humour. His being acquainted with the old poets and balladists, such as Charles d'Orléans, Colin Muset,[1] Marot,[2] Villon[3] and Ronsard[4] is evidenced by his *Poems and Translations*. Yet, on the whole, they had, it seems, but little influence on the general bulk of his work. His intimacy with them rather reveals in Synge a quaint habit of exploring the unfrequented nooks and by-ways of literature. It was with the same insatiable curiosity that he tackled the minor Elizabethans—Nashe, Beaumont,[5] Greene, Peele, Marston and others—still but little known at the time—although, as we shall later indicate, a certain harsh masculinity in their writings and also a distinct linguistic kinship may have accounted for this predilection.

Synge's sympathies were mainly with the classics. They appealed to his essentially, though not apparently, academic mind. When Mr. Yeats first met him he was planning a critical work on Racine—then and always one of his favourite writers—and had just been reading Corneille. He liked to see the classics earnestly interpreted. He saw some of Molière's[6] plays at the Comédie Française, notably *The Rogueries of Scapin* ; and when the comedy was

[1] ii. 248. [2] ii. 216.
[3] ii. 201, 203, 245-7. [4] ii. 203, 214, 225.
[5] ii. 225. [6] i. 135; iv. 54.

first performed at the Abbey Theatre, Dublin, on April 4, 1908, in Lady Gregory's " Kiltartanese " version,[1] he was the stage-producer. It seems plausible to assert that he derived much in the way of general craftsmanship and method from the French writers of the seventeenth century. This would apply, in the first place, to his knowledge of the " architectonics of drama "—to use a phrase of Matthew Arnold's —as revealed in the *facture* and construction of his plays, which Irish judges themselves consider superior to that of the average Irish play. It may also account for the extreme finish and compactness of his style.

We regret to find ourselves at variance with Mr. Yeats when he repeatedly and emphatically declares that Synge knew nothing of the modern writers.[2] That he did know them seems indubitable. Although he scoffed at Swinburne's glorification of Victor Hugo's *Les Misérables*, he greatly praised the scene in which Jean Valjean paces his room. On the other hand, we have seen that in the years 1898–9 Synge reviewed books by Anatole le Braz and Maeterlinck, who were then amongst the most up-to-date men of letters. But, besides these, Synge had read a

---

[1] *The Kiltartan Molière: The Miser. The Doctor in Spite of Himself. The Rogueries of Scapin.* Translated by Lady Gregory (Dublin : Maunsel, 1910).

[2] Letter to the London *Nation*: " I urged him vainly to read the prints of his own time." Preface to Synge's *Poems and Translations* (Cuala Press, 1909): " Knowing nothing of new books and newspapers, reading the great masters alone."

great many more, whom we shall now venture
to classify.

In the first place, he was very closely acquainted with the so-called "realistic" school
of novelists and prose-writers. He knew a great
deal of Balzac, whose vocabulary he found
technical and difficult to understand. He was
a constant reader of Flaubert and Maupassant,
being temperamentally related to them by his
introspective habits, his relish of "human turpitude,"[1] and also by the *labor limæ* to which a
somewhat lapidary quality in his style testifies.
Although he repudiated Zola's "joyless and
pallid words"[2] and Huysmans' "ugly crew,"[3]
their naturalistic *manière* strikingly accorded with
his own formula of Art—which we may provisionally define as an art deeply rooted in reality,
but crowned with a wild imaginative superstructure. The same process is to be found in
Zola, who, as has been frequently noticed, is as
much of a "Hugolesque" Romanticist as a
Realist properly so called.

Much has been said about the way in which
the decadent poets may have operated on Synge's
work. That he knew their verse is beyond

---

[1] A phrase applied to Flaubert by Sully-Prudhomme in one
of his letters (1877).
[2] Preface to the *Playboy* (ii. 4). Synge especially liked the
description of the market-carts in Zola's *Le Ventre de Paris*.
On Zola and Synge, see L. Paul-Dubois, *L'Irlande contemporaine et la question irlandaise* (Paris : Perrin, 1907), p. 409, n. 1.
[3] *The Vagrants of Wicklow* (iv. 12); cf. his review of
Huysmans' *L'Oblat* in the *Speaker*, April 18, 1903 ; also ii. 4.

cavil. Mr. Best had lent him the works of Baudelaire, and it was from Synge that Mr. D. J. O'Donoghue first heard the well-known story of how Baudelaire, in order to startle the public (*épater le bourgeois*), once called on Maxime du Camp with his hair dyed green.[1] Synge the man had certainly nothing Baudelarian in him— except, perhaps, his love of cats[2]; and he found Baudelaire's whole mind "morbid."[3] As to Mallarmé, Synge mentions him in the preface to the *Playboy*; and we have seen that he had read and re-read the *Divagations*. Far from shirking such a delicate question, we beg leave not to discuss immediately whether this possible influence of the decadents on Synge was decidedly injurious, as many Irish critics are inclined to think.

Among the living French writers, two deserve quite a special mention. The first of these is M. Pierre Loti. Synge thought him the greatest living writer of prose, and he used to say that he wished to do for the peasantry of Western Ireland what M. Loti had done for the Breton fisherfolk. When Synge was in London in

---

[1] "The Synge Boom: Foreign Influences," by D. J. O'Donoghue, *Irish Independent*, Aug. 21, 1911.

[2] "Synge me dit son amour des chats, et quelle âme mystérieuse habite, à son sentiment, dans leur corps si souple . . ." (M. Anatole le Braz's notebook).

[3] Preface to *The Tinker's Wedding*. On Baudelaire's influence on Synge, see a somewhat unconvincing statement in *The Influence of Baudelaire in France and England*, by "G. Turquet-Milnes" [Madame André Turquet] (London: Constable; N.Y.: E. P. Dutton, 1913), p. 249.

January, 1903, re-writing his Aran manuscript, Mr. John Masefield saw one or two books by M. Loti lying on his table. On April 18 of the same year Synge reviewed Loti's *L'Inde sans les Anglais* for the *Speaker*. Here we have proof positive of actual influence. There are unmistakable marks of it all through Synge's prose topographies. It becomes still more conspicuous in *Riders to the Sea*, as the mere comparison of texts will, we think, fully reveal.[1]

On the other hand, Synge was steeped in Anatole France, whose easy style and subtle intellect he much admired. He had read *L'Orme du Mail, Le Crime de Sylvestre Bonnard,* and *La Rôtisserie de la Reine Pédauque,* and often quoted the passage in the last-named book in which an old woman says a prayer because it happens to be printed in large type. Synge further found in Anatole France the disillusioned scepticism which was to be the keynote of his plays ; and as Prof. Sherman aptly says,[2] " despite the Frenchman's vastly greater range of culture, the two men were absolutely at one in their aloof, pyrrhonic irony and their homeless laughter—the laughter of men who have wandered all the highways of the world and have found no abiding city." Yet one may point out that whereas Anatole

---

[1] See an article on " Synge and Loti " by the present writer in the *Westminster Review*, May, 1913, p. 532 ; and some excellent comments by Prof. Stuart P. Sherman in the N.Y. *Nation*, Dec. 26, 1912, p. 608, or in the *Evening Post* (N.Y.), Jan. 11, 1913, p. 6.

[2] *Art. cit.*

France's pessimism is often as withering as the
nihilism of Voltaire in *Candide*, Synge's pessimism is exhilarating and relieved by a rich
sense of humour which acts as a mental tonic :
it exalts because it exults.

Synge had a very limited knowledge of French
criticism. He had read and reviewed Jules
Lemaître, but he ignored Brunetière. As a rule
he preferred original works to critical writings.
He would not have read a book on himself—
this one least of all.

This cursory examination of the schools or
men of letters to whom Synge may have been
indebted must naturally conclude with a few
remarks concerning his relation to contemporary drama. "He disliked modern drama
because of its sterility of speech, and perhaps
ignored it," says Mr. Yeats.[1] Yet he did not
entirely ignore it. He was, as we know, familiar
with the German playwrights and with the
"intellectual" movement started by Ibsen and
Maeterlinck. At the same time he much relished
crude melodrama.[2] For example, the present
writer has been informed that when in Paris
Synge saw a "creepy," Grand-Guignol-like
playlet entitled *Leur Sang* at the theatre in the
Rue Blanche (now the Théâtre Réjane) which
made a very deep impression upon him.

---

[1] *Synge and the Ireland of his Time*, p. 12.
[2] Synge, when in Ireland, often went to see the melodramas
at the Queen's Theatre, Dublin (cf. Jack B. Yeats, *With Synge
in Connemara*, ap. W. B. Yeats, *op. cit.*, p. 41).

AND THE IRISH THEATRE

An ingenious attempt has been made by a
Dublin critic, himself a friend of Synge in Paris,[1]
to trace almost all his plays to corresponding
French prototypes. Synge's specific indebtedness to individual dramatists will be fully
examined in connection with the genesis of his
several works, and the list of alleged " sources "
will even be supplemented by the addition of
analogues other than French. Yet let it be at
once remarked that these parallels are valuable
from the standpoint of comparative literature
only. Inquiries tending to establish that a play
must have its origin in a previous one are
generally most ineffectual specimens of genealogical research. A critic, even with the support
of external evidence such as dates and outward
resemblances, must always be cautious in ventur-
ing such assertions. Very often a deterministic
sophism falsely explains what is at bottom an
independent, spontaneous and genuine creation
of Art. Nothing is more common than a plot,
nothing less infrequent than unconscious coinci-
dences between playwrights : has not M. Georges
Polti written a book (published in the *Mercure
de France* series) in which he mathematically
demonstrates that the really fundamental dramatic
situations number only thirty-six ? To select a
typical instance from the Irish school itself. The
writer of these lines has it from Mr. Thomas
MacDonagh, the author of *When the Dawn is
Come*—a sort of Irish " anticipation " or peep

[1] Mr. D. J. O'Donoghue, *art. cit.*

59

into the future, with the scene laid twenty years hence—that, on the first performance of the play (October 15, 1908), critics averred that its subject and very title were borrowed from Verhaeren's Socialistic or Utopian drama, *Les Aubes* (1898), translated into English by Arthur Symons in the same year under the title *The Dawn*. Now Mr. MacDonagh had never read Verhaeren, and yet his play was almost identically the Belgian's. As to Synge, it seems that we can surmise, and only surmise, that he found the root-ideas of his plays in foreign models. Except perhaps in the case of *Riders to the Sea*, Synge's indebtedness absolutely cannot be proven. The subjects of his plays are of such an elemental nature that they necessarily belong to the folklore of many nations, and no one can say with certainty whether the eternal stories and incidents on which they are based have come from the Continent to Ireland, or from Ireland to the Continent, or to both from a common origin. Criticism can only make conjectural *rapprochements*. But even if Synge had actually adopted or adapted his dramatic themes from alien sources, it would by no means detract from his greatness or his originality as a playwright. All great dramatists have been arch-plagiarists, and there are stale loans in Molière, who said : " Je prends mon bien où je le trouve." Synge's actual indebtedness might only call in question the objective value of his plays as *Irish* plays. This ushers in the third and last problem suggested by this review of

Synge's relation to Continental literature : Was the foreign influence for good or bad with regard to Synge's attitude to Ireland ?

The many excellent elements which he derived from abroad, mainly in point of style and workmanship, are now given unanimous recognition, and have been separately noticed. However, it is part of the legend created in Dublin for the purpose of discrediting Synge's work to say that he was far too much of a foreign scholar. The study of European art and thought, Irish critics contend, led Synge to the adoption of a standpoint which is both morbid and exotic. This twofold charge being always laid at Synge's door in a general sense, without specific reference to any of his writings, we can discuss it before examining Synge's works themselves—nay, as a sort of introduction to the works.

The alleged morbidity of Synge's *Anschauung* is generally ascribed to Baudelaire and the decadents. Only their influence, it is argued, can explain Synge's extraordinary craving for the abnormal. An Irish critic [1] goes even to the length of seriously representing Synge as a sort of literary Frankenstein, " hunting for slimy, clammy, hideous things "—*La Charogne*, presumably—" gleaning odds and ends of humanity from graveyards and dead-houses and making a monster " ! Although Synge never was the ghastly, *macabre* creature pictured in the above

---

[1] " Synge as a playwright," by " Che Buono " (the late William Bulfin).

excerpt, there is no shirking the fact that he has, in a certain sense, taken moral freaks and pathological cases as characters in some of his plays, and that he always revelled in all that was pungent, truculent and savage. But this bizarre instinct was due, we think, to a personal factor which has been lost sight of, not to any literary influence. It was very deeply rooted in Synge's own physical nature. There was in his low vitality a natural predisposition to grimness. Although his mind was fundamentally sane, his impaired bodily health had distorted his vision from the beginning. He saw life and Irish life both with and through eyes that were diseased. His was such an intense, supersensitive temperament that he naturally clutched at extreme types of existence with all the hectic greediness of a consumptive. To him life was not characteristic unless exaggerated, hypertrophied. No doubt Baudelaire and the decadents were strikingly in accordance with this natural bent of Synge, and possibly reinforced it ; but they did not create it. What was with them a literary fad was with him a vital need. Had Synge never read them he would have had exactly the same outlook.

As to Synge's exoticism, it can scarcely be contested that the Gallic element in him is somewhat at odds with the Gaelic. European culture moulded Synge's mind in such a fashion that certain excessively, almost provokingly un-Irish elements intruded themselves into his Irish brain.

Yet, in spite of all, he remained fundamentally Irish.[1] On the whole, the extraneous imports as compared with the solid Irish substance of his genius are practically negligible. Yet they do exist, and the statement of certain Irish critics, to the effect that Synge's mind was entirely untouched by alien influence, is a ludicrous exaggeration. In Synge, however, the combination of the two elements is particularly felicitous. He was one of the few Irish writers who europeanized Ireland without degaelicizing it —who allied the depth of an intense national spirit to the width of a broad-minded international culture. Literary cosmopolitanism enabled Synge to express Irish life so completely that his peasant characters are lifted from the narrow boundaries of their petty Robinson-Crusoe-island provinciality int a kind of universal and dateless dreamworld which makes them representative of human nature everywhere. In vain does Mr. Yeats contend that " no man, even though he be Shakespeare, can write perfectly when his web is woven of threads spun in many lands " :[2] the study of foreign literatures

---

[1] He even opposed European influence when it threatened the literary independence of Ireland : "Once, when in later years, anxious about the educational effect of our movement, I proposed adding to the Abbey Company a second company to play international drama, Synge, who had not hitherto opposed me, thought the matter so important that he did so in a formal letter " (Yeats, *op. cit.*, p. 12).

[2] Quoted by K. L. Montgomery in *Fortnightly Review*, September, 1911, p. 560.

equipped Synge with a vastness of perception and bearing not to be found in such Irish writers as remain unacquainted with them.

Above all, the various elements introduced by foreign influence were so fully absorbed and welded themselves with his own personality in so thorough a manner that the influence as such was practically overcome and might almost be said to vanish. As Mr. George Moore once very wittily expressed it to the writer, "An original author assimilates and the influence disappears ; the plum and the peach influenced the nectarine, but the nectarine is a fruit in itself." So was it with Synge, who had so clear-cut an individuality that he could not well be said to be, in the strict and literal meaning of the word, beholden to any one. The foreign element was imbibed immediately and mingled with the substance of his inmost temperament ; and in many cases there seemed to exist a sort of pre-established harmony which facilitated the blending and made the two terms practically indistinguishable.

It is the whole drift of the present essay to link up as it were Synge's life with his art. Synge's personality, as we have had and shall still have occasion to note, pervades with a peculiar autobiographical flavour the whole bulk of his *opus* and gives it oneness through all its growth. Both are therefore to be studied in their mutual conjunction and interaction. The foregoing pages already contain many scattered instances of Synge's idiosyncrasies. It is now time that we should, as an appropriate conclusion to this chapter, take a general view of the man himself.

At the time we have just considered (1903), Synge was thirty-two years of age ; and we are in a position to draw a full-length portrait of him. There exist several good pictures, drawings and photographs of Synge at different ages.[1] He stood some five feet eight or nine inches high. Though he was big of frame, and had a neck of unusual thickness, he did not look particularly strong. The man (Mr. Thomas MacDonagh remarks) bore a curious likeness to certain portraits of Oliver Cromwell. The head was large and massive, with long, dark—rather brown than black, almost auburn—tossing hair. Synge looked much older than his age. The swarthy complexion [2] of his grave, deeply-lined face, with delicacy and pain written over its expression, and a force of iron will peeping out through the

---

[1] See list in Appendix B.

[2] Mr. Bernard Shaw once picturesquely, but not inaptly said to me that "Synge had a face like a blacking-brush." M. Anatole le Braz, in the unpublished diary already referred to, has the following admirable portrait of Synge : "La figure de Synge est typique : une tête longue, un peu carrée, aux traits tourmentés et, par moments, quasi douloureux, pas belle, mais singulièrement expressive. La moustache châtaine voile à demi les lèvres épaisses ; une manière de goître enfle le côté droit du cou. Il se montre d'une courtoisie charmante, pleine d'aménité, de douceur, légèrement timide. L'intelligence est ouverte, accueillante. L'homme n'a pas cette morgue enfantine qui m'a frappé chez beaucoup de ses compatriotes, aucune ' pitrerie ' non plus, mais un grand sérieux, une foi profonde dans la vitalité du mouvement irlandais, un enthousiasme contenu qui,

hazel-grey eyes, seemed to "put on" years to his appearance. The cheeks were drawn and seamed, the jaws square-set. The bushy moustache partly concealed the wide mouth, on which there was a great play of humour. The chin was clean-shaven, but for a little tuft of hair, smaller than an ordinary goatee, and answering rather to the description of what is known as a " smeg " (" smeggeen," " smiggin ") in Anglo-Irish. The voice was hoarse and quick and often difficult to catch, with hardly any mellifluous Irish brogue in it. On the whole, Synge did not look particularly Irish.[1] There was rather something Scotch and even slightly foreign about him.

It would be a total misconception to represent Synge as a gloomy misanthropist, or, as ninety per cent. of the people in Ireland fancy him to be, as a sort of monster sent here below to blacken the good name of Irish character. If he maligned his country—a question which we shall impartially examine—it was without malice prepense or mischievous intention, but simply, we believe, owing to some natural bent which he could not resist, or because he saw in the Irish peasant a picturesque setting for his strangely "morbid" trend of thought. Some

---

parfois, illumine le regard, affermit la voix, le sentiment aussi, général chez ses congénères, que ce qui s'accomplit en ce moment en Irlande est un phénomène historique unique au monde et dont les fastes des autres nations ne contiennent pas d'exemple."

[1] A friend of his, however, maintains that in the Wicklow glens you often meet Synge in the person of roadside beggars.

J. M. SYNGE
From a photograph by James Paterson, R.S.A. (1908)

friends, who think his plays " cynical," wonder
at the apparent contrast in the dual personality
of man and writer in Synge. We are not at
present concerned with discussing whether the
writer was " cynical " ; but we can emphatically
deny that the man was.

Those who knew him personally liked him
for his gentle, unobtrusive character. There
are but few *ana* to be told of him. He was a
soft-spoken, shy-mannered, somewhat uncouth[1]
person of a retiring disposition and entirely
lovable nature. In a social circle he generally
remained an inscrutable listener until drawn out
of his shell of reserve. Casual acquaintances
found him dull ; others thought that he led an
intense inward life. He certainly had no conversation in Mr. Bernard Shaw's or Mr. George
Moore's sense of the word. He had neither the
Irish brilliancy—he loathed brilliancy—nor the
Irish self-consciousness. His feelings were far
too deep to be lightly shewn. He talked but
little, and least of all of himself. His constant
effort seemed to be to make others forget that
he was there, so that he might observe them
without their knowing it. Nor was there any
romantic attitudinizing in the mystery wherein
he seemed to enwrap himself ; it was mere
unaffected simplicity which even his literary
fame and the world-wide success of his plays
never spoiled.

When he did talk, all perceived that there

---

[1] Dr. Lynch describes Synge by the German adjective
ungeheuer.

really was something very companionable about him. He was full of an ironical gay vitality, and would tell things of a rare charm—mainly quaint stories and sayings which he had heard in out-of-the-way places. All that he said smacked of life. All that he cared for was concrete experience. A man of few opinions, with no bent for philosophic generalizations, he was content to watch life from an exclusively artistic standpoint.

No one ever heard him utter any word of bitterness or flattery. He had neither the Irish "blarney" nor the Irish wickedness. Unlike so many of his fellow-countrymen, he did not retail petty gossip. He was not one of the chorus in the Irish "whispering-gallery." When some malicious anecdote was told in his presence he would laugh at it in a round, hearty laugh; but he himself never gossiped. In brief, by his descent, his culture, his outlook—physically and temperamentally, he was in seeming contrast to the traditional Irishman. A sensitive and brooding man of subdued energy, always sincere in his enthusiasm, he stood at the opposite pole to the burly and sanctimonious Irish type of the Thomas Moore order, as well as to the rollicking, happy-go-lucky, devil-may-care "Englishman's Irishman."

And yet this was the man who, having discovered modern Europe, had at the same time recovered ancient Ireland—whither we must now follow him.

CHAPTER IV

SYNGE'S OBSERVATION OF IRISH IRELAND

"When I was a young man we'd have given a lifetime to be in Ireland a score of weeks; and to this day the old men have nothing so heavy as knowing it's a short while they'll lose the high skies are over Ireland, and the lonesome mornings with birds crying on the bogs. Let you come this day, for there's no place but Ireland where the Gael can have peace always."

THESE words, spoken by Fergus in the second act of *Deirdre of the Sorrows*,[1] Synge's last tragedy, might as well be taken as a retrospective confession of Synge himself. Synge in Paris and elsewhere on the Continent was little short of a literary *déraciné*. He might have achieved criticism, though it had many drudgeries which he was perhaps too lazy to overcome ; but, had he not discovered Ireland, he would never have really discovered himself. Like all geniuses, he was contradiction incarnate : he resided abroad because he could find himself at home only in his native environment. Foreign influence moulded and perfected but the outward form or manner of his art ; the solid human matter remained to be found in Ireland. It is this profound social reality which underlies all his later work that we must now investigate.

---

[1] ii. 156.

JOHN MILLINGTON SYNGE

With the exception of Borrow's romances, we know of no " books of errantry " more delightful and attractive than the four series of prose essays which embody the results of Synge's exploration of Erin. Although they were written at various dates, and describe widely different districts of Ireland,[1] we may be permitted to take them as a whole, for they represent either Synge's early initiation to the ways and humours of Irish peasant folk, or the subsequent observations whereby he freshened his memories and first-hand knowledge of things Irish.

It will be at once noticed and possibly wondered at that in these sketches of travel Synge writes only of rural Ireland. A double reason accounts for this general limitation of Synge's field of social inquiry. On one hand, it is to be borne in mind that Synge had grown weary of the conventionalities of town life, which he could escape only by an almost Wordsworthian return to nature. "One wonders," he writes, " why anyone is left in Dublin, or London, or Paris, when it would be better, one would think, to live in a tent or hut with this magnificent sea and sky, and to breathe this wonderful air, which is like wine in one's teeth." [2] Further, the well-known fact that the distinction between town

---

[1] Apart from the four districts described in the prose essays—Wicklow, Aran, Kerry, and Connemara—Synge also knew Donegal, to which he refers in *Between the Bays of Carraroe* (iv. 173).
[2] *In West Kerry* (iv. 81).

and country is perhaps less marked in Ireland than anywhere else is not to be overlooked. Barring the few large centres, which are English or Scotch rather than Irish, and of which Synge never speaks, Irish towns are but small towns,[1] merged in an indistinct provincial atmosphere. Ireland remains essentially an agricultural island, a nation of peasants. To find Ireland, Synge had to ramble in the country ; and Abbey Theatre plays are typically Irish because they do not as a rule deal with urban life.

There is ample reason to believe that it was in Wicklow—which was, if not his native county, his home during the longer portion of his youth—that Synge commenced his study of Irish life and scenery. The supposition is borne out by characteristic passages shewing that the Wicklow papers must have been written long before their publication (1905–8).[2] At all events the observations themselves undoubtedly date back to a very early period of Synge's life.

In this day when " regionalistic " literature is so much talked of, it is noteworthy that almost every modern Irish dramatist has a definite geographical area which he takes as the locale

---

[1] *The Small Town* (iv. 232).

[2] Synge re-wrote them several times. Cf. *The People of the Glens* (iv. 37) : " I came back from France two months ago." In *At a Wicklow Fair* (*ibid.* 47–8) we find the origin of *The Tinker's Wedding*, which was first written about 1902. We may mention by the way that Synge contributed to the *Gael* (April, 1903, p. 117) an unreprinted Wicklow sketch entitled " An Autumn Night on the Hills."

of his plays. Thus Mr. Pádraic Colum writes
of the Irish Midlands ; Mr. S. Lennox Robinson
and Mr. T. C. Murray, of their native county
of Cork ; Mr. Joseph Campbell, of Donegal ;
Mr. William Boyle sets his delightful comedies
amidst Co. Louth surroundings[1] ; and the Ulster
Literary Theatre shews its provincial limitations
by its title. Synge, likewise, is inseparable from
the Irish countryside where he first lived. The
Wicklow peasant had all his heart ; and to some
extent it was the Wicklow peasant that he was
to put on the stage, even when he professed to
portray Western Gaeldom.

We need not in our turn re-tell the miscellaneous experiences that Synge encounters " on
the road."[2] In these Wicklow notes we are
confronted with a number of wayside incidents
which would seem trivial, were they not told in
such graphic though unaffected style that the
memory of them haunts one for many days.
Exception may perhaps be taken to the strange
way in which Synge derives his information from
wholly untrustworthy guides—tramps, tinkers,
ballad-singers and other vagrants who, like the
proverbial Irish jarveys,[3] are apt to misinform
the inquisitive visitor. Yet it is charming to
listen to the humorous, and oftener tragic stories
that Synge's chance acquaintances narrate, in the

[1] Or at least is closely connected with Co. Louth, where
he was born. See his charming volume of humour and
pathos of country life in that county, *A Kish of Brogues*
(London : Simpkin Marshall, Hamilton, Kent ; Dublin : Gill
and O'Donoghue, 1899).

[2] iv. 20.   iv. 210.

familiar and genial way so highly characteristic of the Irish nature.

In one of the Wicklow papers Synge states his standpoint of observation with forcible lucidity. " In all the circumstances of this tramp life," he says, " there is a certain wildness that gives it romance and a peculiar value for those who look at life in Ireland with an eye that is aware of the arts also."[1] His is less the curiosity of the professional sociologist, with his statistics and frequently pseudo-scientific methods, than of the intuitive æsthetician who realizes the collective consciousness by abrupt self-identification. Synge does not present us with a comprehensive gallery of Hibernian types—such as, for instance, the *Silhouettes Irlandaises* so exquisitely delineated by Mrs. William O'Brien in another part of the country[2]—but rather a selection of arresting trick-characters that possess a picturesqueness of their own and stand out in bold relief. It so happens that those " variations from the ordinary types of manhood "[3] especially appealed to the morbid side of Synge's nature. Yet in this first series of impressions he also depicted other phases of life, less shabby and abnormal, though flavoured as it were with a peculiar zest which made them suitable material for his art.

It was this right kind of local colour, this

---

[1] *The Vagrants of Wicklow* (iv. 12).

[2] *Silhouettes Irlandaises. Au Pied de Croagh Patrick.* Par Madame William O'Brien (Sophie Raffalovich). (Paris : Guillaumin, 1904.)

[3] iv. 12.

differentiating essence or "virtue" of the Irish temperament, that Synge was primarily bent on disengaging. No wonder, then, that these records of rambles in Co. Wicklow—although, in our judgment, by far the best written of all Synge's sketch-books—should have but a minor importance as compared with the rest. Just as the Ulsterman is more Scotch than really Irish, the Wicklow peasant is more or less Anglicized ; the typical Gael has been driven by the invaders from the Eastern to the Occidental seaboard, unless, pursuing his westward course, he has fled to the Hy-Breasail confines of "Greater Ireland"—America. It was therefore in the half-barbarous "Western World," in yonder self-contained microcosm where the people talk of all that is outside their immediate vicinity as a detached unknown thing called *an domhain mor*— "the big world"—that Synge was to find the genuine Celt, with his dreaminess, his imaginative exuberance, his puzzling combination of mysticism and practicality.

We have seen in a previous chapter how Mr. W. B. Yeats's clear-sighted advocacy had led Synge to betake himself to the Isles of Aran, a triad of treeless rocks in the Galway Bay, about ten leagues out to sea. Personal inquiries made on the islands (the results of which do not substantially differ from the facts already recorded in the excellent Introduction compiled for the American edition [1] of Synge's book by Mr.

[1] John W. Luce Company, Boston, 1911. The book is got up with the characteristic illustrations by Mr. Jack B. Yeats.

AN ARAN ISLANDER

CHILD WITH PIG REFERRED TO IN ARAN BOOK

Photographs taken by J. M. Synge in Aran

Edward J. O'Brien, who has had the advantage of supplemental information furnished by the little colony of Aran Islanders now residing in the United States) enable us to give particulars of Synge's mode of life on this sequestered Atlantic outpost.

Synge's first visit to Aran was paid in May, 1898, and lasted exactly six weeks. It was during this first residence that he began his book,[1] which he slowly completed during his subsequent sojourns, being at pains to re-write it in France, Wicklow and London in the meantime. There are but few accounts of life in Aran;[2] and Synge's own production, if perhaps too much of a diary, is an incomparable store-

---

[1] " *The Aran Islands* was begun before any of the plays. He told me himself, and there is no doubt of it " (Mr. John . Masefield in a letter to the writer).

[2] The opening of Charles Lever's novel, *Luttrell of Aran*, takes place in Inishmore ; cf. also *Grania : The Story of an Island*, by the Hon. Emily Lawless (London : Smith, Elder) ; and *Hurrish: A Study*, by the same (London : Methuen ; N.Y. : Harper) ; "Vers l'Occident : à travers l'Irlande," by Henri Potez (*Revue de Paris*, Sept. 1, 1901) ; one chapter in E. Œ. Somerville and Martin Ross's *Irish Yesterdays* (London : Longmans, eleventh thousand, 1908) ; *Smuainte ar Árainn* (Sketches of Aran Life), by "Una ni Fhairceallaigh," M.A. [Miss Agnes O'Farrelly], published by Clódhanna for the Gaelic League, Dublin ; the latter portion of *Bilder aus Irland*, by Prof. Hermann Osthoff (of Heidelberg), reviewed in *Revue Celtique*, vol. xxix, 1908, p. 89 ; *Leabhar an Athar Eoghan* (The O'Growney Memorial Volume), by Miss Agnes O'Farrelly, M.A. (Dublin : Gill ; London : Nutt, 1904), pp. 137, 138, 170, 174-5, 372 ; "The Aran Islands," by Maude Radford Warren (*Harper's Monthly Magazine*, May, 1910) ; "The Edge of the World," by Miss Ethel Rolt-Wheeler (*English Review*, March, 1913).

house of entirely novel experiences, and contains
many a page worthy of the greatest stylists.   It

A CHRONOLOGY OF SYNGE'S SUCCESSIVE VISITS TO ARAN

(i) May, 1898 : *The Aran Islands*, Part I.
    A fortnight on Inishmore (iii. 1–10) at Thomas Con-
    cannon's inn at the Seven Churches.
    One month on Inishmaan (10–92) : "In France a
    month from this day" (p. 16), at Patrick MacDonagh's
    cottage.
    Outing to Inishere (p. 92).
    Back to Galway (p. 100).
(November, 1898—May, 1899 : Paris (90 Rue d'Assas), publishes "A Story from Inishmaan" in *New Ireland Review*,
November, 1898, p. 153.)
(ii) September, 1899 : *The Aran Islands*, Part II ("After an
    absence of many months," p. 107).
    Three or four weeks on Inishmaan (105–25) at
    MacDonagh's.
    Outing to Inishmore (125–33).
    Returns on October 5, 1899 ("eve of the Parnell
    celebrations," p. 136).
November, 1899 : Paris ("A letter has come from Michael
while I am in Paris," p. 143).
(iii) Autumn, 1900 : *The Aran Islands*, Part III.
    Autumn, 1901 (had published "The Last Fortress of
    the Celt" in the *Gael*, April, 1901, p. 109.
    Inishmaan (145–70), at MacDonagh's ("September,"
    p. 152).
    Inishere ("a few days" : 170–7) at Michael Powell's.
    Inishmaan (177) at Thomas Connelly's "inn" (p. 192).
("I told them I was going back to Paris in a few days to sell
my books and my bed" (p. 178); actually gives up Paris
towards end of 1902.)
(iv) Autumn, 1902 : *The Aran Islands*, Part IV.
    Inishmaan (196–225).
    Inishere (225).
End of 1902 : London (4 Handel Street, W.C.), (cf. Masefield, *art. cit.* : "I first met John M. Synge . . . on a Monday
night of January, 1903 . . . A week, or perhaps a fortnight,
later, I met him again").

is to be remembered that M. Loti's influence had probably something to do with its literary merits. On the whole, the book as it stands is the best possible return that Synge could make to his island friends for their " kindness and friendship " [1]—though they do not themselves think so.

It would be simply criminal on our part to attempt a *résumé* of a book so full of interesting details. Moreover, we are concerned with Synge, not with Aran. However great may be what we shall venture to term the geographical, archæological and social guidebook value of *The Aran Islands*—which the present writer has had ample occasion to test for himself—there is no need of our dwelling at length on this side of the subject. The book has many aspects in common with Synge's other travel sketches, as we shall later point out. All that is needed at present is an analysis of the especial note or element that appealed to Synge in Aran.

The central impression is, we think, one of utter primitiveness.[2] Primitive life is of par-

---

Publishes " A Dream of Inishmaan," in the *Gael*, March, 1904, p. 93.

Publishes " An Impression of Aran," in the *Manchester Guardian*, January 24, 1905, p. 12.

April, 1907 : *The Aran Islands* first published in book form.

[1] *The Aran Islands*, Introduction.

[2] " The life is perhaps the most primitive that is left in Europe " (iii. 10). This is what Synge calls "the real spirit of the islands " (49), "their distinction " (56).

ticular interest to sociologists, on the one hand, with whom Australian and other savages have of late become great friends ; and, on the other hand, to artistically-minded travellers : witness R. L. Stevenson's *Vailima Letters*, which he wrote in Samoa, or Alexander Smith's *A Summer in Skye* and André Savignon's Ushant book, *Filles de la Pluie*—two works, by the way, singularly analogous in subject, if not in treatment, to Synge's own. Synge, by living in common with Aran fishermen and observing them in his own peculiar manner, was tilling practically virgin soil. He touched the rough grain of peasant nature. He got down to the bare elemental substance of a basic humanity ignorant of the world-made man and of the man-made world alike. And the prehistorically childlike quality of the Aran aborigines was felt by Synge all the more acutely as he was coming straight from over-civilized countries. He could not help comparing notes, and perceiving that, though the two social types are at bottom one and the same, the wilder one possesses a kind of aristocratic superiority.[1] The daily toil and struggle for existence of those " beings who feel their isolation in the face of a universe that wars on them with winds and seas," [2] the sheer conflict of Man and Nature left to confront each other without a single barrier between them, transcends the combatants into legendary supermen.

How this *leitmotiv* of primitiveness is harped

[1] iii. 33. [2] iii. 52.

EVICTION DESCRIBED IN ARAN BOOK

THE "POLIS" AT THE ARAN EVICTION

Photographs taken by J. M. Synge in Aran

upon and diversified throughout Synge's impressions of the Aran Islanders, with their endless talk of war,[1] their insensibility,[2] their fairy superstitions,[3] their perpetual mingling of the natural with the supernatural [4]—any reader of the book will be able to discover for himself. Inversely, it may be of interest to place on record the islanders' impressions of Synge. First, we are in a position to fix Synge's whereabouts in Aran,[5] and to lift the veil of disguise which he has thrown with such gentle delicacy over the identity of his island friends.[6] It was primarily to learn Irish again that Synge had gone to the islands.[7] And yet the people felt that he was peculiarly different from the many Irish scholars who had visited Aran before him. To-day, if

---

[1] iii. 20, 119.   [2] iii. 218.

[3] iii. 5 and *passim*.   [4] iii. 149.

[5] Cf. *supra*, p. 76 : chronology of Synge's visits to Aran.

[6] See *The Aran Islands*, Introduction. " Pat Dirane," the old story-teller who could tell " as many lies as four men " (99), is Pat Doran, now dead, but distinctly remembered by Aran folk—especially by Miss Costello, the daughter of the cess-collector who lives in Kilronan, Inishmore. The " old man " and the " old woman " are Patrick MacDonagh and his wife. Mr. MacDonagh had visited a relative of Synge's in Dublin when he first left Inishmaan as a cabin-boy (186). " Michael " (16–7) is Martin, his younger son, now married, and residing on the island. His elder brother has married an Inishere woman who does not remember Synge, and lives with her in America. As a rule the islanders say that *The Aran Islands* would have been a better book if Synge had spoken less of the people and more of Nature. (Cf. Edward J. O'Brien, *loc. cit.*)

[7] He did not come as a total stranger, as his family was known to the islanders, and a relative of his had spent some time on Aranmore forty-two years ago (iii. 9).

one asks them, they say that the man they called John was so strange and silent that no one actually knew him. He would wander about by himself, or lie on the rocks, basking in the sunshine for hours at a time or looking out over the heaving Ocean. Yet all greatly appreciated his gentleness. One islander shewed us his own photograph, which had been taken by Synge. Another exclaimed with delight: "He used to play the fiddle, and was a great conjurer." In the book we find him shewing them gymnastic feats, going a-shooting with them, and even rocking the cradle of the "old woman"'s little grandson.

That Synge, nurtured on the heady brew of Continental art, should not have hesitated thus to settle on rock-bound Inismeadhoin, and, despite his bad health, "rough it" amidst the ruder conditions of a life "almost patriarchal"[1] and so utterly estranged from his own, is indeed highly meritorious. Yet at first sight one finds it hard to realize how a writer endowed with such refined European culture could well adapt himself to those primal realities—could, indeed, at all understand the mind of the wild islanders. We are already but too familiar with the "littery gent" who brings his own store of æsthetic conventionalities and sophistications to bear upon an alien world, and with the artificial descriptions which generally follow. Not so with Synge. His European learning did not

[1] iii. 181.

hamper his perception of Aran life, or of Irish life at large ; nor did it make him artistically insincere. He did his best to feel at one with the people, to "start afresh" and live a new fashion of life altogether. Whether he quite succeeded is, however, a little doubtful.

Indeed, though he loved the Aran Islanders and was *with* them, he keenly felt that he was not *of* them. Not that his purely æsthetic standpoint was synonymous with unemotional detachment or objective lack of sympathy ; but simply because he was cultured, and they were not. "I feel," he says, "that I am a waif among the people. I can feel more with them than they can feel with me, and while I wander among them, they like me sometimes, yet never know what I am doing."[1] And again : "Below the sympathy we feel there is still a chasm between us."[2] Just as the Wicklow peasant considered him as one of the "quality" and addressed him as "your honour," in Aran they regarded him as a *duine uasal*—"noble person." And this sense of social distance and psychological incomprehension naturally made him very sad.

Curiously enough, we know for certain that the islanders took exception to several passages in Synge's book. For instance, they strongly resented the anecdote recorded by Synge of how Old Mourteen, on passing the slated house where the schoolmistress lived, said to him, "Ah, master, wouldn't it be fine to be in there and to

---

[1] iii. 120.   [2] iii. 122.

be kissing her ? "[1]   Likewise, I am told that for a long time " Michael " had a grudge against Synge (he afterwards forgave him) for having quoted *in extenso* the letters which he had addressed to him.   Mr. Yeats and Lady Gregory often conferred with Synge on the subject before the publication of the book, pointing out to him that people as perceptive as the Aran Islanders would surely object to being used as literary material, and that despite Synge's precaution to change the names of the inhabitants and to disguise their real identity, their very fewness would always make them easily recognizable. The fact is that however dearly the Aran Islesmen cherish the memory and regret the early death of the man who first made them famous, on the whole they rather dislike Synge's book. This is indeed bound up with a general state of mind in Ireland—a curious supersensitiveness to adverse criticism in the foreign Press.   Nobody likes to be written about, and the Aran Islanders have been so victimized in this respect — especially by American lady journalists — that they have everybody's sympathy.   I find an interesting example of that feeling in the sad scathing which some unhappy gentleman, whose crime was that of recording personal impressions of the Aran Islanders, received in a little book of Irish small-talk entitled *Mion-Chomhrádh : Leabhar Cainte Gaedhilge-Béarla*, by Mr. Tomás Ua Concheanainn (known as Tomás Bán),

_____
[1] iii. 13.

crowned at the Oireachtas in 1901, and published by the Gaelic League in 1904. The dialogue[1] shews a fine fury which would not be disowned by the enemies of the *Playboy*, were the passage intended for Synge himself, which it is not. Here it is in all its vigour—

"Chuala mé go raibh aon ghlincín amháin a sgríobh ag na páipéir, agus ag páipéir Shasana freisin, ag stealla-mhagadh faoi mhuinntir na n-oileán."

"A' ndeir tú sin liom?"

"Deirim maise."

"Tumadh maith faoi'n sáile badh cheart a thabhairt do'n chladhaire, agus barr na bróige 'san mása i ndiaidh an fholctha."

"Shaothruigh sé go maith é."

"Tá na mílte fáilte roimhe gach aon 'san oileán, acht creid mé ann nach gcuirfidh muid suas le masladh ná tarcuisne." . . .

"Creid mise ann go mbeidh súil agam-sa i ndiaidh an bhuachalla úd a rinne magadh fúinn ins na páipéir."

Which, being literally interpreted, signifies:

"I heard there was one 'ghlincín' [silly person] who wrote to the papers, and to the English papers at that, hurling ridicule on the islanders."

"Do you tell me so?"

"I do indeed."

"A good ducking under the salt water the

---

[1] *Op. cit.*, pp. 74–6.

coward should get, and the top of a boot in the tender part after the bath."

" He well deserved it."

" There are thousands of welcomes before everybody to the island ; but, believe me, we will not put up with insults." . . .

" Believe me, *I* shall have an eye after that boy who ridiculed us in the papers."

The adventures Synge met with in 1903, during his tour in West Kerry and Blasket Island, do not materially differ from those he encountered in Aran. Needless to say, he had to put up with very doubtful comfort in the wilds, and suffered hardships which may have impaired his health. This third series of impressions, however, deserves a brief notice, not only because of its beautiful style, but also as throwing a flashlight on Synge's methods of observation. He now tried—whether attending a performance at a country circus[1] or watching the quaint humours of Puck Fair[2]—to see the people in the mass. And this slight change must be borne in mind as a transition to Synge's subsequent attitude.

He later continued to explore the Irish hinterland by starting with Mr. Jack B. Yeats on a tour through the Congested Districts (June 3 to

---

[1] *In West Kerry*, iv. 74.

[2] *Ibid.*, 120 *et seq.* For another description of Puck Fair see Mr. Robert Lynd's *Rambles in Irish Places* (London : Mills & Boon, 1912). Cf. also Mr. Jack B. Yeats's *Life in the West of Ireland* (Dublin : Maunsel, 1912).

J. M. SYNGE DRIVING ON A CAR IN CONNEMARA

From a water-colour by Jack B. Yeats

July 2, 1905), the routes followed being from Galway to Gorumna and Carna, then from Athlone to Ballina and Belmullet. Mr. Jack B. Yeats kept diaries of the excursion which we expect have been preserved, and he has set down his memories of his travelling companion—who, he informs us, being the elder one, was in command of the trip—in a short but charming essay entitled *With Synge in Connemara*.[1] As to the twelve papers in which Synge himself has recounted his experiences on the mainland, they are distinctly journalistic, and, perhaps, did not quite demand republication.[2] Yet they are interesting in view of the fact just referred to— Synge's slight swerving from his original standpoint. *In the Congested Districts* consists of articles rather loosely strung together, and intended for the English readers of an English newspaper, most of them unacquainted with social conditions in Ireland. Synge therefore adopts the less artistic and more distinctively

---

[1] *Ap*. W. B. Yeats, *op. cit.*, pp. 39–43. Mr. Jack B. Yeats had already exhibited at 9 Merrion Row, Dublin, from October 23 to Nov. 2, 1901, a series of sketches of life in the West of Ireland (cf. *Samhain*, No. 1).

[2] It is because of the reprinting of the articles that Mr. W. B. Yeats withdrew his introduction to the Collected Edition, now published separately as *Synge and the Ireland of his Time*. The Executors said that a scrap of paper had been found with a sentence by Synge to the effect that selections might be taken from the Congested Districts series. The Wicklow and Kerry articles alone were intended for republication : " I have a lot of Kerry and Wicklow articles that would go together into a book " (Synge in a letter to Mr. W. B. Yeats, May 4, 1908, printed in *op. cit.*, Preface).

sociological attitude of the descriptive reporter, investigating with real economic insight the causes of pauperism in this distressed country-side. He directly interviews the peasantry, and is almost overwhelmingly impressed by the countless evils—the greatest of all being emigration—that the Gael is heir to in these so-called "uneconomic holdings." He delves into the reports of the Department of Agriculture and Technical Instruction,[1] or describes with unsparing exactness social life as such in the typical small town of the West.[2] And, to conclude, the thoughtful Synge goes even to the length of suggesting "possible remedies."[3]

This is the place to say something of Synge's politics. In the Connemara papers he avowedly subscribes himself a Home Ruler,[4] and although the Irish wail or whimper against English oppression is practically never given vent to in his works,[5] yet his leaning to the national side was indubitably sincere. Still he never was—and this is another trait which distinguishes him from the common Irishman—politically inclined. There is a consensus of opinion among his friends on the point. "Synge seemed by nature unfitted to think a political thought," writes Mr. W. B. Yeats,[6] "and with the exception of one sentence,

---

[1] iv. 189.   [2] iv. 232.   [3] iv. 239.
[4] iv. 245. Synge "indoctrinated" his nephews, causing them to become Nationalists "without their knowing it." Synge was an ardent Parnellite.
[5] Synge said he had given up reading Irish history "because it made him sick."   [6] *Op. cit.*, p. 11.

spoken when I first met him in Paris,[1] that implied some sort of Nationalist conviction, I cannot remember that he spoke of politics." Mr. J. B. Yeats describes him in the margin of Mr. Warren Barton Blake's copy of the *Playboy* as "an ardent Home Ruler and Nationalist . . . yet so little pugnacious that he never declared his opinions unless under some sort of compulsion. A resolute peaceful man." [2] In the words of Lady Gregory, "he seemed to look on politics and reforms with a sort of tolerant indifference."[3] "He was," says Mr. John Masefield,[4] "the only Irishman I have ever met who cared nothing for . . . the political . . . issue." This puts the truth admirably. Synge was a man of practically no opinions in an opinion-ridden country. Had he taken an interest in politics, it would have been the interest of the man who watches a dispute for the fun of the thing, and, with a mischievous wisdom, forbears from taking sides.[5]

---

[1] In Paris Synge had been intermittently Socialist. He felt that things went wrong. But he violently disagreed with the methods of French nationalism and anti-semitism, which he called "une fumisterie."

[2] W. B. Blake, "John Synge and his Plays," *The Dial* (Chicago), January 16, 1911, p. 38.

[3] *English Review, art. cit.*

[4] *C. R., art. cit.*

[5] "One night when we were still producing plays in a little hall, certain members of the company [most patriotic in those days] told him [Synge] that a play on the Rebellion of '98 would be a great success. After a fortnight he brought them a scenario which read like a chapter out of Rabelais. Two

JOHN MILLINGTON SYNGE

Even the sharp contrast between his æsthetic attitude in the Wicklow essays and in the Aran book and his more or less sociological standpoint in the Kerry and Connemara papers is only apparent ; for, if we examine the latter more closely, we find that the " remedies " he advocates are remedies coming from within, not from without ; in other words, that he essentially relies on the old resources of tradition and conservatism, not on wholesale transformations based on up-to-date ideals.   One perceives him a little incredulous even of the Gaelic League[1] which, however, was perhaps the only one of all present-day Irish " movements " that he personally patronized.   His view is that " one's first feeling, as one comes back among these people . . . where nearly everyone is interesting and attrac-

---

women, a Protestant and a Catholic, take refuge in a cave, and there quarrel about religion, abusing the Pope or Queen Elizabeth and Henry VIII, but in low voices, for the one fears to be ravished by the soldiers, the other by the rebels.   At last one woman goes out because she would sooner any fate than such wicked company " (W. B. Yeats, *op. cit.*, p. 11).   When Lady Gregory's *White Cockade* was first produced in December, 1905, Synge said that her method " had made the writing of historical drama again possible" (Lady Gregory, *Irish Folk-History Plays*, Putnams, 1912, ii. 194).   Very characteristic of Synge were the lines by Raleigh which he was wont to quote and which he inscribed on one of his portraits (cf. Appendix B, No. 7) :

"If Church and State reply,
Give Church and State the lie."

[1] iv. 245.   Synge loathed the idea of "movements" or "schools."   He wanted individual writers, and said that one of his young Irish fellow-dramatists had lost a good deal of his talent by joining the Gaelic League.

tive, is a dread of any reform that would tend to
lessen their individuality rather than any very
real hope of improving their well-being."[1]   Of
course, " it is part of the misfortune of Ireland
that nearly all the characteristics which give
colour and attractiveness to Irish life are bound
up with a social condition that is near to
penury."[2]   But this is " the desolation that is
mixed everywhere with the supreme beauty of
the world."[3]   Nay, it is " the utter loneliness
and desolation of the place that has given these
people their finest qualities."[4]   And we daresay
that, had Synge been given the choice between
the local note of distinction and the peasant's
material welfare, there is little doubt that, for all
his abundant sympathy, he would have chosen
the former.

The gist of the matter lies in the fact that,
even in this last series of articles wherein Synge
professes to deal with contemporary social
problems—and this mainly, if not solely, for the
sake of his English reader—he remains more profoundly interested in the Ireland of the past.[5]
By placing his confidence, not in radical legisla-
tion, but in the common sense and deliberate

---

[1] iv. 158.   [2] *Ibid.*
[3] iv. 71.   [4] iv. 98.
[5] Cf. Synge's remark in the introduction to *The Aran
Islands* : " The other islands are more primitive, but even on
them changes are being made, *that it was not worth while to
deal with in the text.*"   Cf. also the synopsis of persons in *The
Well of the Saints* : " Scene—some lonely mountainous district
in the east of Ireland *one or more centuries ago.*"

procrastination of the peasant, he shews that he is a man with the " ould knowledge." Below the primitiveness of the Irish countryman of to-day, he finds the old-world civilization of the ancient Gael. Modernness to him means un-Irishness.[1]

It is significant in this connection that Synge throughout his prose observations hardly gives us any idea of perhaps the most striking feature of the Irish peasant : his intense Catholic piety. One would never suspect, on reading these essays, that the Irish country-folk are Christian worshippers whose religious feeling is often carried to an absurd excess of superstition and almost to fetishism. To Synge, the Irish peasant is a latter-day Pagan, on whose old-time heathendom the Christian faith has been artificially and superficially grafted—

" Before they covered the coffin an old man kneeled down by the grave and repeated a simple prayer for the dead. There was an irony in these words of atonement and Catholic belief spoken by voices that were still hoarse with the cries of pagan desperation." [2]

This was at a funeral in Aran. But in West Kerry [3] also Synge met people who believed in the Tir-na-nOg, the Elysium of pre-Christian

---

[1] He detested all influences modernizing the Irish peasantry : " I saw him visibly moved once to sadness when someone told him how tourists had spoiled the country people in Ireland " (John Masefield, *art. cit.*). Synge added : " The Irish peasants spoil quickly because they are so simple."

[2] iii. 52.   [3] iv. 131.

Ireland. It therefore becomes evident that the Irish peasantry as portrayed by Synge in his essays is closely akin to the aboriginal Gaedhealtacht ; in other words, that Synge's solely artistic preoccupations led him to take an interest in the modern Irishman almost only in so far as he typifies a survival of the dateless Irishman of the sagas.

This attempt of Synge to cut himself adrift from current associations and to disentangle the antique Irish race from the formidable complexus of present-day life is, in the first place, a national service. But it is simultaneously a means of self-expression. Ireland is to Synge what the colours on a palette are to a painter, a something wherewith to depict one's own soul. He does not perhaps so much use himself to interpret Ireland as he uses Ireland to interpret himself. And this is the general import of these *Reisebilder* : they are both a revelation of Synge's intimate nature and a direct preparation to his art.

On the one hand, the typical Irish scenery is in strange unison with his individual outlook. Synge is a man of many moods ; and the temperamental scenery of the West, in its alternate sunny gaiety and rain-soaked sullenness, with the red dresses of the women ever and always dotting the background, awakens an equally varied response. Sometimes, as in that wonderful sentence in which Synge describes himself as " existing merely in his perception of the waves and of the crying birds and the smell of seaweed," [1] the harmony is so supreme that his feeling for Nature is almost carried to the pitch of a neurotic hyperæsthesis. Very seldom indeed is the scenery painted for its own sake—but rather to convey some psychical essence or human atmosphere. Nearly all the descriptions of Wicklow landscapes are meant to carry with them the baleful " shadow of the glen " and give the reader a sense of the " oppression of the hills." [2] At the same time Nature is freed from all glamour and meretricious romance ; nothing is unduly prettified, and Synge, in deliberately brushing past externals themselves to grasp the inner significance of the scene, hints at and suggests rather than fully develops his landscape, generally confining his descriptions to succinct and so to speak parenthetical asides. " Bars of purple cloud stretched across the sound where immense waves were rolling from the west, wreathed with snowy phantasies of spray. Then there was the bay full of green delirium, and the Twelve Pins touched with mauve and scarlet in the east." [3]

But the typical Irish peasant equally fits in with his subjective humour. Not that he sees him whole in his mind's eye ; on the contrary, these essays can in a way be taken as actual documents ; but with his singular gift of vision, and his constant comparative attitude, he succeeds in

---

[1] iii. 153.   [2] iv. 13.   [3] iii. 113.
[4] Throughout the prose essays he compares the people and the scenery of one district of Ireland with those of another

implicitly fusing all the provincial types he has
seen into an average mental representation of the
Irish peasant. The peasant as he conceives him
is characterized by his essential gloominess. He
is as different from the " ragged, humorous type
that was once thought to represent the real
peasant of Ireland "[1]—the dare-devil, harum-
scarum peasant of Anglo-Irish fiction—as London is from Aran. No wonder that Synge's
picture of his fellow-countrymen should be so
pessimistic, since he is treating of old Ireland in
its decadence, not of young Ireland in its san-
guine expectations. Moreover, his nature draws
him to the darker side of Irish life, not—to
borrow a phrase from " Fiona MacLeod "—to
the " blither Irish Celt." In Wicklow or Kerry,
in Mayo or Aran, the peasant's extraordinary
wildness and the mad scenes met with in those
parts are congenial to Synge's ironical brooding.
" Some incident of tramp life gives a local
human intensity to the shadow of one's own
mood." [2] But the impression culminates in
what may be styled the spirituality of the Irish
countryfolk. They are born poets, the descend-
ants of the ancient bards that were chased to
the West. Hence the " affinity between the
moods of those people and the moods of varying
rapture and dismay that are frequent in artists
and in certain forms of alienation." [3]

district or of Continental Europe (iii. 136, 148, 179, 181,
etc.).

[1] iii. 173.　　　　[2] iv. 6.　　　　[3] iii. 49.

JOHN MILLINGTON SYNGE

In brief, Synge discovers mirrored in the
scenery and people of his native soil all that
lies concealed within himself. But it is not
only the food his soul hungers for that he finds
in Ireland ; it is also the material exactly suited
to his literary genius. And we may now conclude by drawing attention to the three elements
of interest common to all these prose topographies, wherein all his later work is as it were
virtually contained.

There is, to begin with, the linguistic interest.
What Synge finds in the cabins of his Eastern
and Western friends is good talk. We are told
that he took down curious phrases wherever he
went,[1] and in these note-books of day-to-day
experiences we find him listening to the bewil-
dering speech of the people [2] and making countless remarks and comparisons about their intonation and way of pronouncing.[3] It is not
only his knowledge of Gaelic that he improves
by roaming through the country ; it is also his
familiarity with Ireland's English speech. The
peculiarities of the Irish peasant's broken English are reproduced with painstaking accuracy.
Very likely Synge would never have achieved
much through the medium of ordinary English ;
only dialect, and dialect used in a fashion hitherto
unknown, could serve his artistic purpose. This
he discovered in the wilds, and the reader of
these essays more than once comes across whole

---

[1] W. B. Yeats, *op. cit.*, p. 31.
[2] iii., 1 and *passim.*   [3] iii. 8, 180, etc.

sayings, tirades and fragments of dialogue that will, with very slight alterations, be found in Synge's plays.[1]

Next, there is the folklore interest. Synge hears from the lips of the peasants stories as fresh and rude as anything in the literature of the Middle Ages, and these he records just as they are told. These narratives are by far the best things in the travel notes, being remarkable not only for their variety and picturesque extravagance, and the vivid style in which they are couched, but also for the aptness with which Synge, possessed of wide European learning, likens them to similar tales that can be heard in other lands and presents us with short studies in comparative folk-literature.[2]

Last, but not least, there is the specifically dramatic interest. The prose essays are the raw material out of which Synge will fashion all his plays, the matrix in which the dramas, comedies and farces remain like jewels not yet cut, polished and set. All his plots, or incidents which will be incorporated in the scenarios of the plays, have their germs in the folk-tales just referred to. The odd characters he meets are understudies for

---

[1] Thus the place-name " The Stooks of the Dead Woman " in the *Playboy* (ii. 13) was borrowed from *In West Kerry* (iv. 119); Michael James asking Christy's name (ii. 26) recalls to mind the Blasket Islander asking Synge the same question (iv. 90); the publican's eugenic condemnation of bachelordom (ii. 99) is but an echo of Old Mourteen's remarks in *The Aran Islands* (iii. 133), etc.

[2] *e. g.* iii. 30–1.

his future personages ; it seems as if the playwright and his *dramatis personæ* were in anticipation rehearsing off the stage.[1] It will be interesting to compare in due time the sources of the plays as they are found in the journals with the dramatized versions. Still this question of "origins" is comparatively immaterial. What is far more important is to find in these impressions of rambles characteristic observations which clearly announce the awakening of Synge's dramatic propensities. Thus, in *Wicklow*, he remarks that "if a playwright chose to go through the Irish country-houses he would find material, it is likely, for many gloomy plays that would turn on the dying away of the old families, and on the lives of the one or two delicate girls that are left so often to represent a dozen hearty men who were alive a generation ago."[2] In *The Aran Islands* he strikingly refers to "the dramatic emphasis of the folk-tale,"[3] and he perceives infinite dramatic possibilities in the contrast between "the strangely reticent temperament of the islanders" and "the passionate spirit that expresses itself at odd moments only with magnificent words and gestures."[4] Again, in *The Congested Districts*, he informs us that the Geesala district "has, unexpectedly enough, a strong branch of the Gaelic League, and small

---

[1] Compare, for example, Pegeen Mike of the *Playboy* with the little Hostess of *In West Kerry*.
[2] iv. 53. This has been achieved by Mr. Edward Martyn, *e. g.* in his play *Grangecolman*.   [3] iii. 110.   [4] iii. 82.

Irish plays are acted frequently in the winter." [1]
The texts here speak for themselves, and bear
witness to an irresistible calling.

With good reason, then, Synge will write in
the preface to the *Playboy* that "all art is a
collaboration." [2] His collaborators are the whole
Irish peasantry. A nation will speak through
him. And it will speak in the dramatic way,
which best of all can express the profuse vitality
of these prose observations — of the people
observed and of the observer himself.

---

[1] iv. 222. Cf. his letter (August, 1906) on Gaelic plays *ap.*
Lady Gregory, *art. cit.*, p. 564.
[2] ii. 3.

JOHN MILLINGTON SYNGE

CHAPTER V

THE IRISH DRAMATIC MOVEMENT BEFORE SYNGE AND HIS RELATION TO THE ABBEY THEATRE SCHOOL

I

A PRELIMINARY retrospect of the literary and sociological evolution of the Irish theatre has been thought indispensable for a full and proper understanding of Synge's own dramatic standpoint.

The history of Irish stage literature remains hitherto unwritten ; yet one feels tempted to sketch it. Ancient Ireland, strange to say, never knew drama proper.[1] Yet the dramatic substance is abundantly, though implicitly, present in all her literature. On the one hand, the nearest approach to drama in ancient Ireland consists of dialogues in Gaelic[2] — the most

---

[1] Cf. Georges Dottin, "La Littérature Gaélique de L'Irlande," *Revue de Synthèse Historique,* vol. iii, p. 63 ; Yann Morvran-Goblet, " La Littérature celtique au XXᵉ siècle," *La Revue,* Sept. 15 and Oct. 1, 1908 : " Le théâtre, ce genre si peu celtique et surtout si peu irlandais " (p. 145) ; A. le Braz, *Essai sur l'Histoire du Théâtre Celtique* (Paris University thesis : Calmann-Lévy, 1904), ch. ii, pp. 46–7.

[2] Cf. Douglas Hyde, *A Literary History of Ireland* (London : T. Fisher Unwin, 1899), p. 511 ; Eleanor Hull, *A Text-Book of Irish Literature* (Dublin : Gill ; London : Nutt, 1906), vol. i.

famous instance being *Agallamh Oisín agus Phádraic* (the Colloquy between Ossian[1] and St. Patrick),[2] in which the Pagan or heroic and the Christian views of life are dramatically contrasted. This and other later dialogues[3] are vividly interpreted on platforms by Irish speakers even at the present day. On the other hand, the old Irish epics afford proof that the Irish genius is not lacking in dramatic powers. Remarkable fecundity in the conception of plot and incident is one of the chief characteristics that differentiate the early literature of the Gael from that of the mournful and uninventive Anglo-Saxon ; dialogue, carried on with a terseness, wit and flexibility unknown to the formal epic manner is an amazingly copious element ; and some of the finest tragic themes—the legend of Deirdre for example—are to be found in the

---

[1] Usheen.

[2] Published in the *Transactions of the Ossianic Society*, vol. iv. Dublin, 1854–61 ; re-told in Part III of Miss Alice Milligan's dramatic triology, *Oisín and Pádraic ;* in J. H. Simpson's *Poems of Oisín, Bard of Erin* (M'Glashan & Gill, 1857), pp. 61–184 ; cf. also Jeremiah Curtin, *Myths and Folk-Lore of Ireland* (Boston : Little, Brown & Co., 1900), pp. 327–42 ("Oisin in Tir-na-nOg") ; and Mr. W. B. Yeats's *Wanderings of Oisin*. On the MSS. and printed recensions of this dialogue, cf. *Revue Celtique*, vol. xxxiii, No. 1, p. 4.

[3] Such as the dialogues between a sinner and Death (*An Bás*) or an old man and Death ; note also how the dialogue method obtains in recent Irish work like *Seádna*, by Canon O'Leary (an tAthair Peadar), *Two Men from the Country*, and the numerous dramatic recitations between two lovers of different creeds (see W. P. Ryan, *The Pope's Green Island* (London : Nisbet, 1912, ch. xxiv).

JOHN MILLINGTON SYNGE

sagas, throughout which scenarios are scattered.[1] This dramatic substratum of old Irish epics is best exemplified in Ireland's greatest romance, the *Táin Bó Chuailgne* (Cattle-raid of Cooley or Quelney), of which several translations [2] are now available.

The tardy flowering of the Irish drama strikes one therefore with great surprise, and it can but be wondered at that the dramatic form proper has not been precipitated or worked out long ago. The Gaelic epics—which in their turn probably represent the outcome of a previous lyrical age [3]—are comparable to an indistinct protoplasmic mass containing dramatic germs or possibilities, and out of which tragi-comic life would fain leap forth. Yet it does not do so.[4]

---

[1] See an article by Prof. Vida D. Scudder, of Wellesley College, in *Poet-lore*, vol. xvi, p. 46 ff.; A. le Braz, *op. cit.*, ch. i; *Encyclopædia Britannica* (11th ed.), *s. v.* "Celt," p. 627.

[2] Prose translation by Miss Winifred Faraday, M.A. (London : Nutt, Grimm Library, No. 16, 1904); blank-verse rendering by Mrs. Mary A. Hutton (Dublin : Maunsel, 1910); French translation by d'Arbois de Jubainville (*Revue Celtique*, vols. xxviii–xxxii); German translation by E. Windisch (*Irische Texte*, extraband, Leipzig, 1905). Cf. *Readings from the Táin*, by John Strachan (published by *Eriu*, the journal of the School of Irish Learning). Mr. David Nutt announces *The Ancient Irish Heroic Tale : The Cooley Cattle Raid*, the first complete English translation from the Irish of the Book of Leinster and allied versions, by Prof. John Dunn, of the Catholic University, Washington.

[3] Cf. Ernest Bovet, *Lyrisme, Épopée, Drame : une loi de l'histoire littéraire expliquée par l'évolution générale* (Paris : Colin, 1911).

[4] Gustave Cohen, "La renaissance du théâtre breton et l'œuvre de l'Abbé le Bayon" (*Mercure de France*, Dec. 16, 1911 and Jan. 1, 1912) : "Toujours est-il que les dialogues si nombreux dans l'épopée irlandaise n'ont point abouti à des drames."

Why, then, does the history of the Irish theatre, for upwards of nine centuries, remain a total blank ? The causes are numerous. In the first place, the mysticism and undemonstrative contemplativeness of the Irish Gael—though less pronounced in him than in the Scots Gael—conceivably hampered the free development of his dramatic impulse. Next, the literature of ancient Ireland is mostly narrative ; there were professional story-tellers, the *fili*[1] and, more especially, the *shanachies* or *seanchuidhe ;* and the narrative relation of events, from a literary point of view, is the very opposite of their dramatic externalization or visualization. Besides, had the Irish had a drama of their own, they could not have got it printed under the régime of oppression enforced on Ireland by her successive invaders. But there is one reason deeper than all, which lies in the fact that Irish history, for a considerable number of years, was itself the most poignant of tragedies. Ireland, living through real drama, had no time nor desire for dramas of imagination. The " play-activity," which is the essence of all art, and which extracts literary fiction from actual life, could not possibly exist in Ireland as long as drama and life were one and the same thing.[2]

---

[1] *Encyclopædia Britannica, loc. cit.,* p. 625.

[2] Likewise, for a long time, it was impossible to publish a humorous paper in Ireland : there is so much real humour in Irish life ! Similarly, in ancient Scotland, the Highland chieftains warred against each other, and there was no need for fictitious stage-fights.

JOHN MILLINGTON SYNGE

The Irish people, being unable to develop a native drama, became the dramatic providers of other nations. But drama itself may be viewed from two distinct standpoints: that of acting and that of playwriting. That the Irish were not lacking in the former power there is ample evidence. Even a Celtophobe will own that many of the great so-called English actors have been either Jews or Celts[1]—more particularly Irish Celts. Ireland gave the English stage such names as Macklin, Peg Woffington,[2] Spranger Barry, Sheridan Knowles,[3] Mossop, Macready, senior, the Blands, the Glovers, the Boucicaults and Mrs. Henry Irving; to America she gave the elder John Drew,[4] Virginia Earl,[5] Ada Rehan and James O'Neill.[6] Such a list—which

---

[1] Cf. *The Green Room Book*, ed. by John Parker (London: T. Sealy Clark, 1909), p. 633: "Footlight Families," by J. M. Bulloch (Editor of the *Graphic*). Prof. York Powell ("Irish Influences on English Literature," *Freeman's Journal* (Dublin), April 8, 1902 (a lecture delivered before the National Literary Society, Dublin, April 7, 1902), republished in Oliver Elton's *Frederic York Powell* (Clarendon Press, Oxford), vol. ii, pp. 297–301), shews that the "English" theatre would have been in a sorry plight without the Irish playwrights, from Roger Boyle and Sir John Denham downwards.

[2] Cf. Charles Reade's comedy, *Masks and Faces*, or his novel, *Peg Woffington*.

[3] Cf. Jules Douady, *Vie de William Hazlitt l'essayiste* (Paris: Hachette, 1907), p. 235.

[4] Art. by Acton Davies, in *Munsey's Magazine* (N.Y.), Feb. 1906, p. 630.

[5] *Munsey's Magazine*, April, 1904, p. 147.

[6] Art. by Herbert N. Casson on "The Irish in America," in *Munsey's Magazine*, April, 1906, pp. 97, 100; *The Irish in America*, by Patrick Higgins and F. V. Conolly (The Irish

could be considerably lengthened—testifies to an extraordinarily vital histrionic instinct among the Irish.[1] Dramatic talent runs wild all over the Emerald Isle. Nay, the theatrical propensity or vocation (which is conspicuous in the very gesticulation with which the average Irishman punctuates his speech) assumes the proportions of a real Hibernian trait, of a veritable sociological phenomenon in Ireland past and present. The Irish, who have been born missionaries, born soldiers, born orators, born politicians, born " poets and dreamers,"[2] born musicians, are also born actors. One cannot open an Irish newspaper without finding some mention of private theatricals even in the remotest districts. Dramatic societies have spread all over the land ; presumably they represent the typically Irish form of club life, understood as the gregarious life of such social units as the sporting societies of England, the religious assemblies of Scotland, or the musical gatherings of Wales. Gaelic pieces are acted in the tiniest villages by pupils in schools and by church brotherhoods. Parish priests are becoming dramatists, and turn out diminutive masques and plays for their congrega-

Library, vol. iv ; London : John Ouseley, 1909), p. 93. Cf. " The Irish People and the Stage," by Floyd Davis, in the *Green Book Album* (Chicago), August, 1909.

[1] Cf. W. B. Yeats, *Samhain*, 1904, or *Collected Works* (Bullen), vol. iv, p. 133.

[2] The title of a well-known volume by Lady Gregory (Dublin : Hodges & Figgis ; London : John Murray, 1903).

tions to present. Charming anecdotes[1] relate how swift and sensitive, especially in perception of ideal suggestions, is an Irish audience.[2]

It seems plausible to assert that the influence of religious conditions has had much to do with the preservation of the native Irish dramatic instinct—which, not being at liberty to develop under the check of the oppressor, would have of itself fast died out, had it not been fostered by some external factor. The fact just referred to of Irish priests arranging theatrical entertainments in the rural districts, and as it were taking the lead of the modern Gaelic dramatic movement, is, we think, peculiarly significant. Some dramatic "virtue" seems to be inherent in the Roman Catholic worship.[3] "If Calvinism," writes Francis Grierson,[4] "has made the Scotch mind more metaphysical than æsthetical, the symbols of Catholicism have helped to keep the Irish character mystical and poetic." "Dramatic" would perhaps be more exact than "poetic." There is an avowedly spectacular, almost theatrical, element in the Roman Catholic service: at Mass, the priest, as

---

[1] Cf. W. B. Yeats, *loc. cit.*

[2] "Like the Japanese, the Celts were always quick to take an artistic hint; they avoid the obvious and the commonplace; the half-said to them is dearest" (Kuno Meyer, *Selections from Ancient Irish Poetry* (London : Constable, 1911), p. xiii).

[3] It is significant in this connection that specimens of the choræographic Scotch-Gaelic drama are to be found only in the Catholic islands : the "Wee-Frees" have killed folk-art.

[4] *The Celtic Temperament* (London : George Allen, 1901), p. 38.

one might express it in an untranslatable French phrase, *joue la scène de la cène.* This scenic element is perhaps still more pronounced in Roman Catholicism as it is practised in Ireland, where the extreme piety of the people is apt to over-emphasize the concrete, ritualistic side of the service.

Given this presumable influence of Catholicism on the Irish drama, one will ask why there have been so few mystery plays [1] in fifteenth and sixteenth century Ireland, at a time when these were numerous all over the rest of Europe. This, in our judgment, is due, first, to the unsettled state of the country at the period, then, and chiefly, to the precise, almost literal Catholic orthodoxy of the Irish people, which makes them think the representation of the divine mysteries on the stage profane and sacrilegious. We remember being present at a Gaelic Passion play in Dublin [2] at which the producer felt the necessity of coming before the curtain to explain the wholly edifying purpose of the performance, lest the audience should consider it blasphemous.

It has been thought interesting to recall this interdependence of religion and the theatre as a possible explanation of the survival of Ireland's stage-acting instinct. But we must now turn to

---

[1] Cf. James J. O'Neill, "Irish Theatrical History: A Bibliographical Essay," in *An Leabharlann,* vol. ii, No. 2, p. 115; "The Irish Stage," by Geraldine M. Haverty, in *The Gael,* July, 1900, p. 218, and subsequent issues.

[2] *Cluiche Tri-Rannach,* by Pádraic MacPiarais (Abbey Theatre, April 7, 1911).

the other aspect of the dramatic problem: playwriting. This, again, is a vast field to survey.
Irish plays are numberless. But classification
will facilitate our study. What is an Irish play?
   The phrase may designate either an Anglo-
Irish play or a Gaelic play. An Anglo-Irish
play is a play written in English on an Irish
subject. A Gaelic play is a play in Irish Gaelic
on an Irish subject.
   Mention should also be made of plays written
by Irishmen for the English stage, with no
specially Irish intention—just as there have been
and ever will be Irish-born actors in plays English both in language and subject. Congreve's,[1]
Farquhar's, Goldsmith's, Sheridan's and Oscar
Wilde's comedies, and most of Mr. George
Bernard Shaw's stage-conversations, belong to
this third class of plays, which might also, in a
way, be labelled " Irish." It would indeed be
an attractive study to examine from a specifically
Irish standpoint these " English " plays by Irish-
born dramatists, in order to discern whether any
trace of their authors' peculiar Irish idiosyncrasies could not, after all, be detected in their
" English " characters—and whether, generally
speaking, apparently anglicized Irish men of
letters, who are usually " stolen " as " English "
writers by English critics who think them
worth stealing,[2] do not remain Irish in spite of

---

[1] Congreve was English by birth ; but he had spent all his
youth in Ireland.
[2] Thus Macaulay " stole " Swift in his well-known essay.

themselves. Of course, such an inquiry does not concern us here; yet we dare say that the answer to it would very likely be positive, and, in particular, it would not be very difficult to shew that Wilde's or Shaw's humour is of an Irish, not of an English, quality; but, again, we must be contented with throwing this out as a suggestion merely.

Anglo-Irish plays of the older school—whether wholly taken up with an Irish theme, or only containing certain Irish characters in a non-Irish plot[1]—all had in common a particular conception of the Irish temperament embodied in the so-called "stage Irishman," a type against which the present-day Irish dramatic movement stands in professed reaction, but which—as we shall see in Synge's own case—it has not perhaps quite succeeded in rooting out.

To outline the genesis of the stage Irishman,[2] and classify the Tudor, Stuart, Jacobite, eighteenth-century and modern varieties of the type, would require a dissertation. One finds him not only in drama, but in fiction; he has been evolved both by anti-Irish Irishmen, English-

[1] Cf. W. J. Lawrence, "Irish Character in English Dramatic Literature (*Gentleman's Magazine*, Aug. 1890, pp. 178–91); "Irish Types in Old-time English Drama" (*Anglia*, Bd. 35, 3. Heft, p. 347–56). Of course, we need not refer to foreign plays on Irish subjects, such as Calderon's *El Purgatorio de San Patricio* and Lope de Vega's *El Mayor Prodigio*.

[2] Cf. W. H. Gratton-Flood, "The Inventor of the Stage Irishman" (*New Ireland Review*, April, 1905); "The Evolution of the Stage Irishman," by W. J. Lawrence, Belfast, in *The Gael*, January, 1903, pp. 13–15.

men and Americans, and by totally unprejudiced writers belonging to the three nationalities, just because he had been handed down to them as a ready-made, stereotyped mental image. Shakespeare,[1] Ben Jonson,[2] Dekker [3] and Ford,[4] and later Smollett,[5] Sheridan,[6] Thackeray,[7] Maria Edgeworth,[8] George Meredith [9] and Shaw,[10] have all portrayed stage Irishmen ; so have Farquhar,[11] Lover,[12] Lever,[13] Carleton [14] and especially Dion Boucicault ; [15] or, in America, Andrew Mack and Chauncey Olcott [16]—to name no others. Add to this the influence of the music-hall songs [17] and of the cartoons in *Punch*,[18] and you have gathered in a nutshell all the

[1] Captain MacMorris in *Henry V*, iii. 2.
[2] *Irish Masque ; New Inn.*
[3] *Old Fortunatus.*
[4] *Chronicle History of Perkin Warbeck.*
[5] O'Regan.
[6] *The Rivals* (Sir Lucius O'Trigger) ; *St. Patrick's Day.*
[7] *Irish Sketch-Book.*
[8] *Comic Dramas in Three Acts.*
[9] *Diana of the Crossways* (Mr. Sullivan Smith) ; *Celt and Saxon.*
[10] Tim Haffigan in *John Bull's Other Island.*
[11] *Foigard in the Bosti.*   [12] Handy Andy.
[13] Mickey Free, *Harry Lorrequer.*
[14] Paddy-Go-Easy.
[15] *The Colleen Bawn ; The Shaughraun ; Arrah-na-Pogue ; The Lily of Killarney.* Cf. G. B. Shaw, " Dear Harp of my Country " (*Saturday Review*, Feb. 1, 1896), reprinted as an appreciation of the *The Colleen Bawn* in *Dramatic Opinions and Essays* (London : Constable, 1907), pp. 326–32.
[16] *O'Neill of Derry.*
[17] Such as those of Denis O'Sullivan in America.
[18] Robert Lynd, *Irish and English : Portraits and Impressions* (London: F. Griffiths, 1908), p. ix.

THE STAGE IRISHMAN
By Jack B. Yeats

leading factors in the creation, growth [1] and transmission [2] of that popular type.

Now as to the type himself. By striking an average between all stage Irishmen, or rather picking out the pre-eminently notorious representatives of the personage, one is led to sketch the figure in about the following terms. The stage Irishman habitually bears the generic name of Pat, Paddy or Teague.[3] He has an atrocious Irish brogue,[4] makes perpetual jokes, blunders and bulls [5] in speaking, and never fails to utter, by way of Hibernian seasoning, some wild

---

[1] William Barrett, " Irish Drama ? " (*New Ireland Review*, March and April, 1895), p. 38 ; " Irish Drama : A Symposium " by Angus Mackay, Blake O'Connor, Jas. J. Scanlan, *ibid.*, p. 104.

[2] " Three Centuries of Stage Literature," by W. A. Henderson, *New Ireland Review*, 1897, p. 168 ; "Footsteps of the Colleen Bawn," by T. E. Galt-Gamble, *ibid.*, vol. vi, p. 27 ; Robert Lynd, *Home Life in Ireland*, pp. 178–9, 280.

[3] Irish *Tadhg* (*Anglicè* Timothy).

[4] See a letter to the Editor of the N. Y. *Nation* on " The Irishman's Brogue," by Albert Matthews, July 21, 1904, pp. 52–3.

[5] On Irish Bulls, see the *Essay on Irish Bulls*, by R. L. Edgeworth and Maria Edgeworth (London, 1802) ; *Edinburgh Review*, July, 1803, p. 398 ; *Chambers's Journal*, Aug. 26, 1866, p. 539—Nov. 1, 1879, p. 702 ; *Every Saturday*, vol. vi, p. 273 ; *The Book of Bulls*, ed. by G. R. Neilson (London : Simpkin, Marshall, 1898) ; *Irish Life and Humour in Anecdote and Story*, by Wm. Harvey (Stirling : Mackay ; London : Simpkin, Marshall), pp. 213–41 ; Mr. J. C. Percy's *Book of Bulls* (Dublin and London : Mecredy, Percy & Co., 1912). The Irish bull is not to be confused with the English malapropism : as a rule it is not sheer nonsense, but (as the Irish novels by Somerville and Ross fully shew) an impressionistic statement evading the ordinary methods of logic and language.

screech or oath[1] of Gaelic origin at every third word ; he has an unsurpassable gift of " blarney " and cadges for tips and free drinks. His hair is of a fiery red ; he is rosy-cheeked, massive and whisky-loving. His face is one of simian bestiality, with an expression of diabolical archness written all over it. He wears a tall felt hat (billicock or wideawake) with a cutty clay pipe stuck in front, an open shirt-collar, a three-caped coat, knee-breeches, worsted stockings and cockaded brogue-shoes. In his right hand he brandishes a stout blackthorn or a sprig of shillelagh, and threatens to belabour therewith the daring person who will " tread on the tails of his coat." For his main characteristics (if there is any such thing as psychology in the stage Irishman) are his swagger, his boisterousness and his pugnacity. He is always ready with a challenge, always anxious to pick a quarrel ; and peerless for cracking skulls at Donnybrook fair. *Au demeurant, le meilleur fils du monde.*

This preposterously funny conception of the Irish character, which has done duty for centuries on the English, American, and even Irish stage, is not altogether a fictitious convention. Whether the figure has been drawn from actual prototypes, or whether a few Irish car-drivers have found it advantageous to copy it in their own lives with the help of occasional touches of eccentricity, in order to please the

[1] Bedad, begorra, alanna, asthore, arrah, by chrish la, etc.

English tourist's imaginary notion of the Irishman, there is no doubt that the stage Irishman
is met with in certain districts, even nowadays.
Irish audiences accept the stage Irishman with
amusement on the comic music-hall or concert
platform. They find that the picture has done
Ireland very little harm in the long run.[1] One
may indeed urge in defence of this somewhat
absurd or extravagant representation of the son
of Erin that, if one traces it back to its *fons et
origo*, it is but the outcome of the necessity for
all drama to exaggerate or caricature national
types in order to make them typically national
and (in the hackneyed phrase) " racy of the soil "
—just as a stage-manager is apt to overdo his
local colour lest it should not be " local " enough.
If we may be pardoned an apparent truism, the
dramatic Irishman is a " stage Irishman " only
because he is an Irishman on the stage. The
burlesquing of a national character is a per-
missible form of entertainment. There is a
stage John Bull in the Parisian theatres, just as
there are stage Frenchmen in the London
musical comedies. Yet nobody takes offence,
and the French accent in the stage Frenchman's
English is inimitably funny to a French hearer.

However, of late years, the Irish people have
begun to express violent aversion to the traditional
Teague.[2] " On this side of the water," writes an

[1] Cf. W. B. Yeats, *Samhain*, 1905 (*Collected Works*, vol. iv,
p. 195).
[2] Cf. " Crusade against the Stage Irishman," in *The Gael*,
May, 1903, p. 145.

JOHN MILLINGTON SYNGE

American critic, Mr. Horatio Sheafe Krans,[1] alluding to incidents that took place at the St. Louis Exhibition in 1900, when some Irish actors refused to act in a piece in which the Irishman appeared as a buffoon, " disapproval of the stage Irishman has recently expressed itself in showers of eggs and storms of hisses—a form of protest that oddly combines rowdyism and solicitude for the national character." That the stage Irishman should thus be driven off the boards of the serious theatre is not altogether incomprehensible. He is found fault with on the score of his being but an incomplete or one-sided portrayal of the Irish nature. The common-place traits of the Hibernian character are certainly over-accentuated. Its brutal and more odious aspect is brought into undue prominence ; its gentle, sentimental and melancholy side is almost entirely overlooked. There are no re-deeming features. Irish life is reduced to a huge whiskified joke. No wonder, then, that the Irish public mind should loathe and resent the whole picture. And the portrait is taken excep-tion to all the more keenly as the Irish, like all unhappy nations, have grown extremely sensitive and " touchy " about their racial characteristics. " For centuries the Irish have been politically overwhelmed by the English, and the Jews have been persecuted by almost every other nation. It is only natural that both should be sensitive.

---

[1] *Irish Life in Irish Fiction* (N.Y. : The Columbia University Press ; London : Macmillan, 1903), pp. 224–6.

But if Ireland is to have a literature the Irish must allow themselves to be dealt with as freely as any other nation in the world." [1] Add to this that Ireland, a nation in the making, cannot afford to be publicly misrepresented on the stage—a thing which the strong, independent nations like France or England can easily tolerate.

In brief, the stage Irishman has been banned simply because Ireland has at last awakened to a sense of her ethnical dignity, to patriotic self-consciousness. We may note in passing that this has been the work not merely of the united historical forces, but, mainly, of the Gaelic League, which, by concentrating Irish nationalism on the very concept of nationality, has helped Ireland's national regeneration and ushered in as it were the dawn of an Irish *Aufklärung*. Attention must here be paid to the all-important changes brought about in the status of Irish drama by this shifting of the point of view in national self-criticism.

The whole transformation in the data of the problem may be summarized by saying that, in the main, Irish nationalism has intellectualized or spiritualized itself. Three successive stages may indeed be distinguished. The materialistic nationalism of the Fenian, " Physical Force " period, with the revolutionary and agrarian agitations that ensued in the 'eighties, gave way

[1] W. B. Yeats, *ap. Current Literature* (N.Y.), Dec. 1911, p. 676.

to an era of political or rather polemical nationalism, during which the whole dramatic energy
of the Irish race seemed to be spent in oratory,
with its gestures and *mise en scène*. The dramatic
thrill was then afforded only by the perfervid
rhetoric of the street-corner demagogue. At
that phase " the Irish question did not pass into
history because it did not pass out of politics." [1]
Still, in this transitional period the brute element
of the foregoing anarchic decade had already
been done away with ; there remained but the
half-spiritual power of eloquence. A third and
final change was brought about by the break-up
of the political movement with the so-called
" Parnell split" in 1890,[2] which turned the
country's attention from the instinctive violence
of the tactics that had obtained so far to more
rational methods of social readjustment. The
old rancours having gradually died down, the
nation gave a powerful impetus to scholarship
and began to take an interest in disinterested
learning. Fifty thousand Gaelic text-books
were sold in one year, and " the sons and
daughters of the landlords and officials began to
read." [3] The political issue passed into the background ; the cultural issue was brought to the
fore. As there had been in other countries an

---

[1] Lord Rosebery, *ap.* Michel F. J. MacDonnell, *Ireland
and the Home Rule Movement* (Dublin : Maunsel, 1908),
p. xi.
[2] Cf. W. B. Yeats, " The Irish Literary Theatre," *Literature,*
May 6, 1899, p. 474.
[3] *Ibid.*

age of "enlightened" despotism, this was one of "enlightened" Irish nationalism. Ireland at last realized that her national reconstruction would be effected not by brute force, but by intuitive or discursive intellect.

It is not difficult to shew how this resurgence of Gaelic spirituality asserts itself in all the manifestations of present-day nationalism. The most material of all problems, the land problem, is now stated in the purely intellectual terms of statistical sociology. The Irish Agricultural Organization Society has for its leaders a learned economist, Sir Horace Plunkett, and a thinker of many-sided mental activity,[1] Mr. George W. Russell ("Æ"), whose primary ideal is a psychological regeneration of the Irish peasant. The extremist party in politics, now known as the Sinn Féin party, is a body of keen dialecticians who appear to confine themselves to constructive speculation, without doing anything in the domain of practice. Its leader is Mr. Arthur Griffith, an incisive writer whom some have no hesitancy in comparing with Swift and John Mitchel.[2] Then there is the Gaelic League, with its organized and enthusiastic revival of the old Irish tongue, the old Irish dances, folklore, songs and sports, its bold educational ideal of

[1] Mr. George W. Russell is a poet, a playwright, a journalist, an art critic, an agriculturist (Editor of the *Irish Homestead*), a painter, a mystic, and a genial and admirable conversationalist.

[2] *e.g.* Mr. "George A. Birmingham" [Rev. James O. Hannay], "The Literary Movement in Ireland," *Fortnightly Review*, December, 1907, p. 957.

building up a national character,[1] which makes it not so much a language movement as a thought movement. Last, but not least, a literary renascence, itself an offshoot partly of the Gaelic League and partly of the previous patriotic Anglo-Irish school of writers headed by Thomas Davis, J. C. Mangan and Standish O'Grady, expresses most adequately the intellectualistic cravings of twentieth-century nationalism.

It was inevitable that the literary movement in its turn should be not only poetic, fictional or historical, but, first and foremost, dramatic. For "the drama was not dead but sleeping."[2] And the awakening was all the more intense as the sleep had been long. The Irish theatre, both in its Gaelic and Anglo-Irish aspects, was from the first extraordinarily prolific. There is no need here to consider the Gaelic drama. As has been pointed out, it is primarily educational or propagandist in its aim, and its literary value is small—at any rate up to the present. There are, however, some very good plays in Gaelic by Dr. Douglas Hyde (the President of the Gaelic League), Mr. W. P. Ryan, Eadmon MacNeill, Canon O'Leary, and Fr. Dineen.

It may be objected at the outset that an Anglo-Irish national theatre, or, to put it more accurately, an Irish national theatre in English,

[1] Sydney Brooks, *The New Ireland* (Dublin and London : Maunsel, 1907), p. 2.
[2] George Moore, *Hail and Farewell: I. Ave* (Tauchnitz, No. 4314), p. 47.

is little short of a contradiction in terms.[1] Should
not Irish plays be written in Gaelic only ? There
is no 'shirking the fact that the objection is
serious and, at bottom, justified. No doubt the
multitudinous shades of the Gael's thought and
feelings are ultimately incommunicable in the
rigid idiom of the " Sassenach "—unless, perhaps,
the latter be rejuvenated and unstiffened through
its being handled by the Gael. Still, it may be
urged in defence of the present Anglo-Irish
experiment that, should the modern dramatists
assimilate the Gaelic language, they would *ipso
facto* renounce their vast cosmopolitan public,
who would no longer understand them.[2] " We
are preparing, as we hope, for a day when
Ireland will speak in Gaelic, as much as Wales
speaks in Welsh, within her borders, but speak,
it may be, in English to other nations of those
truths which were committed to her when " He
set the borders of the nations according to His
nagels, as Dionysius the Areopagite has written." [3]
" Our desire is . . . to use English as a universal
language, and to save our own as a medium for
some future literature," [4] for, " from universal
use and journalism, the English language in fifty
years will be as corrupt as the Latin of the

---

[1] Cf. D. P. Moran, *The Philosophy of Irish Ireland* (Dublin :
Duffy and *Leader* Office, 1905), p. 106.

[2] Mario Borsa, *The English Stage of To-day* (London and
N. Y. : John Lane, 1908), ch. viii.

[3] W. B. Yeats, *Ideals in Ireland*, ed. by Lady Gregory
(London : at the Unicorn, 1901), p. 90.

[4] George Moore, *op. cit.*, p. 47.

eighth century, and will become . . . a sort of
Volapük, strictly limited to commercial letters
and journalism."[1]   This philological pessimism
and this provisionally bilingual ideal of Irish
drama seem to us, in a way, but a transposition
of the political problem of Home Rule, which
either means a limited autonomy—an Ireland
purely and simply represented at Westminster
by some hybrid compromise—or total severance
from England, such as the rigorous separatism
advocated by Sinn Féin.   The former of the two
stages in the dramatic as well as political question
may be but the transition to the future advent
of the latter ; but, at present, the Irish national
theatre must needs stay half-way and, " for the
next generation at least, the national literature
must be written in English."[2]   Very likely the
coming of complete Home Rule will determine
in the end the creation of a national drama in
Gaelic only.

This fundamental objection having been discussed and allowed for, we may now proceed
to recall the history of the modern Anglo-
Irish dramatic movement.   It was in 1899
that Mr. W. B. Yeats,[3] Mr. Edward Martyn,[4]
Mr. George Moore,[5] and Lady Gregory founded
the Irish Literary Theatre in Dublin under

---

[1] George Moore, *op. cit.*, p. 49.
[2] Stephen Gwynn, *To-Day and To-Morrow in Ireland*, p. 92.
[3] Cf. H. S. Krans, *W. B. Yeats and the Irish Literary Revival.*
[4] Cf. George Moore, *Hail and Farewell: I. Ave.*
[5] Cf. Lucien Maury, *Portraits Littéraires.*

the auspices of the National Literary Society
(created in 1891). The name chosen for the
new venture was peculiarly significant. It indicated a direct reaction against the unliterary
mercantilism of the British theatre, run on
strictly business or industrial lines, which had
hitherto unnaturally dumped down in the Irish
metropolis the absurdest specimens of English
"society" drama, acted by mediocre London
touring companies. Here again, in this disinterested attitude of the founders of the Irish
Literary Theatre, we seem to find a kind of
parallel to the economic state of affairs—the
contrast between Irish impecuniosity, favourable
to artistic production, and Anglo-Saxon inartistic
and even anti-artistic opulence. In the second
place, the plays had to be Irish in substance, in
contradistinction to the works of the Irish-born
playwrights, who, through an intellectual training that was both classical and English, had lost all
their racial characteristics, and wrote on English
subjects for English audiences. In fine, the
Irish Literary Theatre was broadly national, and
it did not aim at making money. It started
with a list of guarantors [1] on which figured
ardent Nationalists like John O'Leary, William
O'Brien and Miss Maud Gonne, and staunch
Unionists like Lecky, the historian, Lord Ardi-

[1] Full list in *The Gael*, June, 1899, p. 78, and *ap.* George
O'Neill, "Recent Irish Drama and its Critics," *New Ireland
Review*, March, 1906. The first £50 was the gift of Mr.
John Quinn, the brilliant New York lawyer.

laun, Lord O'Brien (the Chief Justice of Ireland),
and Lord Dufferin (formerly Ambassador of
H.B.M. in Paris). The theatre had its own
occasional organ, *Beltaine*, edited by Mr. W. B.
Yeats.

At first, as a company of native Irish players
could not be procured, English actors, enlisted
by Miss Vernon, had to be resorted to. When
the opening performance was given on May 8,
1899,[1] at the Antient Concert Rooms, with Mr.
Yeats's *The Countess Cathleen*, " a play possessing
all the beauties of the *Princesse Maleine*, and the
beauty of verses equal to the verses of Homer," [2]
Miss Florence Farr acted as general manager,
Mr. Ben Webster as stage-manager, and Miss
May Whitty and Mr. Trevor Lowe figured in
the cast. Cardinal Logue took offence at the play
on the ground of its alleged anti-Catholicism ;
public feeling ran so high that the police had
to be brought in, and the unlooked-for attacks
were renewed five years later in a virulent
pamphlet published by an ex-M.P.[3] Moreover,
it appeared that this self-dubbed " Irish " piece
was based on an Irish legend derived from
French sources,[4] a fact which angered some

---

[1] The dates of first performances are given in P. P. Howe,
The Repertory Theatre, Appendix II.

[2] George Moore, Introduction to Edward Martyn's *The
Heather Field* and *Maeve* (London : Duckworth, 1899),
p. xx.

[3] *The Stage Irishman of the Pseudo-Celtic Drama*, by F. H.
O'Donnell (London : John Lane, 1904).

[4] See the notes at the end of Mr. Yeats's *Poems* (London :
T. Fisher Unwin, 1901) ; " The Countess Kathleen O'Shea,"

narrow-minded patriots. There was no such difficulty, however, with the subsequent plays. Real successes were Mr. Edward Martyn's *The Heather Field*[1] (May 9, 1899) and Mr. George Moore's five-act comedy *The Bending of the Bough*[2] (February 19, 1900, at the Gaiety Theatre), a pungent satire on Irish political life, dramatized from a story by Mr. Martyn, since published as *The Tale of a Town*.[3] But the latter play owed its good fortune mainly to local and personal allusions; again, it was acted by English actors, and was the work of an Irishman who was out of touch with his native land. Little enthusiasm was raised by Miss Alice Milligan's *The Last of the Fianna* (February 19, 1900) and Mr. Martyn's symbolical play *Maeve* (February 20, 1900). In the third and last year of its existence the Irish Literary Theatre had again to rely on English companies, such as that of Mr. F. R. Benson in *Diarmuid and Grania*, a fine legendary drama first written in French[4] by Mr. George Moore and Mr. W. B. Yeats, which was somewhat unsuccessful (October 21, 1901). Fortunately, each performance was followed by *Casadh an tSúgáin* ("The Twisting of the Rope"),

in *Fairy and Folk-Tales of the Irish Peasantry*, edited and selected by W. B. Yeats (London : Walter Scott, The Scott Library, N.D.), pp. 232-5.
[1] London : Duckworth, 1899.
[2] London : T. Fisher Unwin, 1900.
[3] Published at Kilkenny by Standish Hayes O'Grady.
[4] See the end of *Hail and Farewell: I. Ave*, by George Moore,

" the first Gaelic play produced in any theatre," [1] in which the author, Dr. Douglas Hyde, himself acted with admirable insight.

However, on the whole, the experiment remained a failure. On the one hand, the incongruity of English professionals in Irish parts was self-evident.[2] On the other hand, with very few exceptions, the plays were almost as foreign as the players. Continental influences, notably those of Maeterlinck, Ibsen and the French symbolists, had not been quite embodied and " Irished " in the personalities of the playwrights. Irish playgoers wondered at the *peregrinitas* of the stage creations presented to them. The neo-Irish school, which had begun to write under the pressure of the intellectual movement then stirring to life in Dublin, and in reaction to the conventional stage Irishman, had now shrunk too much from the materialistic coarseness of the ancient conception and gone to over-spiritual, over-idealized types. This opposite excess was to become still more conspicuous in the subsequent plays.[3]

The Irish Literary Theatre lasted three years. It was then that, while rehearsing the Gaelic-

---

[1] As stated in a booklet issued by the Abbey Theatre Company in connection with their performances at the Grand Opera House, Harrogate, May 18, 1911. Cf. W. B. Yeats's " Stories of Red Hanrahan " (*Collected Works*, vol. v, pp. 213–24).

[2] Thanks to Mr. Martyn's liberality, the Irish Literary Theatre had enough money to pay them.

[3] *e. g.* in Lord Dunsany's semi-Maeterlinckian, semi-Oriental fantasies.

speaking actors for *Casadh an tSúgáin* at the
Gaiety Theatre, Mr. Frank J. Fay and his brother-
actor, Mr. William G. Fay, an electrician who
had become an elocutionist and comedian of exceptional parts, quite comparable with Coquelin
Aîné, first conceived the idea of forming a company of Irish-born players. Scraping together a
few pounds from sympathizers, they started at
once. Mr. Frank J. Fay had just read an article
published in the *Morning Leader* (August 18,
1900), in which Mr. William Archer, review-
ing a volume of Norwegian dramatic criticism,
explained how Ole Bull, the great Norwegian
violinist,[1] had formed the Norwegian National
Theatre for seven or eight amateurs, who had
answered his advertisement for people wishing
to make a profession of singing, dancing and
acting. Just as Ludvig Holberg had driven the
Germans from the Danish stage, so Ole Bull
had driven the Danes from the Norwegian
stage. Mr. F. Fay felt that the time had come
to train a troupe of Irish actors to act Irish
plays—instead of having English players who
" put on " a brogue, mainly with the object of
being funny to the English section of the audience : second-rate minds always think " funny "
an accent or idiom different from their own.
Mr. Frank Fay mentioned his idea to his
brother, and wrote about it to the *United Irish-*

---

[1] Mr. Archer also wrote about Ole Bull and the Bergen
Theatre in an article entitled " Ibsen's Apprenticeship," which
appeared in the *Fortnightly Review*, January, 1904, p. 25.

man (now *Sinn Féin*), going on to explain how the Norwegian National Theatre had hatched Ibsen ; how from the amateur Molière had grown the great stage of France ; how Racine had written his most famous tragedies for school-girls ; how L'Illustre Théâtre had been at the outset merely a collection of amateurs ; and how Antoine, the amateur of genius, was not thought fit by Got to enter the Paris Conservatoire.

Mr. W. Fay had been for some years a professional actor, but had left the stage ; and the two brothers kept a company of amateurs,[1] with whom they used to act for their own amusement at the Coffee Palace, Townsend Street, Dublin, St. Teresa's Hall, Clarendon Street, at Dalkey and Kingstown People's Concerts, at bazaars, and wherever a chance was given them. Through writing for the *United Irishman*, Mr. F. Fay got to know Mr. James H. Cousins (" Seumas O'Cuisin "), who told him that Mr. George W. Russell (" Æ "), who had seen the company perform Miss Alice Milligan's *The Deliverance of Red Hugh* at the Antient Concert Rooms for the " Daughters of Erin "[2] Society, wanted to shew him a play on *Deirdre* which he had just written. Mr. Frank Fay heard Mr. Russell read his play, and liked it so much that he brought his brother to hear

---

[1] Two members of which, Messrs. P. J. Kelly and T. Dudley Digges, are now professionals in New York.

[2] Cf. *The Gael*, August, 1902, pp. 257–60 : " Inginidhe na h-Éireann : The Daughters of Erin," by John J. Reynolds.

F. J. FAY

W. G. FAY

it too, and they soon decided to produce it. This was done on April 2, 1902, by Mr. W. G. Fay's " Irish National Dramatic Company " (so the new body called itself) at St. Teresa's Hall, Clarendon Street, Dublin. Mr. W. B. Yeats had given them his patriotic one-act play, *Kathleen ni Houlihan*, which was performed with triumphal success on the same night, with Miss Maud Gonne in the title-rôle.

During the show one evening Mr. Frank Fay suggested that the amateur players should keep together and rehearse a little. This was done in October following, when *Deirdre* and *Kathleen ni Houlihan* were repeated at the Samhain Festival under the auspices of Cumann-na-nGaedheal, a Nationalist organization. The Irish National Dramatic Company had now re-moved to permanent quarters, the Antient Concert Rooms, where four new pieces were staged : *The Sleep of the King* (October 29, 1902), a blank-verse poem-play on the legend of King Conor by " Seumas O'Cuisin " ; *The Laying of the Foundations* (October 29), by Mr. Fred Ryan, a satire on town-council robbery which was, so to speak, *The Pillars of Society* of Ireland's dramatic movement ; *A Pot of Broth* (October 30), a farce by Mr. W. B. Yeats on the Irish peasant's gullibility ; and *The Racing Lug* (October 31), a sea-tragedy by " Seumas O'Cuisin."

Messrs. Fay's valiant enterprise had now fully succeeded, and the Irish National Dramatic Company developed into the Irish National

Theatre Society, whose first presidency was offered by the founders to Mr. W. B. Yeats. The company's modest headquarters were the Molesworth Hall, Camden Street, Dublin. Eight plays were produced, two of which— *In the Shadow of the Glen* and *Riders to the Sea*, performed on October 8, 1903, and February 25, 1904, respectively—were the work of J. M. Synge, who made there a fairly successful *début*.

The Irish theatre movement had now arrived at a turning-point of its history. In 1904 Miss A. E. F. Horniman, "an Englishwoman, of course,"[1] whose name is associated with the creation of a dramatic system known as the Repertory Theatre,[2] which has bestowed its benefits all over Britain, stepped forward with assistance, not only allowing the Irish National Theatre Society a small annual subsidy,[3] but undertaking at her own expense the renovation of the old theatre of the Mechanics' Institute in Abbey Street, Dublin, adjoining the river Liffey, and lending it rent free for six years to the Society. The entire restoration and decoration of the "Abbey Theatre" was the work of Irish hands. The architect was Mr.

---

[1] G. B. Shaw, Preface to *John Bull's Other Island*.

[2] On which see P. P. Howe, *op. cit.*

[3] Withdrawn in Dec., 1910. Miss Horniman handed over the playhouse (on which she had expended £13,000) to the "Abbey Theatre Company" for £1,000. The "Abbey Theatre Endowment Fund," and the annual tours of the company in America (1911, 1912) have since produced a large part of the £5,000 necessary to carry on the work.

AND THE IRISH THEATRE

Joseph Holloway, C.E., of Dublin ; the stained-glass windows in the vestibule were designed by Miss Sarah H. Purser, A.R.H.A., an Irish artist who has successfully revived that lost industry ; [1] and the brass frames were supplied from the Irish workshops at Youghal, Co. Cork.

The Abbey Theatre is now a fixture in Ireland's dramatic renascence. Its official as well as unofficial history so far remains untold ; and, indeed, it is much too soon to attempt a record of its achievements, or form a mature judgment of its merits. " We stand too close to the picture, . . . and clear vision is reserved for unborn eyes." [2] Despite its overwhelming vitality, as evidenced by the some sixty Irish plays it has brought forth during these first eight years of its existence, and the tremendous impetus it has given to the Irish,[3] Scotch,[4] and Welsh [5] sections of the neo-Celtic drama, the theatre is as yet in its infancy. Moreover, most of the playwrights are still living, and it is

---

[1] See a letter (Jan. 9, 1903) by Prof. York Powell in Oliver Elton's *Frederic York Powell* (Clarendon Press, Oxford, 1906), vol. i, p. 358.

[2] W. J. Lawrence, " Dublin as a play-producing centre " (*Weekly Freeman*, Christmas No., Dec. 14, 1907, p. 25).

[3] Other Irish dramatic organizations are : the Ulster Literary Theatre, the Theatre of Ireland (Cluithcheoirí na nÉireann), the Pioneer Dramatic Company, the Leinster Stage Society, the National Players, the Gaelic Repertory Theatre. There are also dramatic societies in Cork and Waterford.

[4] The Glasgow Repertory Theatre ; Mr. Graham Moffat's company of Scottish players.

[5] A prize for the development of Welsh drama has recently been founded by Lord Howard de Walden.

always unadvisable to venture even provisional opinions on uncompleted literary careers. J. M. Synge is the one dramatist susceptible of monographic study, and the annals of the Abbey Theatre must be left to be compiled by some more expert hand. All we need at present offer is a summary of the theatre's methods of acting and playwriting as they have been established from the start. This only can lead us to a thorough appreciation of our author's own position.

First, as to the acting. The movement started, as we have seen, in the wake of André Antoine's Théâtre Libre, and was also curiously parallel to kindred English undertakings such as the Independent Theatre, the Stage Society, and the Repertory Theatre. Like all these, it aimed primarily at greater truthfulness and simplicity in stage production. Whereas the industrial British theatre makes the average English actor an unbearable " mummer," the Irish amateurs went direct to the great school of simple acting—the French school. It is remarkable how the Irish theatre movement is impregnated with French influence. The Fay brothers, who formed the Abbey Company, are enthusiastic admirers of the French stage ; they never miss an opportunity of seeing the touring French companies [1] and, when possible, taking their Irish fellow-workers to see them too ; and one of them has made quite a special study of

[1] Such as M. Roubaud's, who often comes to Dublin.

the modern French style of acting, and has been a painstaking collector of all documents relating to the subject.

One of the principal Irish reforms was suggested by the acting of *Tartuffe* by Coquelin Aîné at the Gaiety Theatre, Dublin. Messrs. Fay had noticed how in the first scene all the actors stood in a line parallel to the footlights, and how those who had nothing to say kept their eyes fixed on those who were speaking. On the English stage the idle ones would be doing all they could in the background to attract attention to themselves away from the speakers. The Irish players were taught to obliterate themselves as much as possible in order to concentrate the onlookers' attention on the speakers. Also, they were made to stand almost stock-still and not move about or indulge in unnatural gesticulation and stage " business " after the absurd fashion of English actors who, when they have to deliver a long speech, " pace the stage like lions in a zoo." [1]   " When they do move, it is with very spontaneous clumsiness." [2]   The next point was to lower the pitch of voice—" to act pianissimo, in a tone hushed as if in a sick-room, all grave and as it were careworn." However, the distinctness of the elocution was paid extreme attention to. [3]

---

[1] C. E. Montague, *Dramatic Values*, p. 54.

[2] Cf. A. B. Walkley, *Drama and Life*, pp. 309–16.

[3] The players read a novel aloud among themselves, and the reader was stopped whenever the pronunciation became indistinct.

Thirdly, there were no " stars " in the company :
apart from seniority, all actors were equal ; all
might have to play inferior parts, and none was
allowed to monopolize the stage. Lastly, when
the curtain fell, the theatre did not remain
dark for a certain length of time, as a broad
hint to continue the applause ; and when it
rose, the actors did not stand stiff, but bowed
and smiled.

In short, whilst English acting may be defined
as the art of shewing off one's self, the Irish
actors are used to shew off the plays. In their
dread of over-acting, they are apt to under-act.
Hence their occasional amateurishness. Their
art's essential object is artlessness. Of course,
one may detect some affectation in this punc-
tilious seeking after simplicity. " They have
something of the self-importance of children
surpliced for service at the altar or ' dressed up '
for a grand domestic occasion." [1] But, of course,
the stiffness of the " deliberately adopted " style
of acting of which they boasted in one of their
first programmes will disappear in due time and
has indeed almost disappeared.[2]

These simple methods of acting are, as it were,
conditioned by the very nature of the Abbey
Theatre. In the first place, like the modern

---

[1] A. B. Walkley, *loc. cit.*
[2] A school of acting, on the lines of the Paris Conservatoire,
has lately (Nov. 23, 1911) been founded at the Abbey Theatre
under the direction of Mr. Nugent Monck, a disciple of
Mr. William Poel.

Breton stage, the Alsatian drama, the Bohemian Theatre, the Spanish " Zarzuelas " and " Sainetes," the German Volkstheater, a good portion of the contemporary Russian drama, and such specimens of Sicilian or Japanese plays as have been produced in France and England, the modern Irish drama is a national (not to say Nationalist [1]) drama. Nationality in Ireland being largely synonymous with rusticity, there are as yet but few Irish plays dealing with town life, middle-class problems, or industrial questions. The Abbey Theatre, so to speak, is of an essentially agricultural type. On the other hand, the playhouse itself is of a diminutive kind (562 seats in all), and its resources are limited. Hence stentorian voices, or tawdry stage appliances, would be totally out of place. Everything has to remain humble and sincere. The scenery, in almost all cases, is elementary—the usual cabin-interior with the typical half-door. Stage mechanism is remarkable for its absence.[2] The back-cloth has been so designed that it sets out the characters in the cast without in

[1] The Abbey Theatre was the only theatre in the United Kingdom that did not close at the time of King Edward VII's death.

[2] However, for the more symbolical plays, the colour designs associated with the names of Mr. Gordon Craig and Prof. Max Reinhardt have been used by Mr. Robert Gregory and others at the Abbey Theatre. Cf. Edward Gordon Craig, *On the Art of the Theatre* (Edinburgh and London : T. N. Foulis, 1905 ; new edition, London : Heinemann, 1912) ; *Towards a New Theatre* (London : Dent, 1913).

any degree competing with them in importance.[1]

Again, the actors themselves can but be
simple. They are, or rather were, for the
most part, clerks, tradesmen's assistants, typists,
artisans, railway servants, coming straight from
the prosaic life of shop and factory, from the
rank and file of the average working-class. At
first they received no salaries from the theatre ;[2]
they supported themselves independently of the
stage, which was in the position of a recreation
merely. As a rule they were of peasant stock—
though most of them still have no Gaelic—so
that their competent stage-managers had no
difficulty in fashioning them into performers of
plays dealing with country life.

Such were, summarily described, the general
outward conditions amidst which Synge began
to write for the Irish stage. Let us now consider the inner development of his own views on
the drama, in their relation with, and antagonism
to, the conceptions of the other Abbey Theatre
playwrights.

II

Synge does not confront his interpreter with

---

[1] Cf. W. B. Yeats, "The Theater of Beauty," *Harper's
Weekly*, Nov. 11, 1911.

[2] The actor-stage-manager was the only one who drew a
small pay from the theatre. Later, when Miss Horniman
granted her subsidy to the society, all the players began to
receive a salary. Cf. W. J. Lawrence, "The Abbey Theatre :
its History and Mystery," *Weekly Freeman*, Christmas Number,
Dec. 7, 1912, p. 11.

the initial difficulty stated by Mr. G. K. Chesterton, at the opening of his book on Mr. G. B. Shaw [1]—that of writing a preface on a copious and incorrigible preface-writer. Unlike Mr. W. B. Yeats, he did not profess to expound the leading principles of the Irish literary school ; unlike the lamented "Irish" essayist, Lionel Johnson,[2] he never indulged in learned criticism ; nor did he, like "John Eglinton," the analyst, discuss with keen dialectical acumen Ireland's literary ideals. The theorizing tendency was, we have seen, practically non-existent in him ; his art creed, and the main requirements he sets forth as essential to drama, are to be found not in some perfervid manifesto, but only in three short introductions,[3] and in a few poems. Although these were written at various periods of his life, Synge's expositor has a right to condense, for clearness' sake, the material available for an elucidation of his æsthetic standpoint ; indeed, it may be safely maintained [4] that the ideas embodied in these writings were always implicitly or expressly present in Synge's mind.

---

[1] G. K. Chesterton, *George Bernard Shaw* (London and N.Y. : John Lane, 1910), p. 7.

[2] Works published by Elkin Mathews, of London. Johnson was English, not Irish, by birth. He wrote a fine prologue in verse for the first performances of the Irish Literary Theatre in 1899.

[3] Prefaces to *The Tinker's Wedding* (i. 135), *The Playboy of the Western World* (ii. 3), and *Poems and Translations* (ii. 201).

[4] Despite Synge's assertion that most of the poems were written "before the views just stated, with which they have little to do, had come into my head" (ii. 202).

JOHN MILLINGTON SYNGE

He stands, it appears, in a twofold reaction. On the one hand, he opposes the mystical lyricism of the Yeatsian drama. The Irish revolt against materialism had become over-idealistic. At its inception it had resulted in a re-birth of the philosophic spirit, which caused such Irish men of letters as those grouped around " John Eglinton " in the tiny " Hermetic Society " to take Emerson to heart in Dublin in the very days (1886) when Maeterlinck was studying him in Ghent. The transcendentalist philosophy in its turn had led to spiritualism—nay, even to occultism. This was not simply a spontaneous reawakening of the visionary instinct in the Celtic nature ; it was also the product of combined outside influences. Mr. Yeats, at that time a student of magic white and black, conversant with the Kabala, Jacob Böhme, William Blake, Dr. Steiner, and the Rosicrucians, and a disciple of Madame Blavatsky's theosophy,[1] had turned a veritable wizard, and evolved in his elusive poem-plays stage-types of infinite artistic value, but, at the same time, of almost inhuman aloofness from reality. Ireland in his hands had become again Inisfail, the Country of the Two Mists, of the " Celtic Twilight." [2] " Æ," temperamentally a seer of a very high order, had delved into books on Swedenborgianism and Hindoo lore

---

[1] Cf. *Madame Blavatsky and her " Theosophy "* : *a Study*, by Arthur Lillie (London : Swan Sonnenschein, 1895).

[2] The title of one of Mr. Yeats's best-known prose essays.

and worked out a kind of symbolic cosmogony. On the whole, the pre-Synge Irish peasant as he was portrayed in the plays of these two masters and their followers appeared as a dreamy, ecstatic creature of psychic fantasy, who almost seemed to live in a perpetual trance.

As might be expected, the admirable spirituality of the Yeatsian school found its favourite and congenial material in the legendary history and mythology of ancient Ireland. The more or less supernatural arsenal of wan deities, *sidhe* [1] and *belles dames sans merci*, had been ransacked and displayed on the stage. Synge, as was natural, was repelled by the contemplation of this type of artistic beauty, which was " too far away from life to appease his mood." [2] He was to express his contempt for the unearthly, aërial figures which meant so much to his fellow-workers. After looking at a picture by " Æ," he would exclaim— [3]

> Adieu, sweet Angus, Maeve and Fand,
> Ye plumed and skinny shee,
> That poets walked with hand in hand
> To learn their ecstasy.
>
> We'll stretch in Red Dan Sally's ditch,
> And drink in Tubber fair,
> Or poach with Red Dan Philly's bitch
> The badger and the hare.

This note of naturalistic rebellion which

---

[1] Fairies (pron. " shee ") : literally, " the others."
[2] W. B. Yeats, Preface to Synge's *Poems and Translations* (Cuala Press).
[3] *The Passing of the Shee* (ii. 215).

Synge uttered, and which was so genuinely his, must in a more general way be profoundly Irish, for we hear it struck even in our own day by another great Dublin poet, Mr. James Stephens, in his *Insurrections* [1] : may such insurgents never be pacified ! But, whilst Mr. Stephens revolts against the social environment, Synge protested against the Yeatsian art shibboleth. Mr. Yeats's influence had acted on Synge in a positive manner, as a powerful intellectual incentive which had brought him to self-realization. But there the influence ended ; or, more exactly, beyond that point, it became what might be styled a negative influence. [2] Beside the Yeatsian lyrical conception of life and art, there was room for the Syngean dramatic conception. Synge felt that both were equally legitimate ; but he chose to break away from the former

---

[1] Dublin : Maunsel, 1909.

[2] " I never knew if he cared for work of mine, and do not remember that I had from him even a conventional compliment " (W. B. Yeats, *Synge and the Ireland of his Time*, p. 23). " I never knew what he thought of my work " (W. B. Yeats, diary, *ap.* Lady Gregory, *art. cit.*, p. 558). Synge's relation to Yeats will be touched upon in the third volume (*Vale*) of Mr. George Moore's tripartite autobiography, *Hail and Farewell* (London : Heinemann). Of course Synge always admired Yeats both as a man and writer. It was of Yeats that he spoke when he said to Mr. Masefield (*art. cit.*) : " No one in Ireland understands how big he is." Oscar Wilde once said : " Good artists don't care for each other's work," and Synge had his own art ; but he knew that Yeats was the backbone of the movement, and that they were working together, with their different gifts, to create vehicles for the mind of their country.

for reasons which must be sought in his personal
vehemence, in the gloominess of his individual
outlook, and in his life among a peasantry used
to the brutal tragedy of existence, not to the
æsthetic other-worldliness of an ethereal and
somewhat impalpable symbolism.

The peasant's life, we have seen, had become
so much part and parcel of Synge's own consciousness that this no doubt largely accounts for
his total swerving from the general direction
followed by his compeers. Being accustomed
to the Gael's grim sufferance of his lot, he was
too virile to make much of an art that took
refuge and consolation in the cloud-swept and
enchanted empyrean of Irish myth. He was
bound to introduce a more independent and
more human note of " astringent joy and
hardness." [1]

Synge's realism—if realist he truly is—is of a
kind peculiarly apart. It is not, as some would
have it, the uninspired realism of squalid ugli-
ness, misnamed truth, and invented sheerly for
the sake of averting " the deadly blight of
sugariness and the sweetly pretty "; but rather
a realism selective of the more significant phases
of life, in contradistinction to those trivial and
ineffectual by comparison. The starting-point
must therefore be a reality rich and powerful :
social humanity [2] and, more especially, personal

---

[1] W. B. Yeats, Preface to *Poems and Translations.*

[2] Cf. Synge's theory of art as a collaboration in the preface
to the *Playboy.*

or autobiographical experience.[1]   When Synge
himself speaks of Maeve and Fand, as in *Queens*[2]
—a poem meant to burlesque the whole movement started by Mr. Yeats—it is to turn to the
woman he loves, and give her the palm in the
end—

> Yet these are rotten—I ask their pardon—
> And we've the sun on rock and garden;
> These are rotten, so you're the Queen
> Of all are living, or have been.

But common and "brutal"[3] actuality must only
serve as a root or substructure; the poetic or
dramatic edifice must rise from it to a loftier
level.   Primordial submission to fact has its
necessary counterpart in artistic transcendence
of fact.   Reality must flower into humorous and
imaginative "exaltation."[4]   Humour in its turn,
as Synge conceives it,[5] is not the manufactured
gaiety of the musical comedy,[6] but the something fierce and laughter-compelling—though
pessimistic at bottom—which purifies and bites.
The pre-Synge type was notable for his utter
mirthlessness: on the stage, Synge contends,
"one must have reality and one must have

[1] "Many of the older poets . . . used the whole of their
personal life as their material" (Synge's Preface to *Poems*).

[2] ii. 203.

[3] "It may almost be said that before verse can be human
again it must learn to be brutal" (Preface to *Poems*).

[4] Preface to *Poems*.

[5] Cf. Preface to *The Tinker's Wedding*.

[6] "The absinthe or vermouth of the last musical comedy"
(Preface to *The Tinker's Wedding*); "The false joy of the
musical comedy" (Preface to the *Playboy*).

joy." [1] As to imagination, it is part of reality, since in Ireland it is, " for a few years more," [2] inseparable from life. In short, artistic exaltation is not artificial elation, and can only be maintained if touch is kept with very homely earth.

Synge's second—and secondary—reaction is against dramatic didacticism. This can be dismissed in fewer words. He compares the drama with the symphony [3]—an analogy significant in a musician like him—urging that neither of them proves or teaches anything. Synge is not a man with a message who believes that the theatre is a " criticism of life." He avowedly repudiates the ethical or sociological problem-play inaugurated by " Ibsen and the Germans," [4] who, it may be recalled, had found a few disciples among the early Abbey Theatre dramatists. He also, we think, implicitly alludes to the danger which threatens a self-styled national theatre : that of confusing the literary with the political standard, Nationalist logic-chopping and propaganda with drama proper. Synge has no wish to change or reform anything ; his contention is that the theatre, even in a land of controversy like Ireland, must remain in its purely artistic sphere.

Another point which he omits in his little prefaces, but on which he is known to have emphatically insisted in private conversation, is

---

[1] Preface to the *Playboy*.   [2] *Ibid.*
[3] Preface to *The Tinker's Wedding.*   [4] *Ibid.*

the necessity of a satisfactory technical structure.
He had learnt abroad the mechanics of drama,
and his plays, in our judgment, bear the hallmark of a stagecraft defter than that of Mr.
Yeats and Lady Gregory, and the modern Irish
playwrights generally. The native genius and
formative culture of Mr. Yeats has resulted so
far in a theatre which (with the exception of
Deirdre) is poetic rather than truly dramatic
in treatment and presentation.[1] Indeed, this is
his peculiar and, we dare say, unsurpassable
achievement. His literary output consists of
lyrical, not dramatic, writings ; and even Yeats
the playwright will endure as a lyrist—quite
possibly the greatest of all contemporary lyrists
in the English tongue. Lady Gregory's case is
different : though she has an admirable sense of
dialogue, hers are dramaturgic methods of an
essentially anecdotal kind ; her playlets may be
defined as more or less discursive narratives put
into action. If Mr. Yeats is a reincarnation of
some ancient mystic, she who has justly won the
right of being known as the " Irish Malory "
bears a distinct likeness to the *shanachies* of old.
As a rule, the average Irish play remains technically uncouth [2] and amorphous, as though the

---

[1] The late Lionel Johnson used to say that Mr. Yeats wrote
for the stage "rather from a desire to hear his lines finely
spoken than from a strong bent for the drama."

[2] No doubt this is largely due to the fact that the Irish plays
ought really to be played (as Shakespeare was played) on a
" platform stage " with the audience round three sides of it.
Drama so primitive is half pageant, and demands a closer

extremely fine sense of life ever present in these Irish productions refused to be imprisoned within the narrow compass of artistic rules. Ethnological critics are inclined to ascribe this curious deficiency to the Gael's lack of those architectural powers which are as indispensable to build a drama as to mould a nation. A gifted Irish poet, Seosamh MacCathmhaoil, expresses this natural or affected intolerance of intellectual discipline in the somewhat cryptic formula " Mud or Death." No wonder, then, that the Hibernian theatre should still be in its tentative stage. It exhibits the dramatic elements in juxtaposition rather than in sequence, frequently in a single scene which, like Browning's " dramatic lyrics," [1] depicts the crisis alone, leaving it to the spectator to infer past and future. But the crisis itself is oftener a state than a struggle of volition, an exhibition of character in situation in lieu of character in action. It was Synge's distinctive merit to avoid this glaring shortcoming.

As has been hinted at in a previous section, there is no doubt that Synge possessed the true dramatic gift. English critics, overlooking the fact that imaginative vision is as necessary to the playwright as to the writer of verse, have

---

touch with the audience. Recent experiments at the Abbey Theatre have marvellously proved this.

[1] In an article on " The Personal in the New Poetry," contributed to *An Macaomh*, Mr. Thomas MacDonagh shews that the dramatic lyric is almost as old in Irish as poetry itself (*Studies* (Dublin), March, 1913, pp. 816–7).

averred that he was first and foremost a poet. We should feel inclined to retort that even in his poems—which are exquisite little studies in atmosphere, emotionalism, or characterization— Synge remains first and foremost a playwright.[1] Ballad-poetry—which he was intent on reviving —is essentially dramatic. Above all, Synge had the right dramatic perception of life's growth and becoming. " He was one of the people to whom something is always happening because they know how to see things happen. To such a man life is a Chinese play. He has but to choose when he will raise or drop the curtain." [2]

His dramatic instinct he owed partly to the racial talent of the Irish, partly to his Continental training, and partly to the environment which he found in Dublin. Yet, despite Mr. Yeats's asseveration that " Mr. Synge is a young writer and a creation of our movement,"[3] he was not a product of the Abbey Theatre. It did not create him as it created others ; nor did he create it. Personally he loathed the idea of " movements " and of " schools " ; and in this as in other cases, his individual independence may be safely vindicated. He did not catch the mannerism—nay, not even the manner—of the Celtic Renascence ; he was simply caught up in

---

[1] It is noteworthy that Synge did not insert any verse of his own in the prose of his plays.

[2] Chas. Tennyson, " Irish Plays and Playwrights," *Quarterly Review*, July, 1911, p. 228.

[3] *Samhain*, Oct., 1903 (No. 3), p. 7 ; or *Collected Works* vol. iv, p. 112.

it. It so happened that, by some fortunate or unfortunate synchronism, he found in Dublin a stage to produce his plays, actors to perform them, and a public somewhat noisily critical. One might even go to the length of saying that in the Irish *Pléiade*—which is probably the one strongly organized school at present in Europe—community of ideals never blots out the personal originality of the writers. Each of them follows his own definite line of research ; there is hardly any interaction ; and Synge's lonely detachment is the rule.

We are now in a position to measure the distance covered by Synge in the course of his artistic evolution. He began by seeking self-expression in music and painting ; but he found the fine arts too difficult or too vague. Next he turned to journalistic criticism ; again, he wandered over Ireland and wrote descriptive essays ; but even these remained external attitudes. Synge, despite his intuitive methods,[1] saw life through the often-distorting prism of literature, or pictured his countrymen's ways and doings necessarily from without. At last he placed himself at the core of existence by writing of himself in a few of his poems ; and this inner mental development, always nearing life as it advanced, found its natural terminus in the drama.

---

[1] "When we talked about writers (modern French and ancient English writers) it was not about their writings that we talked, but about the something kindling in them, which never got expressed" (John Masefield, *art. cit.*).

CHAPTER VI

THE PLAYS

IF faith is to be placed in a French critic's [1]
dictum that no exceptional work of art is ever
penned by anyone before reaching the age of
thirty, then Synge's artistic achievement in his
drama must be supremely great, for it was not
until he was thirty-two that he came before the
public as a playwright—a late beginning for a
dramatist whose life was to end so early.

The logical order of his dramatic writings
coincides with their chronology. Synge has left
in succession two one-act plays, *In the Shadow of
the Glen* and *Riders to the Sea*; one two-act play,
The Tinker's Wedding; and three three-act plays,
The Well of the Saints, *The Playboy of the Western
World*, and *Deirdre of the Sorrows*. These we
shall first separately examine from an historical
and critical standpoint—studying them in their
plots, genesis, stage-production and relation to
Synge's personality, and also as illustrative of the
artistic methods of Synge *quâ* playwright and
of the growth of his dramatic technique. We
shall then consider how far his plays may be
regarded as really Irish.

---

[1] Emile Faguet.

I

Synge always told his friends—and Lady Gregory has recently confirmed this—that *In the Shadow of the Glen*[1] was composed before *Riders to the Sea*, but only just before[2]; the two plays were practically finished by the end of 1902. " When I heard them read aloud in London in January, 1903,"[3] says Mr. John Masefield, " at the rooms of one who was always most generously helpful to writers not yet sure of their road,[4] the *Shadow* was complete and the *Riders* not quite complete. A lady read the plays, very beautifully.[4] Afterwards we all applauded. Synge learnt his *métier* that night. Until then all his work had been tentative and in the air. After that he went forward, knowing what he could do."[5]

In the Shadow of the Glen, as we know, was first produced before small audiences by the Irish National Theatre Society at the Molesworth

[1] *In the Shadow . . .* or *The Shadow . . . [ad libitum.]*

[2] This may be due to the fact that Synge heard the shadow-of-the-glen story during a stay in Aran previous to the one during which he was told of the incident on which *Riders* is based. Such at least is the order in which Synge has recorded them in the Aran book.

[3] Letter to the writer.

[4] *C. R., art. cit.* (The rooms were Lady Gregory's, Queen Anne's Mansions, London, S.W. The lady was Lady Gregory. Mr. Arthur Symons, Mr. and Miss Brimley Johnson, Miss Florence Farr, and probably also Miss Pamela Coleman Smith were present.)

[5] Letter to the writer.

JOHN MILLINGTON SYNGE

Hall, Dublin, on October 8, 1903, together with
Mr. Yeats's *On the King's Threshold*. It has now
been performed in various cities of Great Britain
and America,[1] and in a Czech version at the
Theatre, Smíchov, near Prague.[2] A copy of
the Bohemian playbill hangs framed in the vestibule of the Abbey Theatre, where it is treasured
as a memorial.

The play is a bitter sketch of the loveless
marriages of the Irish country-folk. Matrimony
among them is a matter of commercial bargain-
ing rather than of elective affinity. A young
peasant-woman, Nora, is the wife of Dan Burke,
a gruff and well-to-do old farmer. They in-
habit a lonesome cottage at the head of a desolate
Wicklow glen, where solitude almost drives one
to distraction with the tedium of seeing " nothing
but the mists rolling down the bog, and the mists
again and they rolling up the bog, and hearing
nothing but the wind crying out in the bits of
broken trees were left from the great storm, and
the streams roaring with the rain."[3]   Dan,

---

[1] The play was made known in America by Mrs. Fiske
prior to the tour of the Abbey Theatre players through the
United States in 1911–12. See Appendix D.

[2] Cf. W. B. Yeats, *Samhain*, No. 5, p. 4. The performance
at the Smíchov Theatre took place in August, 1907. Afterwards the play was produced at the Royal Bohemian National
Theatre, Prague, with Pan Karel Mušek, the translator, in the
part of the tramp.

[3] This famous passage (i. 19) has been the origin of an
amusing skit on Abbey Theatre plays and their dialect, entitled
The Mist that does be on the Bog, by " Gerald MacNamara "
(Harry Morrow), first produced by the Ulster Literary

doubting the fidelity of his wife, who used to talk gladly with one Patch Darcy, a herd whose body has just been found in a ditch, "eaten by the crows," feigns death that he may spy upon her and her supposed lover. A tramp comes knocking at the door ; Nora kindly lets him in, gives him whisky to drink, one of Dan's pipes to smoke, and a needle and thread to mend his coat. She has hardly stepped out to fetch Michael, a young farmer, who will go and tell abroad that " himself " is dead—for Dan has put a curse on her if she touches his body or lets anyone touch it save his own sister, who lives ten miles away—when up rises the mock-dead man, to the tramp's infinite bewilderment and terror. Dan asks him to give him a drink, and hand him his stick, which he conceals in the bed ; then, hearing his wife return, hastens to die again. Nora comes in with Michael ; she tries to get rid of the tramp by inviting him to rest in the next room ; but he insists on staying ; so, turning their backs to him, they begin to discuss plans of marriage over a cup of tea, incidentally casting reflections on Dan. Thereupon

---

Theatre at the Abbey Theatre on Nov. 26, 1909. The piece tells how a beautiful young actress and her aunt go down to the West of Ireland to pick up local colour, and there meet a poet disguised as a peasant, and also searching for local colour. The actress and the poet then fall in love with each other. It was rumoured at the time of the playlet's production that the poet was meant for Synge, and the actress for Miss Maire O'Neill, his *fiancée*. Whether the identification was correct or not we cannot say.

Dan, sneezing violently, resuscitates anew, and giving vent to the savage and sinister passion that lurks in the sullen depths of his nature, grips his blackthorn and bids his wife leave the house at once. Michael, a coward by nature, who would marry Nora for money's rather than for love's sake (just as Nora herself has married Dan for his " bit of a farm " only), begs her to intercede with her husband on his behalf, as " he always did what she bade him." Then, as if refusing to go away with Nora now she is deprived of everything, he remains silent. But the tramp readily volunteers to accompany her on the roads, where she goes forth to a hard life, but, at all events, to a life she will enjoy. And the little tragicomedy concludes with a perfect touch of ironical humour, when Dan, instead of striking Michael, sits down with him to a glass of whisky.[1]

Such is the bare intrigue or incident of the play. But Synge, despite his care in technique, is more profoundly interested in the inner development of his characters than in the outer frame of action. Nora is certainly the most vitally arresting figure. Hers is less the love-yearning of the woman who knows the world sexually [2] than the poetic desire [3] for the some-

---

[1] Curiously enough, the *Playboy*, as we shall note, concludes in the same fashion : " We'll have peace now for our drinks."

[2] Miss Maire O'Neill's interpretation of the part.

[3] The interpretation of Miss Maire nic Shiubhlaigh [Mary Walker], who created the part of Nora. Cf. a very interesting article on the acting of Miss Walker by Mr. John Masefield (written after the performance at the Abbey Theatre on

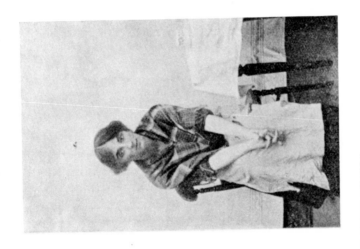

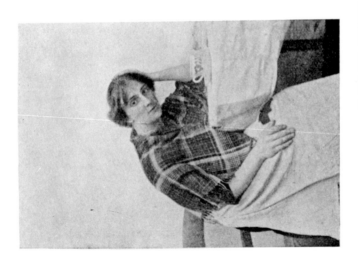

MAIRE NIC SHIUBHLAIGH AS "NORA BURKE"

(In the Shadow of the Glen)

thing new or exciting which may relieve the oppression of solitude. She has a poetic soul and is " a grand woman to talk." But the free expansion of this soul is checked by her distressing surroundings and by life in company with " an old fellow wheezing, the like of a sick sheep, close to her ear." The shattered ideals and thwarted aspirations of all humanity speak through her as she sits an inscrutably sad woman above the ruins of her world.

It would be easy in this connection to misconstrue the little piece into a plea for free love, more precisely, into an Ibsenian problem-play with an Irish setting. No doubt Synge's work is a little suggestive of what Hedda Gabler [1] or the Lady from the Sea might have done, had they lived in Wicklow instead of Norway. The " moral" of *In the Shadow of the Glen*—if there is any such thing—is probably that a woman has a right to follow the man her soul inclines to. But this interpretation, this undue intrusion of " opinions" into the play, would be totally untrue to Synge's non-didactic methods, and need not detain us.

This craving for poetry in the young woman discontented with her lot finds a satisfier in the

Dec. 27, 1904) in the London *Daily News*, Jan. 4, 1905, p. 6 ; and his fine unsigned appreciation of "The Irish National Theatre" in the *Manchester Guardian*, Jan. 2, 1905.

[1] Supposing that *Hedda Gabler* is a " play with a purpose" —which Ibsen himself denied (see Count Prozor's preface to the French edition of the play, and W. Berteval, *Le Théâtre a'Ibsen* (Paris : Perrin, 1912), p. 256).

typical, though by no means symbolical, tramp.
Like Nora, he has "a fine bit of talk." We
already know how Synge used to fall in with
tramps and suchlike vagrants in the course of
his rambles through Eastern Ireland, and what
artistic significance he attached to the type.
The point is worth labouring, for not only in
Synge, but in the whole contemporary Anglo-
Irish drama [1] we find a romantic glorification of
the tramp and the fiddler, not unlike, it seems,
that in M. Jean Richepin's *Chemineau*.[2] Some
angry-minded critics, whom this tramp-worship
exasperates, allege that the outlaw or beggar
who "goes the roads" is thus taken as representative of the whole Irish race by the Abbey
dramatists simply because they generally belong
to the upper classes, and can only get the black-
guardly vagabond to tell them of "the wonders"
and of the quaint bits of folklore on which their
plays are based, not the honest and respectable
Irish peasant who, as a rule, is loath to speak to
the "quality." Tramps are certainly much more

[1] *e.g.* "Rutherford Mayne"'s *The Turn of the Road*;
Mr. Pádraic Colum's *The Fiddler's House*; Seumas O'Kelly's
The Shuiler's Child (the word "shuiler" literally means
"walker"; in Co. Louth it is applied to tramps coming from
other counties in contradistinction to local tramps); Lady
Gregory's *The Travelling Man*, etc. There is a tramp in
Mr. Yeats's farce, *A Pot of Broth*. In Mr. Paddy Kelly's *The
West Wind: a playlet in two scenes*, published in the *Irish
Independent*, Christmas No., December 2, 1911, a wanderer
reminiscent of Synge's own tramp tells an old couple about the
romance of his roving life.

[2] First produced at the Odéon Theatre, Paris, Feb. 16,
1897. Synge, who was in Paris from October, 1896 to May,
1897, might have seen Richepin's play.

unpopular in real Irish life than on the Abbey stage ; they are commonly regarded as thieves to whom alms should be grudged. However, it is undeniable that the type has a marked artistic and dramatic value. Tramp life—which, we have seen, personally appealed to Synge—may be taken as expressive of the poetic revolt against settled existence, as the free escape into some ideal dreamworld of the artist who finds the daily fare of life unbearably insipid and wearisome. It is the roughest, crudest and least sophisticated life that man surrounded by civilization can live.[1] All this poetic longing for rude primitiveness which, as has been noted, was such an essential tendency in Synge's art, is to be detected in the tramp he presents in this first one-act play.

We have so far considered the piece as it stands, and it is time that we should inquire into its sources and mental working out. The indubitable origin of the playlet is a folk-tale which " Pat Dirane " [Pat Doran] told Synge in 1898, during his first stay in the middle island of Aran.[2] The story—which belongs to the common folklore of Ireland, having been heard in Munster by Mr. Curtin,[3] and by Mr.

[1] Cf. W. H. Davies, *The Autobiography of a Super-Tramp*, with a preface by Bernard Shaw (London : Fifield, 1908) ; *The True Traveller* (London : Duckworth, 1912).
[2] As Synge himself writes in a letter to the Editor of *The United Irishman*, Feb. 11, 1905, p. 1.
[3] Mr. Jeremiah Curtin, the American scholar mentioned in *The Aran Islands* (iii. 4). The fact is stated by Mr. W. B. Yeats in *Samhain*, No. 5, and *The Arrow*, No. 3.

JOHN MILLINGTON SYNGE

Fournier d'Albe in Tory Island [1]—is recorded in Synge's *Aran Islands*,[2] and it is interesting to compare the primitive anecdote with his own dramatic selection from it.

The narrator of the original Gaelic tale— "always speaking in the first person, with minute details to shew that he was actually present at the scenes that are described "[3]— corresponds to the tramp in the play. As may be pointed out, Synge in his play has shifted the scene of the story from Aran, or rather from the vague region in the Irish Midlands [4] where the incident is supposed to take place, to Co. Wicklow, for reasons which will be

---

[1] As mentioned by Mr. W. B. Yeats in a letter to the Editor of *The United Irishman*, Feb. 4, 1905. Miss Alice Milligan has heard the story in Donegal. Another parallel to the tale will be found in the story of the Roman Earl, at the end of Dr. Douglas Hyde's *Love-Songs of Connacht*.

[2] iii. 42–6. The book was still in typescript at the time. Mr. Yeats and Lady Gregory had tried to have it published, and Mr. John Quinn of New York had offered to pay the expense of making plates for it, but Mr. Yeats had said he wanted the book taken on its merits, even if Synge had to wait years for a publisher. At that time Synge often stayed at Coole Park, Gort, Co. Galway, Lady Gregory's residence. On Synge's tribulations to find a publisher, cf. Lady Gregory, *English Review, art. cit.*—A medium whom Mr. Yeats questioned about Synge at a *séance* of spiritualism kept on repeating "large paper," alluding (as Mr. Yeats afterwards discovered) to the "large paper edition" of *The Aran Islands* which he persuaded Messrs. Elkin Mathews and Maunsel to publish jointly for Synge.

[3] iii. 46.

[4] iii. 42 : "One day when I was travelling on foot from Galway to Dublin."

explained further. The plot in the story is practically the same as in the play—at least until the return of the woman (Nora) with the young man (Michael Dara) ; some phrases are actually transcribed.[1] Synge has only added a few unimportant details—such as the tramp stitching his coat [2]—not to be found in Pat Doran's anecdote. But he has quite altered the gruesome end, when the dead man (Dan), on finding the young man lying with his wife in the next room, " hit him a blow with the stick so that the blood out of him leapt up and hit the gallery." [3] The *dénouement*, in this as in other plays of Synge's, is strangely evanescent and indeterminate : we find no clear explanation of the exact psychological motive why the glens-woman goes off with the tramp ; the delicate analysis of the characters in this winding up is done in a kind of subconscious mezzotint ; dramatic action seems to pass away into music.

Synge's musical training is here indeed conspicuous. Dramatic composition, in this and subsequent plays of his, becomes closely akin to the art of the symphony ; the very scenario strikes one as the work of a musical composer ;

---

[1] *e. g.* " He that's dead can do no hurt " (iii. 44).

[2] Note also how carefully Synge accounts for the unlikelihood of the mock-dead man not being " tidied or layed out itself " by explaining that Dan has put a curse on whomever would touch his body except his sister. The washing of the body immediately after death is an ancient Irish custom which has survived up to the present time.

[3] iii, 45–6.

drama at this stage seems to compare with a beautiful organ voluntary. To begin with, there is an extremely elaborate symphony and antiphony of *sound* in the very dialect spoken by his characters, revealing the unsuspected musical possibilities of the English tongue, which, as the common phrase goes, " is not a language one would wish to be talked to death in." Prof. Saintsbury and other experts have written books on English prose-rhythm : nowhere is this cadence of the sentence more remarkable than in Synge. Nay more, this sense of euphony is visual as much as auditive. Théophile Gautier it was who talked of a " symphony in white major."   And indeed, in the tramp's descriptions of natural scenery, we are confronted with a fashion of *colour*-symphony not incomparable say with Whistler's *nocturnes*. Synge's study of painting appears, in point of fact, to affect his dramatic technique almost as much as his musical studies may have done. But these are characteristic beauties of Synge's plays on which we shall have occasion to enlarge in our concluding survey of his dramatic output. In *The Shadow of the Glen* they seem to us to accord but imperfectly with the otherwise realistic atmosphere of the whole piece ; and it is only when Dan and Michael sit down together to a glass of whisky that we return from this somewhat disembodied imagination to a reality more convincing and more truly Synge's own.

Very cleverly does Synge incorporate some details of his Wicklow impressions in this originally Western scenario. His tramp, we have seen, is one of those " vagrants of Wicklow "[1] whom he has so affectionately studied. Of course the place-names[2] in the play are mentioned in the prose sketches and enable one to identify with the utmost precision the exact spot where the scene is to be located. The episode of Patch Darcy being " eaten by the crows " primitively occurs in the essay " The Oppression of the Hills "[3]—the very title being reminiscent of the general atmosphere of *In the Shadow of the Glen* and of at least one particular passage[4] in the little play. The details about the herds and their ewes and about the man who would " walk through five hundred sheep and miss one of them, and he not reckoning them at all " is directly borrowed from " At a Wicklow Fair."[5] This minute research into " origins " might be carried further; our sole object in making the enumeration is to shew once more how much the prose essays represent the plays in embryo and by what curious mental process the latter have been evolved out of

[1] iv. 1.
[2] Aughrim, Lough Nahanagan, Richmond Asylum, Rathvanna. " The races beyond " (i. 9) must be the Arklow races (iv. 40). Very likely the play takes place close to Annamoe, where Synge had spent part of his youth.
[3] iv. 13.
[4] " I've heard tell it's the like of that talk you do hear from men, and they after being a great while on the back hills."
[5] iv. 45.

JOHN MILLINGTON SYNGE

Synge's rich mass of painstaking social observations.

We need not therefore surmise—as has been done by Dublin critics—that the play has any other source than its profoundly Irish one. Of course the story of the husband who " lets on to be dead the way he'll catch his wife's goings on " [1] is an old artifice to be found in many a work of fiction or drama. It occurs in Molière's *Le Malade Imaginaire* (Act III, Scene XII) and in Voltaire's *Zadig*,[2] where, " as a close student of French literature, Synge could have found it " ; [3] it also occurs in a recent French playlet, *Octave*, by Yves Mirande and Henri Géroule (1906), whose plot is almost identical with Synge's own, although Synge probably did not know it. But the whole theme at bottom is but a re-telling of the ancient Oriental legend of the Faithless Widow.[4] Still we must take Synge's own word

---

[1] iii. 45.

[2] Chapter II : "Le Nez." Zadig corresponds to Dan Burke, Azora to Nora Burke, Cador to the tramp.

[3] D. J. O'Donoghue, "Synge : A Personal Appreciation " (*Irish Independent*, March 26, 1909) ; "The Synge Boom : Foreign Influences " (*Irish Independent*, Aug. 21, 1911). Synge had a great fondness for Voltaire's *Contes*.

[4] See the controversy between Mr. Yeats and the Editor of the *United Irishman* in the issues of Jan. 7, 1905, p. 5 ; Jan. 28, 1905, p. 1 ; Feb. 4, 1905. On the legend itself, cf. Ed. Grisebach, *Die treulose Witwè, eine orientalische Novelle und ihre Wanderung durch die Weltlitteratur* (Leipzig : W. Friedrich, 4th ed., 1884 ; republished as *Die Wanderung der Novelle von der treulosen Witwe durch die Weltlitteratur*, Berlin, 1886) ; *Irodalomtœrteneti Kœzlemenyek* (a Czech review of literary history), vol. xxi, 1911 : "A Variant of the Ephesian Matron,"

that his play " differs essentially from any version of the story of the Widow of Ephesus with which he was acquainted."[1] The apparent similarity between Synge's Irish play and the non-Irish legend simply shews that these elemental folk-tales are world-wide. And it may be asserted that, however intimate Synge's contact with foreign literatures may have been, the substantial nucleus of his little piece remains principally Irish. In the words of Mr. Yeats, there is no need for resorting to " the assertion made in ignorance but repeated in dishonesty, that Synge had taken his fable and characters 'from a writer of the Roman decadence,' not from his own mind nor that profound knowledge of cot and curagh which he was admitted to possess."[2]

However, *In the Shadow of the Glen* has been and to a certain extent still is unpopular in Ireland. After having been hissed on the opening night, it produced a hot controversy in the papers, and its performance led to something of an internal crisis in the affairs of the Irish National Theatre Society, Mrs. Gonne-MacBride having resigned on account of it. It was objected to mainly

by Weber. As to the idea of the mock-dead man, it already occurred in the wake scene of Dion Boucicault's *The Shaughraun* (1875) and in Crofton Croker's *The Corpse Watchers*. It is an ancient folk-tale. In other versions the man is only a malingerer.

[1] Synge's letter to the Editor of the *United Irishman*, Feb. 11, 1905, p. 1.

[2] *Synge and the Ireland of his Time*, p. 2. The " writer of the Roman decadence " is Petronius.

because of its supposed un-Irishness.   In the first
place, it was (rather wrongly, as we have just
seen) regarded as a work patterned on some
foreign model, and arbitrarily dubbed Irish.   But
the consideration which had most weight was
that the play, without being actually slanderous,
dealt with what after all was but an exception,
and, in so doing, seemed to barter away the
firmest national asset : the unimpeachable chastity
of Irish home life, in contradistinction to the
essential immorality of British " society " drama.
Some Nationalist critics denied with perfect
sincerity " that such a thing could happen at all,
while others who knew the country better said
that it could, but should never have been staged."[1]
All these charges were beside the true question :
Synge's sole intention had been to make not a
play of " ideas," but merely a work of art dealing with Irish life, even in a somewhat unusual
aspect ; and all these arguments, by their methods
even more than by what they actually proved,
or attempted to prove, evidenced utter ignorance
of how real literature and real drama do their
work.

II

Synge's diptych of one-act plays is singularly
illustrative of the two chief aspects of Irish
country-life. *In the Shadow of the Glen* dealt
with pastoral Ireland ; *Riders to the Sea* is taken

[1] W. B. Yeats, *Samhain*, No. 4, p. 13 ; also *Collected Works*,
vol. iv, p. 120.

up with the sombre poetry of sea-faring life. It smacks richly of the Ocean and its saltness; and in its attempt to depict the marine atmosphere on the stage, successfully rivals with— nay, in our view, surpasses—the comparatively few plays in which this difficult experiment has ever been tried.[1]

The date of composition of *Riders* has been already stated. The piece was first performed by the I.N.T.S. at the Molesworth Hall, Dublin, on February 25, 1904, and has since then been acted all over Ireland and in English-speaking countries. Contrary to assertions often made, it has never been produced in Prague or Buda-Pesth.

The site of the play is pitched in "an island off the west of Ireland"—undoubtedly Aran. On wave-bitten, wind-swept Inishmaan Synge had perceived the awe-inspiring tragicality of the seamen's lives, with the shiver of peasant grief at the human toll exacted by the rapacious deep, and the agony of women young and old who can do no more than wait and weep at home. It was on his fourth visit to the Aran Isles that he heard of the case of "second sight" which has suggested the very imaginative title of the tragedy : " When the horses were coming down to the slip an old woman saw her son, that was drowned a while ago, riding on one of

---

[1] To speak only of the Irish school itself, we know only of two sea-tragedies : *The Racing Lug*, by "Seumas O'Cuisin," and *The Storm*, by Hugh Barden. See also Mr. Edward Martyn's Ibsenian play, *The Enchanted Sea*, published in 1902 and produced in 1904.

JOHN MILLINGTON SYNGE

them " ; [1] and he had previously made miscellaneous observations about the islanders' way of riding,[2] the maternal feeling among the women,[3] the fisherfolk's continual dread of the sea,[4] above all about the natives' attitude towards death,[5] that have unmistakably gone to the making of the play.

It will be readily conceded that a tracing of the psychological process by which Synge welded together these many details into a harmonious whole, although a task of extreme interest, would be a somewhat hazardous reconstruction, given the lack of biographical information, and the absence of any *central* " source " as in the case of *In the Shadow of the Glen*.[6] Suffice it therefore to analyze the dramatic moments or stages and the elements of pathos in the finished play.

The thread of material action is easy enough to follow. The scene is the cabin of Maurya, a fisherman's aged wife, whom the sea has already bereft of her husband and four sons. She is awaiting news of another missing son, Michael. A " young priest " has just brought in fragments of clothing found on the body of a drowned man washed up far away on the coast of Donegal, for Maurya's two daughters to identify. They recognize them as having belonged to Michael, and conceal them in the

[1] iii. 222.   [2] iii. 59.   [3] iii. 111–12.
[4] iii. 127, 164.   [5] iii. 208–9.
[6] *Scattered* germs of the play are to be found in the Aran book (iii. 121, 122, 154, 156, 167, etc.).

turf-loft, "the way the old woman won't know of them at all," nor "be getting her death with crying and lamenting." They strive to dissuade their last brother, Bartley, who is about to put to sea in a terrible storm, from undertaking his perilous voyage to the Galway fair. But he remains obdurate even to the entreaties of his mother, who is yet ignorant of her other son's fate, and he departs on horseback without the old woman's blessing.

The dramatic interest here is not one of misgiving or ambiguity, for the moment Bartley goes we feel sure he will never return, and, as Maurya herself declares with terrible prescience, "when the black night is falling I'll have no son left me in the world." Indeed, it is every onlooker's immediate foreboding that the boards bought for Michael's coffin will serve for Bartley's. So great is the certainty that there is not even the excitement of suspense ; and the action, though it will ceaselessly and unobtrusively widen and advance without a jar to the logically fatal and indubitable conclusion, can hardly be said to be progressive.

This extraordinarily deep sense of inevitableness is, we dare say, the richest source of tragic emotion in the play. When Maurya hastens away to bestow her blessing on Bartley, and is prevented from doing so by her otherworld, "spaewife"-like [1] vision of dead Michael riding

---

[1] "Spaewife" is the Scotch for a woman gifted with second sight.

in attendance upon him, this dream, which she
defines with Shakespearean abruptness "the fear-
fullest thing," but expresses our common and
natural foresight of the gloomy end of the
tragedy. From the slow beginning onwards,
we have been more or less unconsciously "pre-
pared" (technically and otherwise) for the
revelation by Synge's subtle and stark realism,
which causes the homeliest details to assume a
fearsome and premonitory significance. Intimate, familiar things like the "young priest"
who is only heard of, the ominous gust of wind
that blows the door open, the turf for the fire in
a corner and the clothes of Michael in another,
the fine white boards from Connemara leaning
against the wall, the forgotten "bit of bread"
which Maurya takes to Bartley, the dropped
stitches in the stocking, are but weird symbols
of an overmastering doom. Seemingly trivial
incidents become as it were dumb actors in a
sort of *arrière-théâtre* which is in eerie unison
with the human drama before us. Expectant
anxiety and imaginative awe gradually steal over
us ; we have before long divined that our pre-
vision is fulfilled ; and yet, when Maurya re-
enters with haunted eyes, a lonely, stately figure
as majestic as the sea itself, her disclosure comes
to us, if not altogether as a surprise, certainly as
an irresistible tragic shock.

It may be well to pause in this breathless
drama to inquire into the exact nature and
origin of Synge's conception of fate. In this

RIDERS TO THE SEA
From an oil painting by John Currie

AND THE IRISH THEATRE

little act we are confronted with an impersonal
note of impending terror—a perception of power
intense, irresponsible, unfathomable, consigning
humanity to utter destruction. Truly are the
characters in their unprofitable strife with the
cosmic forces representative of what a contemporary French playwright[1] aptly terms " le
drame des consciences et du destin." Their
conflict with the Ocean makes them great
because nothing stands between them and the
fierce onset of ineluctable circumstance ; it
actually raises them to heroic proportions.
Synge's fatalism in *Riders to the Sea* is a distinctly Pagan, hence artistic, fatalism. It is, to
some extent, the conception of a destiny akin
to the Anankè which overshadows the beautiful
in the Æschylean tragedy ; it is also, in a way,
the grim Celtic Ankou, the Breton personifi-
cation of death.[2] Possibly Synge derived his
keen mystical sense of doom from the modern
German *Schicksalsdrama*, with which he was
acquainted ; or, if a more adequate parallel be
sought for, from his favourite author Maeterlinck, especially in his play *Interior* (1894)—
which, it may be recalled, figures in translation
in the répertoire of the Abbey Theatre, where
it was produced in Synge's lifetime.[3] A profound and oft-quoted passage in *The Treasure*

---

[1] Henri Bataille.
[2] Cf. A. le Braz, *La Légende de la Mort chez les Bretons
Armoricains*, new ed., chap. iii.
[3] March 16, 1907. Cf. also *L'Intruse.*

163

of the Humble (" The Tragical in Daily Life ")
has it that there is more real drama in " an old
man seated in his arm-chair, patiently waiting
with his lamp beside him, lending an unconscious ear to all the eternal laws that reign
about his house, interpreting, without understanding, the silence of doors and windows, and
the quivering voice of light, submitting with
bent head to the presence of his soul and his
destiny," than in " the lover who strangles his
mistress, the captain who conquers in battle,
or ' the husband who avenges his honour.' "
Synge's minimization of external action, his
psychologizing or interiorizing of the drama
which, we have seen, animates even things by
some all-encompassing but wholly acceptable
symbolism, seems to be contained in this *locus
classicus.* At the same time, the differences must
be pointed out. On the one hand, it is a far
cry from Synge's live, clearly-outlined, flesh-
and-blood personages to Maeterlinck's more or
less sickly *pupazzi*—as Mr. Yeats beautifully
defines them, " persons who are as faint as a
breath upon a looking-glass, symbols who can
speak a language slow and heavy with dreams
because their own life is but a dream." [1] In
other words, Maeterlinck has only atmosphere ;
Synge has atmosphere plus characterization.
Next, whereas Maeterlinck, in this and other
plays of his, would fain wholly spiritualize
dramatic action, state its case in terms of pure

[1] *Synge and the Ireland of his Time*, p. 29.

consciousness, hence make fate entirely imma-
nent, Synge, in *Riders to the Sea*, stays half-way,
and retains a material fatality that altogether
transcends man. The sea is here identified with
doom and death ; it is the sea whose formidable
presence is felt all about the play ; the sea
that lurks behind the stage ; the sea that
throws with loaded dice in the game of human
existence.

This undeniable Maeterlinckian influence remains therefore immaterial as compared with
Synge's direct and vivid contact with the dismal
realities of Aran life. Death as he relentlessly
perceived it amidst his rude island environment
passes through and purifies the whole of his
immortal little act. His sympathetic insight
imparts to him a sense of the grave and overwhelming dignity that impresses one, say, in
Andreef's novels or in Hugo's epic tale of
Gilliat's struggle on the lonely reef with the im-
placable laws of Nature. He himself confesses
in the Aran book that he " could not help feeling
that he was talking with men who were under a
judgment of death."[1] And this acute realiza-
tion by the islanders that the shadow of nothing-
ness is perpetually hovering about them finds its
expression in Synge's play as in actual Aran life
in the half-savage, half-musical melopœia known
as the keen (*caoin*).[2] This lilted recitative, with
all its threnetic appeal, is another very impressive
pathetic note. Irish playwrights know it well—

---

[1] iii. 216.   [2] Cf. iii. 50-2, 212 ff.

witness the dirge in Lady Gregory's *Gaol Gate*—
and Synge the musician also fully grasps its
dramatic efficiency, for he will use it again in
his *Deirdre*. Faintly it sounds from the opening
of the piece, like some " unheard melody " perceived by the spiritual ear alone ; but at the
climax of the tragedy it rises and swells in en-
trancing power, and mingles with the moan of
the Atlantic which one knows without words is
dashing its surf beneath the cabin walls. And,
as we listen to the strange litany of Maurya
chanting the names of her dead men-children,
we remember Synge's wonderful observation as
he returned from the burial of an old woman in
Inishmaan : " This grief of the keen is no
personal complaint for the death of one woman
over eighty years, but seems to contain the whole
passionate rage that lurks somewhere in every
native of the island. In this cry of pain the
inner consciousness of the people seems to lay
itself bare for an instant, and to reveal the mood
of beings who feel their isolation in the face of
a universe that wars on them with winds and
seas." [1]

The wail of the peasant women is renewed
when, by a spectacular and somewhat melo-
dramatic stage-effect which may be thought the
one fault in the play, the corpse of Bartley is
borne into the room. But this slight mistake is
amply redeemed by the singularly august, almost
Greek, solemnity of the play at the close. The

[1] iii. 52.

lyrical fervour of the lament now gives way to a note of resignation which, instead of being bathetic as might be expected, actually heightens and intensifies the tragic effect. Maurya's closing words of half-heathenish, half-Catholic submission, " No man at all can be living for ever, and we must be satisfied," do not mark an anticlimax, but on the contrary, a paroxysm of " exaltation " which lifts the protagonist, in her perhaps overstrained part, above the tragedy itself. The old woman, who is what Synge once styled the " strong central life,"[1] can now almost take pleasure in her last son's death : " There isn't anything more the sea can do to me ; " now that the tale of her loss is complete, she at last secures the ultimate rest and resigned lethargy of a paralyzed heart.[2]

We would fain interpret this concluding note of restraint and ascetic renunciation—which does not in the least debar genuine sympathy for the distress of bereft Aran motherhood—as expressive of Synge's individual stoicism and, in Walter Pater's phrase, " aristocracy of passion." Synge, it must be remembered, ever and always remains a personal author. He told Mr. Pádraic Colum that the reason why he wrote *Riders to the Sea*

[1] A phrase which Synge once used in criticizing Mr. Stephen Gwynn's *Robert Emmet*, which was first written as a play. " It lacked," he said, " the strong central life." *Robert Emmet* was therefore subsequently re-written as an " historical romance " published by Messrs. Macmillan in 1909.

[2] We shall find the same acceptance of foretold fate in *Deirdre of the Sorrows*.

was that he had personally begun to anticipate something of the sadness of old age and death. Yet this autobiographical element does not exclude the influence of two literary works which may have reinforced Synge's precocious sense of human annihilation, and, together with the scenes which he had witnessed in Aran, led him to compose a sea-tragedy.

The first of these external sources of the play, as indicated in a foregoing chapter, is M. Pierre Loti's *Pêcheur d'Islande*. Synge greatly admired Loti, and the novel—which he was re-reading about the time he wrote his two one-act plays and parts of the Aran book—was among the volumes which he had formerly borrowed in Paris from a circulating library in the Latin Quarter at the suggestion of his friend Mr. D. J. O'Donoghue. One may indeed detect a striking parallelism of subject, atmosphere and situation in the two works. Some details and sentences in Loti are quite in keeping with the keynote of Synge's one-act tragedy :

" Ces hommes primitifs avec ces grands silences de la mer qu'on devinait autour d'eux . . ."[1]

" C'était donc possible, c'était donc vrai qu'on allait le lui enlever, ce dernier petit-fils ! "[2]

" C'était bien ce qu'elle avait deviné, mais cela la faisait trembler seulement ; à présent que c'était certain, ça n'avait pas l'air de la toucher.

[1] Ed. Calmann-Lévy, p. 11.
[2] *Ibid.*, p. 17.

. . . Elle confondait cette mort avec d'autres :
Elle en avait tant perdu, de fils ! . . ."[1]

This last touch, the facts just recorded, and
the general juxtaposition of texts afford proof
positive of actual influence. Indeed this is the
sole instance in which it may be asserted with
absolute certainty that Synge was beholden to
some one else, if not for the actual subject
of a play, at least for the external incentive or
stimulus that fostered and vitalized his own
original Irish theme, and ultimately inclined
him to its selection and treatment. On the
whole, Synge's close intimacy with life in Aran
remained a far more important factor in the
genesis of *Riders* than M. Loti's literary influence. In other words, Synge in Ireland felt the
tragedy of the sea just as Loti had felt it in
Brittany. Add to this that *An Iceland Fisherman*, despite its descriptive beauties and psychological merits, and its all-pervading notion of an
impending terror, is a somewhat lax and inor-
ganic narrative, whilst *Riders*, the work of a
genius unhampered by technical awkwardness,
is remarkable for its pithy (some say excessive)
condensation and swiftness.

The other analogue of Synge's play in European literature is Hermann Heijermans' Dutch
four-act *Meerspiel*, *On Hoop van Zegen* (*The Good
Hope*). The original was published in 1900,
and immediately obtained a success in Holland
and in two different German versions throughout

---

[1] Ed. Calmann-Lévy, p. 67.

Germany. Then it was produced in a French
adaptation by J. Lemaire and J. Schürmann at
the Théâtre Antoine, Paris, on December 8,
1902, and subsequently (April, 1903) in
London, in Miss Christopher Marie St. John's
hitherto unpublished English translation, with
Miss Ellen Terry in the part of the old fisherman's wife.[1] Synge met Miss Christopher St.
John at Mr. W. B. Yeats's rooms often enough
between January and April, 1903, but he was
not in town at the time of the first performance,
and anyhow, we have seen that *Riders* was then
finished. In the Dutch play, as in *Riders*, the
tragedy is made the deeper by the old woman's
submission to—nay, acquiescence in—the decrees
of fate ; and the general theme, based on the
universal fact that the sea is very dangerous, and
earning one's life by it, very hard, is practically
the same. But with this common inspiration
the similarity ends ; no particular resemblance
of treatment can be detected ; and on the whole,
as the English translator herself avers,[2] "there
is no way of proving Synge's indebtedness to,
or ignorance of, *The Good Hope.*"

This may be deemed an all too lengthy
comment on this diminutive one-act tragedy.
Tragedy it truly is ; indeed it is "of a new
order of tragedy altogether. It is, perhaps, not
so much tragedy as a fragment of life"—one
might almost say, in the hackneyed phrase, a

---

[1] *The Good Hope* has been revived in November, 1912, by
the Pioneer Players, London.　　　[2] Letter to the writer.

" slice of life "—" set in the atmosphere of tragedy. Even as there is not water in a mist of the hills because it is all moisture, so there is not tragedy in *Riders to the Sea* because it is all tragical." [1] It is elegy all through, but elegy in a highly dramatic form. The reason why we have dealt with it at such length is that it is Synge's absolutely unquestioned and well-nigh flawless masterpiece, the one play by which the general body of his countrymen desire his memory to live. It strikingly exemplifies Synge's unique and felicitous blending of cosmopolitan literature and Irish social experience into a work of heart-rending universal appeal as well as of individual self-expression. His other plays, like *The Shadow of the Glen*, are perhaps more narrowly national, and on this score objected to ; and perhaps it was a mistake to perform (at the time of the now historical row) the broadly human, hence generally accepted, *Riders to the Sea* as a curtain-raiser to the intensely Irish, hence ever-discussed, *Playboy*. Further, the little play illustrates Synge's uncompromisingly veracious and drastic realism— although he here presents a reality altogether destitute of " joy "—, his sense of the elemental and the dynamic, above all, his unsurpassed skill and craftsmanship, which match the play itself

---

[1] Darrell Figgis, " The Art of J. M. Synge " (*Fortnightly Review*, Dec., 1911 ; *The Forum*, Jan., 1912 ; republished in *Studies and Appreciations*, London : Dent ; New York : E. P. Dutton, 1912, pp. 34 *et seq.*), one of the ablest critical studies on Synge.

in its poignancy. *Riders to the Sea*, without in
the least being, as it has been somewhat hyper-
bolically hailed by Irish and English judges, the
greatest tragedy of modern times, remains one
of the most remarkable achievements in British
play-making, and a dramatic episode of exceptional human interest.

III

It is impossible to dismiss these two little
pieces without making a few brief comments on
Synge's professional deftness in the one-act play
as a dramatic *genre*. The art of the one-act
play, which one critic ingeniously compares to
" carving the Commandments on a threepenny-
bit "[1], is analogous to that of the short story.[2]
Both are dependent on a sudden evocation of
atmosphere at the outset ; both are so to speak
literary miniatures, attempts to express a whole
world in epitome, requiring therefore a maximum
of tenseness, terseness, and economy of detail—
limitations with which the lengthier dramatic
productions are unacquainted. Of course this
resemblance is not much to be wondered at, since
Synge's little plays have their origins in short

[1] C. E. Montague, *Dramatic Values*, p. 9.
[2] Cf. the introduction to Mr. H. G. Wells's collection of
short stories, *The Country of the Blind* (Nelson's two-shilling
novels), in which he mentions, among other interesting technical
observations, Mr. George Moore's malicious distinction between
the short story and the anecdote.

folk-stories. However, we do not mean to say that Synge would have made a more efficient short-story-writer than a playwright proper. His work needs no prop from the " might-have-been " ; it is what it is—dramatic in the true sense of the word. Nay, from the very beginning of his career as a playwright, Synge attains an artistic level beyond which he will never go. In these two " one-acters " he tackles drama in all its difficulties, and tackles it with triumphant success.

Such is the significance of the one-act play in its relation to Synge himself. But it may also be taken as indicative of a real need and tradition in the present Irish school of drama. One cannot say whether Synge is responsible for the fact that the other Irish dramatists also write one-act plays ; but as a " collective fact " it is highly interesting. Mr. Yeats has penned many tiny blank-verse dramas, and Lady Gregory entitles her well-known series of comedies *Seven Short Plays*. Possibly this predominance of one-act plays may be regarded as typical of the essential simplicity or humility of the Irish Theatre at its inception—a distinctive trait, we have seen, of its acting and scenery. This fresh exemplification of its radical difference from the English stage, with its long-winded five-act productions, deserved to be parenthetically noted.

173

IV

It is at this juncture that Synge resolutely threw in his lot with the Irish National Theatre Society by becoming identified with Mr. Yeats and Lady Gregory in the direction of the Abbey Theatre from its opening on December 27, 1904. His personal relations with the other two members of the triumvirate presiding over the destinies of the little playhouse by the Liffey were always extremely cordial, and, if Synge was to become the most important, certainly the most discussed, playwright of the theatre, as one of its co-directors he was a complete success. Everybody loved him for his kindly and unassuming ways. Synge preferred not to interfere with the financial affairs of the theatre, which he willingly handed over to its able Honorary Secretary, Mr. W. A. Henderson. He was very nervous about fire, and one day Mr. Joseph Holloway, the architect of the theatre, had to take him all over the scene docks, explaining that in case of emergency it would be easy to escape from all parts of the house. Synge was by nature more especially interested in the staging and rehearsing of the plays. In the former capacity he found a particularly competent collaborator in Mr. W. G. Fay, who acted as stage-manager until 1908. They used to discuss together miscellaneous technical points, such as the exits and entrances of the personages ; and

174

once, as Synge had suggested that the old woman in a piece—*Riders to the Sea* if we are not mistaken—should go out by the back door, whilst Mr. Fay, with his almost telepathic divination of the theatrical requirements of Synge's plays, maintained that it would be better if she entered the bedroom, Synge, with his usual good-humour, readily agreed with him. He was a careful producer ; and before his plays saw the light of publicity he would know all the effects he wanted,[1] and how each word he had written should be recited. In fact, he generally had the text off by heart, and repeated the sentences aloud over and over again till he got the turn of phrase he wished for, and the word-music right.

When the Irish players, having not yet removed to their present headquarters, still rehearsed at St. Teresa's Hall, Camden Street, at the back of a small produce shop, Synge's familiar attitude was to lean on the footlights of the rude slightly-raised platform, at the upper end of the room, with a piece of rough canvas hung up behind him, in order to shut him off from the rest of the hall, where other rehearsals were in progress, or carpenters at work on new scene-frames. Synge would not mind his friends slipping behind the canvas and mutely watching the soft, hushed speech of the performers. On the opening night of the Abbey Theatre Synge was sitting in the large dressing-room over the vestibule—the

---

[1] Observe, in this connection, the extreme precision and terseness of his stage-directions.

Coroner's Court in the then recent days when
the playhouse was a morgue—on the corner of
a white deal table, while the actors dressed for
Mr. W. B. Yeats's *On Baile's Strand*. Mr. John
B. Yeats, coming in, saw Synge and asked him to
keep that position and chat away to him as he
was. The artist took out a note-book and in a
twinkling had created an extremely lifelike pencil-
sketch of Synge, which subsequently appeared
in an issue of *Samhain*, the organ of the I.N.T.S.

Such are the more or less commonplace details
which may be once for all placed on record
relative to Synge's practical association with the
Abbey stage. His dramatic activities had at last
found a fixed and congenial abode ; and, without
any further dwelling on biography, we may now
pursue our critical study of his plays, which
thenceforward succeeded each other with calm
deliberation.

V

Synge informs us in a footnote of his preface
to *The Tinker's Wedding*—the title of a vernacular
Scotch song which he probably knew [1]—that he
wrote his play about the time he was working at

---

[1] *The Tinkler's Waddin'*, by William Watt (1793–1859);
cf. T. F. Henderson, *Scottish Vernacular Literature* (Edinburgh :
John Grant, 1910), p. 457. It is the first song given (with
music) in Robert Ford's *Vagabond Songs and Ballads of Scotland
with many old and familiar melodies* (Paisley : Alexander
Gardner, new and improved edition, 1904 ; originally issued in
two large volumes, the first in 1899, the second in 1901).
See a note on the song and its author on p. 4. Its subject has
nothing to do with Synge's play.

Riders to the Sea and *In the Shadow of the Glen*, and subsequently re-cast it. This was, in point of fact, the very first play ever conceived by him.[1] The present version was arrived at and published only after the *Playboy* riot ; very likely the changes effected by the re-writing were immaterial, although all our knowledge on this point is Mr. Yeats's statement that Synge altered his play " to a more unpopular form."[2] Unpopular it certainly is, remaining Synge's one work so far unacted in Ireland, where the state of religious opinion, together with the probable inequality of the Abbey Theatre directors to the strain of facing another *Playboy* week, will for some time to come render its public production impossible. Synge erred when he prognosticated in his preface that the Irish people would not " mind being laughed at without malice " : we already know how bitterly the Irish national consciousness is apt to resent such treatment. Even in London, where the comedy was first enacted on November 11, 1909 (after Synge's death) at His Majesty's by the Afternoon Theatre, with Miss Mona Limerick in the part of Sarah Casey, the curtain fell amid hissing. The play (we are told) has since been produced in America with equally dubious success.

The obvious and not altogether inconsiderable widening of Synge's dramatic technique from one act to two acts may at once be noted. Presumably the piece was first written as a one-

---

[1] John Masefield, *D. N. B.*   [2] *Op. cit.*, p. 24.

177

act play, and apparently it did not deserve more. But Synge at this period had already acquired the successful dramatist's tendency to become long-winded. Therefore, his play, as a play, is far from faultless.

This disproportion in the comedy becomes more apparent when one considers the rather slender theme with which it is taken up. Synge had heard from a Wicklow peasant that the tinkers were " gallous lads " for " match-making and marrying themselves " ; [1] and a herd at the Aughrim fair had told him the story—literally related in his travel notes [2]—of how two tinkers once asked a priest to marry them for half-a-sovereign and a tin gallon can, but afterwards pretended that their ass had damaged the can in the night, so that the priest refused to have anything to do with such a " pair of rogues and schemers" as they were.

In the main Synge has kept close to the tale in his play, in which Sarah Casey, a young tinkerwoman who leads a loose life with her ditch-companion Michael Byrne, endeavours to change an irregular union by wheedling a *soggarth aroon* into marrying them at reduced fees. When they get to the church—and here is the first slight difference between the folk-tale and the play—they find out that the bridegroom's mother, Mary Byrne, has run away with the can in the night and swapped it for a pint of porter. Then the *dénouement* is entirely

---

[1] iv. 5.   [2] iv. 47–48.

Synge's own invention : at first Sarah Casey insults her would-be mother-in-law; but soon all three side against the priest, who now point-blank refuses to marry them and threatens to tell the police about all their thefts. Suddenly Michael takes off his coat, runs at the priest with the ass's reins, knocks him down into the ditch, gags him, ties him up in a sack,[1] and, as he wriggles about like a worm, is about to run him headlong into a bog-hole. At last the worthy ecclesiastic is released on promising that he will not go " tattling to the peelers " ; but he is hardly on his feet again when, without for-swearing himself, he utters a Latin malediction against the reprobates, who run away post-haste, leaving him master of the situation.

The whole piece may be characterized as broad farce. No one but a stolid, pedantic critic will ever dream of taking it as a social document : is it not obvious that, were an Irish priest assaulted by a bevy of tinkers, the R.I.C.

---

[1] The incident of the tying-up of the priest in the sack was most likely suggested by the following speech of the Lout in " The Lout and His Mother" *ap*. Dr. Douglas Hyde's *Abhráin Diadha Chuige Connacht* (*Religious Songs of Connacht*, London : Unwin ; Dublin : Gill, 1906, ii. 311), a book which Synge read and re-read :

" 'S dá mbeitheá-sa marbh ar maidin amárach
'S go mbéarfainn chum sagairt thú, ceangailte i mála,
Ní léighfeadh dhuit aifrionn gan airgead láimhe."

Translation—
" Sure if you were dead to-morrow morning
And I were to bring you to a priest tied up in a bag
He would not read a mass for you without hand-money."

would readily interfere? Still we rather feel
inclined to regret that Synge ever penned this
immature comedy, which, though it constitutes
a notable addition to the ever-amusing literature
of rascality and vagabondage,[1] distinctly offends
against æsthetic decency and good taste. By its
ludicrous representation of a young tinkerwoman
as an earnest Catholic, its malignant portraiture
of a covetous priest, the grotesque blasphemous-
ness of its language, it has wounded sincere
religious susceptibilities which had a right to
be respected in a country where religion domi-
nates the public mind. Again, technically
considered, the play is by no means perfect.

The sole consideration which may account
for its having been written is that a personal,
rather than a specifically dramatic, interest
attaches to it. It marks Synge's escape from the
joyless reality of *Riders to the Sea* to a vein of
irresistible gruesome fun. The brutal winding-
up of the comedy—which, again, Synge entirely
imagined—is in this respect peculiarly representative of his caustic humour. In it we seem to
find his abnormally loud note of naturalistic protest, his usual relish of the disreputable, not
because disreputable, but because expressive of
a crude and cruel reality more pungent and

[1] Cf. Frank Wadleigh Chandler, *Romances of Roguery : an
episode in the history of the novel* (in two parts, published for the
Columbia University Press by the Macmillan Co., 1899) ; *The
Literature of Roguery* (in the " Types of English Literature "
Series, edited by William Allen Neilson. London : Constable ;
Boston and New York: Houghton Mifflin, 1907, 2 vols.).

THE TINKER'S CURSE
From a water-colour drawing by Jack B. Yeats

exciting than reality itself. This, indeed, is not the gentle, almost harmless, Milesian humour as one commonly conceives it ; it is not, for instance, the amiable humour of the amiable Lady Gregory ; it is a startling, baffling humour which, evading the ordinary sense of the word, leaves one on the borderland between joy and sadness—a fierce, scorching and sinister irony which recalls the Swiftian harshness, the mediæval violence of a Villon, or the picaresque boisterousness of the French and Spanish farces with which Synge was acquainted. Yet, primarily, it strikes the keynote of a temperament.

At the same time, the comedy is illustrative of its author's peculiarly non-religious attitude. Religious belief, we have seen, had practically no influence on Synge ; and though he had been brought up in the Protestant creed, he never had any denominational or sectarian bias. Nor do we concur with some Irish critics in interpreting *The Tinker's Wedding* as the work of a Voltairian or a free-thinking controversialist [1] who had learnt and practised anti-clericalism on the Continent. Synge does not intentionally scoff at things sacred ; he wrote his play not with anti-Catholic forethought, but with a double artistic aim. On the one hand, he wished to depict the life of the tinkers—a tribe of irregular, ribald outlaws as typical of rural Ireland as the gypsies are of

---

[1] (Synge was very fond of Paul-Louis Courier's *Pamphlets*, especially the *Lettre à M. Renouard, libraire, sur une tache faite à un manuscrit de Florence.*)

rural England, or the *gitanos* of rural Spain. In the second place, it was Synge's object to contrast—as has been done, in how different a fashion, in " Lewis Purcell " 's Ulster play, *The Pagan*—the two types of Irish civilization, the Heathen and the Christian—Ireland before and after St. Patrick. Mary Byrne, the degraded tinkerwoman who guzzles and swears, personifies in this connection the undying forces of Hibernian Paganism which, for artistic reasons, were so dear to Synge. The stupendous lewdness of old-time Heathendom lurks in her. Yet this attempt at dramatic antithesis— a process, we have seen, as old as the primitive Irish dialogues —remains on the whole incongruous and unsuccessful : for is not the priest in the play himself a Pagan ?[1]

VI

The Well of the Saints (composed in 1902–3) was first performed on February 4, 1905, to a house of barely two dozen, at the newly-opened Abbey Theatre, where it was repeated for the following six nights. It has since been produced in Ireland, England and America, and in a German version, *Der Heilige Brunnen*, the work of Dr. Max Meyerfeld, at Prof. Max Reinhardt's Theatre in Berlin in 1906, also at the theatre in Munich, August, 1908.[2]

---

[1] On the other hand, why should the priest's malediction frighten the tinkers if they are really Pagans ?
[2] Abbey Theatre, British Association Programme (Sept. 7,

AND THE IRISH THEATRE

The further and this time definitive extension
of Synge's *manière* from two to three acts is the
technical feature which immediately strikes one
in this fourth play of his. The fable, which
is among the simplest and most moving ones
ever chosen by a modern dramatist, has in it all
the searching beauty of an ancient parable. It
is the story of two blind, ugly, weather-beaten
old beggars—husband and wife, Martin and
Mary Doul—whose lifelong sitting at a lonely
cross-roads, " hearing the birds and bees hum-
ming in every weed of the ditch and the swift
flying things racing in the air," has taught them
to replace reality by dreams and physical sight
by imaginative vision. They fancy each other
to be beautiful. As they sit talking beside a
church in ruins, Timmy the smith brings news
that a wandering friar is coming with water
from a holy well in the West that will cure any
complaint. The saint arrives, and, anointing
their eyes with the miraculous water, restores to
them the tragic gift of sight. Very soon, however, they find the actual world in general, and
their own physical persons in particular, less
lovely than the dream-illumined night in which

1908): " *The Well of the Saints* has been played in German
last month with great success in Munich." Mr. Yeats states
in *Samhain* (No. 5, p. 4) that " It has been accepted for immediate production by the Deutsches Theater, Berlin." The
version produced in Munich was a one-act version compressed
from the original. The performance brought Synge (who was
in Ireland at the time) £3 10s. royalties (cf. his letter of Aug.
28, 1908, quoted *ap.* Lady Gregory, *art. cit.*).

they had lived so long enchanted. In course of
time their eyes grow "dim" again and blindness overwhelms them. The saint would fain
miraculously heal them anew, but they are only
too glad to return to their former state and, as
the pious man is about to cure Martin Doul once
more, the blind beggar dashes the holy can from
the friar's hand.

The play has no actual, definite source in
Synge's non-dramatic writings. As in the case
of *Riders to the Sea*, the theme is only distantly
suggested by one passage in *The Aran Islands*,
and scattered details here and there have been
borrowed from the prose observations. Miraculous fountains are numerous all over Ireland ; [1]
Synge mentions seeing in Inishmaan near an "old
ruined church" of the Ceathair Aluinn (The
Four Comely Persons), a "holy well that was
famous for cures of blindness and epilepsy"; and
he records the tale of a child's healing at the
well that was told him by Mourteen, the old
Irish-speaking story-teller.[2] An Inishere story
supplied the saint, and the fierce wrangle of the
Aran couple[3] seems to have suggested the
quarrels between Martin Doul and his wife after
the recovery of their sight. Martin accuses
Timmy the smith of plucking his living ducks ;
this, too, is an observation made on the islands :

---

[1] Cf. Lady Wilde, *Ancient Legends of Ireland* (London :
Ward and Downey, 1888), pp. 236–56 : "The Holy Wells ;"
and the well-known folk-song or carol entitled "Mary's Well."
[2] iii. 13–14.　　　　　[3] iii. 197 ff.

THE WELL OF THE SAINTS
From an oil painting by John Currie

" Sometimes when I go into a cottage I find all the women of the place down on their knees plucking the feathers from live ducks and geese."[1] Again, the oft-mentioned Patch Ruadh (Red-Haired Pat) is one of the Gaelic names heard by Synge in Inishmaan.[2] Lastly, it may be recalled that Synge's first Gaelic teacher in Aranmore had been an old " dark " man.[3] But, as in *The Shadow of the Glen*, the play has been transplanted from Aran to Leinster.[4]

The plot of the play not being contained in Synge's prose topographies, extraneous " origins " may be and have been, in point of fact, sought for. Thus, Mr. D. J. O'Donoghue, Synge's personal friend, avers that Synge got the root-idea of *The Well of the Saints* " in a play by M. Clémenceau."[5] We presume Mr. O'Donoghue alludes to M. Clémenceau's Chinese one-act piece, *Le Voile du Bonheur* (1901),[6] which, in its beginning at least, is actually a little like Synge's own production. But—may we repeat it once more ?—it is manifest that such tales occur in

---

[1] iii. 219. [2] iii. 161. [3] iii. 3, 15.
[4] There are also hints taken from the Wicklow sketches : *e.g.* Martin and Mary Doul's remarks on the dignity of white hair (i. 113, 115) remind us of the old tramp who had spent a month in Kilmainham, and said : " What use is an old man without his white hair ? " . . . (iv. 4).
[5] *Art. cit.* Cf. also W. J. Lawrence, " The Abbey Theatre : its history and mystery," *Weekly Freeman*, Xmas No., Dec. 7, 1912, p. 11.
[6] Produced in an admirable anonymous English version by the " Theatre in Eyre " at St. George's House, Regent Street, London, Nov., 1912.

many, practically all, folk-lores ; and it is inevitable that such broadly human subjects should be handled by various writers in widely distant countries and centuries. We find a re-telling of the fable in the January and May story related by Chaucer in *The Merchant's Tale ;* and, if we deny Synge the right of being an independent and original playwright, whose works must at all costs be traced to non-Irish models, we can as well point out that, as an admirer of Maeterlinck, he might have found a fountain " whose water opened the eyes of the blind " in *Pelléas and Mélisande* (Act II, Scene i) and a treatment of the theme of blindness in *The Sightless.* Also, we have it on the authority of a prominent Abbey Theatre playwright that Synge derived the miracle-idea in his play from Zola's and Huysmans' books on *Lourdes.* But who will fail to perceive the inanity of suchlike genealogical investigations ? We have no coercive proof that Synge wrote his play under the influence of the above-mentioned works, and the literary pedigree of *The Well of the Saints* could easily be lengthened without certainty or profit.[1] If Synge is not to be credited with genuine freedom of invention, let us at least give him the benefit of the doubt.

---

[1] In *Marianela,* a novel by the well-known Spanish writer, Benito Pérez Galdós (7th edition, Madrid, 1888), we find a blind man, Pablo Pénaguilas, who, like Martin Doul, wrongly fancies the woman he loves (Marianela) beautiful ; when he is cured and sees her, she dies.

We must, however, make two concessions—
or rather revelations—to the chemical or recon-
structive school of Synge hypercriticism. In the
first place—a fact as yet unknown to Synge's
closest students—Synge himself did acknowledge
a source [1]—to wit, a pre-Molière French farce,
the name of which he had forgotten, and which
we have failed to identify. In it an old beggar
touched the bones of a saint in a shrine and was
cured, but the cure was not radical, and when
the infirmity returned—we are not sure it was
blindness—he positively refused to be cured
again. Such was the Continental prototype of
The Well of the Saints. But on the other hand—
a fact which will fill the Dublin exegetists with
joy—we have also discovered a most definite and
indubitable, but hitherto undetected, English
origin. It is a short story entitled "The Maid
of Malines" (Mechlin), which forms chapter iv
of Lord Lytton's *The Pilgrims of the Rhine*
(1832).[2]

The tale is fairly long and rich in incident,
but we can sum it up in its relation to *The Well
of the Saints*. Eugene St. Amand, a blind young
French gentleman, is saved from a bolting horse
by Lucille Tisseur, whose natural beauty has

---

[1] He told Mr. Yeats and Mr. Pádraic Colum.

[2] A newspaper critic stated after the first performance of
The Well of the Saints that "the story—a well-known one—
has been treated in our own day by an English novelist"
(*United Irishman*, Feb. 11, 1905, p. 1). We do not know
whether "The Maid of Malines" was the fictional equivalent
of Synge's play thus vaguely referred to.

been marred by small-pox. " It so happened
that Lucille's family were reputed for beauty,
and " [like Mary Doul, who prided herself on
being called " the beautiful dark woman " of
Ballinatone] " vain of that celebrity." St.
Amand is received in the house of Lucille's
parents, and falls in love with her. " Your voice
is very gentle," he says to her, "and that . . . is
the criterion by which I only know the young
and the beautiful "—a remark reminiscent of
Martin Doul's observation that when he " was
a young lad, and had fine sight, it was the ones
with sweet voices were the best in face." At
another time he exclaims, " Ah ! would that I
could see thee ! would that I could look upon
a face that my heart vainly endeavours to
delineate "—just as Martin Doul says to his blind
wife, " I do be thinking in the long nights it'd
be a grand thing if we could see ourselves for
one hour, or a minute itself, the way we'd know
surely we were the finest man and the finest
woman of the seven counties of the east."

Lucille, whose family are Catholic and
" possess the superstitions as well as the devotion
of the faith," hears of the miraculous cure of
a deaf-and-dumb child who has recovered his
voice at the Tomb of the Three Kings at Cologne,
and decides to go there on a pilgrimage, leaving
St. Amand in the company of her parents and of
Julie, who, in Lucille's own words, " is more
beautiful than a dream." " Say not so," answers
St. Amand ; " would I could see that I might

prove to the world how much more beautiful thou art. There is no music in her voice." Lucille tells a priest she meets at the shrine about St. Amand's blindness, and he gives her an introduction to Le Kain, a physician in Louvain famous throughout Flanders for the cures he has wrought among the blind. Lucille returns to Malines with Le Kain. St. Amand is cured and says : " Let me not see her [Lucille] alone ; let me see her in the midst of you all, that I may convince you that the heart never is mistaken in its instincts "—a situation curiously similar to that of Martin Doul trying to find his wife among all the village girls. " Lucille ! " he exclaims, " it is you, I know it, you only ! " He springs forward and falls at the feet of Julie —just as Martin mistakes Molly Byrne for Mary Doul. Disappointed with Lucille, St. Amand marries Julie ; eventually he goes to fight in Egypt against the English, and there becomes blind again, this time for ever, from ophthalmia caused by the sharp dust of the arid plains. Ultimately he restores his affection to Lucille, who has remained faithful to him, marries her, and, like the old couple in Synge's play, enters into " that serenity of mood which mostly characterizes the blind."

Nor is the close resemblance between Lytton and Synge confined to plot and incident ; one of the concluding sentences in " The Maid of Malines " admirably summarizes the whole human meaning of *The Well of the Saints*—

JOHN MILLINGTON SYNGE

" Perhaps after we have seen the actual world,
and experienced its hollow pleasures, we can
resign ourselves the better to its exclusion ; and
as the cloister which repels the ardour of our
hope is sweet to our remembrance, so the dark-
ness loses its terror, when experience has wearied
us with the glare and travail of the day."

Unlike Martin Doul, St. Amand does not get
a chance of being cured again ; the idea of the
second cure, and of its refusal by the patient,
must have been prompted by the pre-Molière
farce. As to the Lytton story, Mr. Yeats repeatedly asked Synge whether he knew it : Synge
always denied having ever read it, and we must
take his word for it. Yet the striking similarity
between *The Well of the Saints* and " The Maid
of Malines" makes it difficult to believe that
Synge was wholly unacquainted with *The Pilgrims of
the Rhine*, which was in every household at the
time of his early boyhood. He might have
read it in his nursery—the nursery to which he
refers in the preface to the *Playboy*—and afterwards become unaware of the fact. However,
the theme of *The Well of the Saints* is so world-
wide that even if Synge was unconsciously influenced by Lytton, "The Maid of Malines"
did not supply more than the bare plot of his
play ; and we have shewn in a previous section
that it is no paradox to maintain that a plot is
by itself almost valueless, and that a creative
artist like Synge can without contradiction be
actually indebted to another writer for his

scenario or outline, and remain at the same time profoundly original and Irish.

The Well of the Saints has often been proclaimed Synge's most perfect achievement. We do not entirely agree with such unstinted praise. Technically, as in *Riders to the Sea*, the action is mapped out from the start : one immediately foresees that the restoration of their sight will only bring misery to the blind couple ; our curiosity is soon at an end, and, in this case, it must be frankly owned that the plot was a little jejune for the three-act form chosen by Synge. Add to this the gross improbabilities in the characters : Martin Doul, immediately on recovering his sight, sees the " green bits of ferns," recognizes Timmy by " the black of his head " and Patch Ruadh by " his fiery hair " : has a cured blind man ever been known to distinguish colours ? Then, is such a saying as " And she after going by with her head turned the way you'd see a priest going where there'd be a drunken man in the side ditch talking with a girl " possible on the lips of an Irish peasant ? Although we by no means concur with the strict censures passed on Synge's play by ultra-Catholic critics at the time of its first production, it is equally clear that in an Irish village, where miracles are still believed in and revered, the cured blind people would have greater social importance than they have in *The Well of the Saints*. Last, but not least, we regard as utterly untrue to the Irish nature Martin Doul's gesture when he dashes the holy can from the saint's hand : an Irish Catholic would no more do "the like of that" than would a priest like Father Hart in Mr. Yeats's *Land of Heart's Desire* consent to hide a crucifix at the request of an evil fairy.

However, *The Well of the Saints* ranks very high in the long series of plays—particularly numerous in Ireland[1]—hinging on the ever-tragic theme of blindness. At the same time it is perhaps of all Synge's dramatic works the one in which we find embodied the truest expression of his pessimistic view, if not philosophy, of life. Nothing can be more pathetic and also more depressing than the two blind people's disillusionment and the complaint of Martin Doul when reference is made to the "grand day" when he was healed : "Grand day, is it ? Or a bad black day when I was roused up and found I was the like of little children do be listening to the stories of an old woman and do be dreaming after in the dark night that it's in grand houses of gold they are, with speckled horses to ride, and do be waking again, in a short while, and they destroyed with the cold, and the thatch dripping, maybe, and the starved ass braying in the yard." One would care in a play for more refreshing ethics—such as, say, the opposite view taken by Maeterlinck in *Sister Beatrice* : Life is worth living ; let us therefore risk to live. However,

---

[1] Cf. all plays—mainly in Gaelic—dealing with the story of Raftery and Carolan, the blind bards ; Miss W. M. Letts's play, *The Eyes of the Blind*, etc.

in this gloomy pathos, in this ascetic pity, we seem to find the dramatic externalization of Synge's inmost consciousness. At the same time the play, with its naturalistic treatment of the supernatural miracle-theme, beautifully expresses (though in a thoroughly un-Yeatsian fashion) the oft-noted tendency in the Celtic temperament to take refuge in a world of dreams, away from the foulness of an actuality transfigured, fortunately, by imaginative illusion.

VII

"The Playboy's real name was Synge ; and the famous libel on Ireland (and who is Ireland that she should not be libelled as other countries are by their great comedians ?) was the truth about the world."

G. B. S., "A Note on Irish Nationalism," Irish Supplement of the *New Statesman*, July 12, 1913, p. 2.

It is not without misgivings that one approaches this notorious, grandly-named comedy, *The Playboy of the Western World*,[1] laboriously written in 1905-6. It has had an extremely stormy career. Wherever it has been produced : Dublin (Saturday, January 26, 1907), London

---

[1] The word "playboy" (Irish *búachaill barra*, literally "boy of the game," a term used in the Irish game of "hurling" (*camánaidheacht*) is Hibernian slang. Its exact meaning (not to be found in Wright's *English Dialect Dictionary* (iv. 543, *s. v.* "play-boy"), which gives only the older acceptations of the word : 1. the devil ; 2. a playful woman) is "hoaxer, humbugger, mystificator (*not* impostor), one who does sham things." Mr. William Boyle, the well-known Abbey Theatre playwright, uses the word in this sense in his comedy, *The Eloquent Dempsey* (Dublin : O'Donoghue, Gill, 1907), p. 18. In Synge's use of

and America, it has occasioned uproarious demonstrations which were *ipso facto* magnificent advertisement for the Irish players. It has been banned by Boards of Guardians, prohibited in Irish towns such as Cork (where we believe it is still tabooed), and denounced in the Press by the school of nondescript epistle-writers whom each revival of the play never fails to set in motion. It has led to the arrest of the Abbey Theatre Company in Philadelphia under the MacNichol law, aimed to prevent "lascivious, sacrilegious, obscene or indecent plays." Needless to add, the case was tittered out of court ; but, most terrible of all, it elicited a trenchant arraignment of the pseudo-Irish organizations in America from the ever-voluble G. B. S.[1]

What is the " comedy " about ? The scene is

---

it, it seems to have three implicit by-meanings : (*a*) one who is played with ; (*b*) one who plays like a player (*i. e.* a comedian and also an athlete or champion : witness the sports in the play) ; (*c*) one who is full of the play-spirit : " a wild dare-devil is called a play-boy [as in Synge's well-known comedy] " (" The Irish Dialect of English," by Mary Hayden and Marcus Hartog, *Fortnightly Review*, April, 1909, p. 779 & n. 1). The word, which is half-humorous and half-poetical, is a very rich one, and (like " philanderer," which, Mr. Bernard Shaw tells me, has its exact equivalent only in Swedish) is exceedingly difficult to translate.—" The Western World " is the English equivalent of the Gaelic folk-phrase *an domhain shiar*, describing the Atlantic seaboard of Ireland as distinguished from the Dublin side, " The Eastern World " (*an domhain shoir*).—The whole title seems to echo that of W. H. Maxwell's well-known volume, *Wild Sports of the West* (London : Richard Bentley, 1838), which may have vaguely suggested it.

[1] Cf. Appendix A, ii, *a* : Books and Pamphlets : Shaw, G. B.

laid in a Mayo "shebeen"—the Irish for a low pot-house—and this little circumstance immediately reveals to the unbiassed spectator the power which the publican—Bung or King Bung as he is popularly called over there—wields in Irish social affairs. "Pegeen Mike," the lively daughter of the shebeener, Michael James, and a matrimonial prize in the district, is about to marry one Shawn Keogh, not because she loves him, but simply because her parent wills it so. We already know from *In the Shadow of the Glen* that marriage among the Irish villagers is less a question of individual liking than a business transaction. As "Æ" has written in "Religion and Love,"[1] the Irish peasant girl "will follow her four-legged dowry to the house of a man she may never have spoken twenty words to before her marriage." Shawn Keogh represents the average *shoneen*, a striking example of the hopeless condition to which rural Ireland is being gradually reduced by emigration which, draining all the good elements away to foreign parts, acts as an inverted form of natural selection resulting in the survival of the unfittest. He is an exceedingly prudish, pusillanimous, spiritless bumpkin, weakly in body and mind, who has a farm and cattle, but no intelligence, character, or vice, and whose one outstanding trait is a maddening terror of Father Reilly. Michael James is about to set out with a few friends to a "wake" (one of the

---

[1] An article published in *Dana*, 1904, p. 45.

well-known Irish midnight feasts offered in honour of the dead), and he suggests that Shawn should stay with Pegeen to protect her at the inn, as there is " a queer fellow lying above in the ditch." But Shawn will hear none of it, and slips out, for a good unmarried Catholic who stops alone with a girl at night incurs excommunication from that extremely Irish person, His Holiness the Pope of Rome.

Such is the initial situation. Shawn Keogh has hardly looked out when the " queer fellow " looks in. A slinking, haggard, unwashed lout, he has fled through the stony fields and boggy holdings to the neighbouring hamlet. At first he is reticent and mysterious ; but little by little the eager questions of the people induce him to relate how he, all his life a poltroon, afraid of every " red petticoat," " the laughing joke of every female woman," but with a quaint poetic strain in his undeveloped, uneducated soul, having endured too long the tyranny of a matter-of-fact father, has had a fight with him and (so he tells) killed his " da " with the blow of a loy.[1] The

---

[1] " Synge gave up his intention of showing upon the stage a fight in a ploughed field between " the Playboy " and his father, because he would not have six large trees, three on each side, growing in the middle of a ploughed field " (W. B. Yeats, " The Theater of Beauty," *Harper's Weekly*, Nov. 11, 1911, p. 11). " He had first planned the opening act in the ploughed field, where the quarrel between Christy and his father took place. But when he thought of the actual stage he could not see any possible side wings for that " wide, windy corner of high, distant hills." He had also talked of the

inflammable Irish imagination is instantly kindled
and Christy Mahon is not only lionized by the
unheroic villagers, but made forthwith potboy in
the shebeen.

Pegeen and Christy, now left alone, become
naturally interested in each other. Not that she
feels any partiality to parricides or assassins of
any kind ; but, in a community where all the
rest—Shawn Keogh first and foremost—are only
cowering blockheads,[1] Christy, for one, *has* done
something, and knows how to tell what he has
done with savagery and romance. Besides, he
says he has slain his father because he would
force him into wedding someone he hates, and
the reason must personally appeal to Pegeen.
The " Playboy " is now surrounded with the
halo of hero-worship in the girl's tempestuous
fancy, and they fall in love with each other.

Gruesome competition sets in among the
peasant-women for the possession of the gallant
murderer. They bring him presents, while
Shawn Keogh tries to pack him off to the States.
But all their endeavours are defeated by the
susceptible and masterful Pegeen. Meanwhile

---

return of the father being at the very door of the chapel where
Christy was to wed Pegeen ; but in the end all took place
within the one cottage room. We all tried at that time to
write for as little scene-shifting as might be, for economy of
scenery and stage-hands " (Lady Gregory, *art. cit.*).

[1] Mr. Ashley Dukes (*Modern Dramatists*, London : Frank
Palmer, 1911, p. 95) very aptly defines Christy's sway over
the Mayo villagers as " the effect of a self-styled giant on a race
of pigmies."

the intriguing Widow Quin insists on the
playboy's joining some races that are being
arranged, and saves him from his father, scotched
but not killed, who has suddenly reappeared,
and whom she maliciously misinforms.

Christy takes part in the sports and is the
victor, whilst the publican and his companions
return from the wake. Michael James, half-
drunk, somewhat reluctantly agrees to sanction
the love between Pegeen and the Playboy with
a promise of marriage. But in has strolled the
never-dying old Mahon, who knocks his son
down and orders him about. Christy's Dutch-
courage and boastful swagger are exposed, and
Pegeen's idol falls shattered to pieces. She, too,
begins to realize that her colossus is clay-footed.
However, the neighbours' worship has so recon-
structed the mock-hero that, goaded to desperation, he strikes his father again. But the very
folk who admired crime when they were simply
told about it in an idealized narrative, now that
they see with their physical eyes the same thing
attempted in earnest, are ready with the rope.
"There is," says Pegeen, "a great gap between
a gallous story and a dirty deed." She herself
scorches Christy's shins with a lighted sod of
turf, while the would-be murderer squirms
round on the floor and bites Shawn's leg. He
escapes hanging only because his "da" has yet
again survived his assault ; and, like Nora and
the tramp in *The Shadow of the Glen*, like the
blind couple in *The Well of the Saints*, the two
198

THE PLAYBOY
By Jack B. Yeats

AND THE IRISH THEATRE

Mahons are doomed to wander forth, unbe-
friended, from the wickedness of the world.[1]

Such are, impartially re-told, the successive
stages of dramatic action in this strange play.
The detailed account of the rowdy and sensational
scenes that took place in Dublin at the time of
the first production belongs to the history of the
Abbey Theatre, and is beyond the scope of the
present essay.[2] Whether the management were
wrong in calling the Imperial police into the Irish
National Theatre, and in enforcing upon the
public a play which they disliked, a foreigner
has no right nor wish to decide. Certain it is,
however, that had the Directors yielded to the
hostility of the audience, and withdrawn the
play, Synge would be utterly unknown nowadays, except to the curious student of Literature's

---

[1] Notice the sameness of Synge's *dénouements*: they are
either—or rather simultaneously, as in the case of the *Playboy*
and *The Shadow of the Glen*—melancholy departures (*e. g.* in
The Well of the Saints) or drinking bouts. However, in *Riders*
and *The Tinker's Wedding*, the protagonist is left to say the
mot de la fin.

[2] The only safe journalistic records of the *Playboy* riot are
the newspapers of the Monday morning after the first performance. Cf. a humorous publication entitled " *The Abbey
Row*, not edited by W. B. Yeats " (a jocular allusion to " *The
Arrow*, edited by W. B. Yeats.") It is said that Mr. Birrell,
on arriving in Dublin about that time, was surprised to find the
city concerned not with Home Rule but with discussing
whether Synge's play was a libel on Irish countryfolk.—Mr.
William Boyle, resenting the piece as a misrepresentation of the
Irish peasantry, withdrew his own plays from the Abbey Theatre
répertoire, but Mr. W. G. Fay at length persuaded him to give
them back.

"bohereens" or by-ways. It is difficult to over-
estimate the service Mr. Yeats rendered Irish
letters at large, and Synge's fame in particular,
by staunchly supporting him and indefatigably
explaining his play to the public during the
memorable week—an act of highly meritorious
generosity and self-sacrifice which has in a way
dethroned or ousted Mr. Yeats from his position
of Standard-Bearer of the Celtic Revival, and
given Synge, possibly with some injustice, the
first place in the Irish movement, which by
unanimous consent had hitherto been Mr.
Yeats's own.

The principal and ever-recurrent objections to
the play itself fall under two main headings. In
the first place, there are particular objections
referring to certain words and episodes in the
comedy.[1] Thus the phrases : " To think I'm
long hearing women talking that talk to all
bloody fools," and " It's Pegeen I'm seeking only,
and what 'd I care if you brought me a drift
of chosen females standing in their *shifts* itself
maybe," produced a nightly turmoil. When the
Irish Company first took the *Playboy* to England
the Censor passed the play, but said that the
sentence " I would not be fearing the loosèd
kharki cut-throats and the walking dead " should

---

[1] At a preliminary reading of the *Playboy* by Mr. W. G.
Fay at a Dublin hotel in Nov., 1906 (Synge was then too
hoarse to read it himself), Mr. Yeats and Lady Gregory found
it necessary to weed out many of the objectionable sentences.
See Appendix A, i, *a*, 1. 4 : Theatre Edition of the *Playboy*.

come out, as all other phrases derogatory to the army. Others took offence at Christy's coarse gesture when he places a looking-glass behind his back, and at the fact that Pegeen is left alone with the Playboy for the night quite unchaperoned—a point which Mr. " F. Norreys Connell," the second producer of the play, made wholly acceptable by the simple expedient of the girl going into an adjoining room and audibly locking the door.

A second and more important class of specific objections concerns the dramatic verisimilitude of certain scenes. The progress of action, with its incidental underplot, is a little clumsy : the conclusion of the second act, in particular, is technically very weak. Nay more, Synge seems to have written the play somewhat at random, without any very definite foreknowledge of its *dénouement*. To select but two instances. In the first act the Playboy arrives harassed and dirty : is it likely that in the third he will be fit to take part in the race ? Again, if Pegeen loves him because he has killed his father, is it so obvious a counterpart that she must cease to love him because he has *not* killed him ?

The objections against the play at large are made on religious, moral and patriotic grounds. The play, it is urged, is a specimen of blasphemous neo-Paganism in view of the continual use of expressions referring to God and the Church, and of the profane travesty on the sacrament of marriage. It must certainly be

JOHN MILLINGTON SYNGE

owned that in the *Playboy* even more than in *The Tinker's Wedding*, Synge, unlike Shawn Keogh, has not been afraid of Father Reilly. The justice of alleging the piece to be immoral— due to the fact that it seems to hold up patricide to admiration—may be questioned. Synge represents an admired murderer, yet in so doing he does not necessarily condone murder. But here we encounter the patriotic objection, which has been raised either by perfectly sincere Nationalists or by political coteries. The exact question is : Would real Irish peasants admire Christy Mahon ?

The Irishness of the piece has been doubted. Mr. O'Donoghue[1] is of opinion that the *Playboy* is but a dramatization of the well-known freak of Baudelaire opening a conversation in a Paris restaurant with the words, "After having assassinated my poor father," to the bewilderment of those present. The supposition is ingenious, but it seems to overlook the anecdote recorded by Synge himself, and the observations he made concerning the Aran Islanders' attitude towards criminals.[2] The Irish peasant's instinct to shield the law-breaker against the English police (the "peelers")—a phenomenon which has its origin in the ancient Gaelic clan-spirit and in centuries of misery and oppression—is an undeniable fact. The well-known case of

[1] *Art. cit.*
[2] iii. 88, 89, 133, 184, 204. Synge was also much indebted to the Kerry sketches, notably as regards the episode of the races in the play.

Lynchehaun in Achill need hardly be recalled.
When Mr. Yeats first went to Aran, the people
were surprised to find that he was only a peaceful
tourist, not a murderer seeking sanctuary ; and an
Irish R.M. told the present writer the story of a
man who had been hidden and protected by the
very relatives of the person he had killed ! Even
the Irish-born policemen sometimes side with
the offender—witness Lady Gregory's *Rising of
the Moon*. Yet what makes the situation in the
Playboy wholly unlikely is that we have to deal
not with "a common, week-day kind of murderer," but with a man who has killed his father.
Patricide is a crime abhorred in all countries ;
and if it is quite certain that Irish peasants would
not inform against Christy, they would not for
all that admire him. Above all, they would not
admire the Playboy *before* he has developed his
supposed deed into a "gallous tale," as is the
case in the comedy.

We are thus led to assume that the play,
while in a way "realistic" and sociologically
accurate, contains a strong element of humorous
or satirical symbolism and allegory. The Playboy
might well have killed both parents instead of
his father only (whom he has not even killed) :
it would not greatly matter. The play as a
whole is Irish in view of its being an extremely
searching study of the Celtic temperament, with
its ever-possible imaginative perversion of ethical
ideals. One cannot say that it is pro-Irish ; nor
that it is deliberately, intentionally anti-Irish,

though we think it very unlikely that the production of the *Playboy* in various cities of England by the Abbey Theatre Company during their annual *tournée* on this side of St. George's Channel should influence English public opinion in favour of Irish Home Rule. The Irish nation as portrayed by Synge in the *Playboy*—which we positively refuse to regard as his masterpiece, in spite of the generally-received judgment and of the somewhat uncritical and conventional eulogies bestowed on the play whenever revived —are anything but fit for self-government. Synge's "comedy," when viewed in this light, certainly constitutes the most tragic exposure of his fellow-countrymen's besottedness. Is it not even rumoured in certain quarters that the management of the Abbey Theatre, which is, as we have seen, largely supported by Unionist finance, is paid to retain the *Playboy* in its repertory, and produce it in England as frequently as possible, so as to indispose against Home Rule the English public mind—which, *a priori*, we may suspect of anything but sympathy towards the idea of Irish autonomy—and thus prevent at any price the passing of the Government of Ireland Bill?

But to return. Synge, sitting in the auditorium of the Abbey Theatre while the row was raging and people shook their fists at him, was overheard to say, " We shall have to establish a Society for the Preservation of Irish Humour ; " and also, " I don't care a rap. It's an extravaganza;" and then he relapsed into silence. Any reader of his preface to *The Tinker's Wedding* will recollect how he complains that some Irish towns are fast losing their humour, a fact which, he maintains, will bring about "morbidity of mind, as Baudelaire's mind was morbid." His intention in the *Playboy* seems therefore to have been to write a kind of humorous burlesque which, like all burlesques, is based on a thorough knowledge of unburlesqued reality—to depict poetically and allegorically, by dint of "exaltation," which in his view was the product of genuine humour, the imaginative, emotional, and sexual self-discovery of a poet's soul, burgeoning at first amidst uncongenial surroundings, and finally expanding into perfect flower of expression in the warm sunshine of public praise. Like all great poets, Christy Mahon is a liar of genius or, at the very least, an embroiderer, in the true lineal descent of Corneille's Dorante, Daudet's Tartarin,[1] Ibsen's Peer Gynt, and Rostand's Cyrano. "It is humbugging us he is." Like all these masters, Synge personifies in his hero the romance inherent in sheer mendacity. Like all his predecessors in European drama, Christy Mahon at first believes in his own lie, and, "in the end of all," falls a victim to it. The admirable gradation in his story proves him to be a true-

---

[1] It may be recalled that the Midi resented *Tartarin* almost as much as some Irish people did, and still do, the *Playboy*.

JOHN MILLINGTON SYNGE

born poet.[1] At the beginning he "just riz the
loy and let fall the edge of it on the ridge of his
[Old Mahon's] skull"; finally, after a series of
careful and subtle transitions which one might
follow throughout the play, he transmogrifies
himself into "a gallant orphan cleft his father
with one blow to the breeches belt." At last
the sheer intoxication of lying and of acting his
lie causes him (like Henri in Arthur Schnitzler's
The Green Cockatoo) to do in actuality what he
has been doing so far only in fancy—namely, to
kill his father, or at least attempt to murder
him. However, at all times, Christy's character
remains highly fantastic ; in a way, he turns out
to be almost as "stagey" and unreal a type as
the stage Irishman of old—the "gossoon" and
the "broth of a bhoy"—while Pegeen, who
very soon becomes his equal, if not indeed his
superior, in the game of imaginative love-
making, distinctly reminds us of certain characteristic features of the Boucicaultian colleen or
"slip of a girl."

Might not one go further still, and maintain
that the *Playboy* is meant by Synge not only as
a humorous and allegorical impersonation of

[1] After having written the play, Synge was very pleased to
find in a ballad entitled "Edward, Edward" (cf. *The Ballad
Book*, edited by William Allingham, London : Macmillan,
"Golden Treasury" series, 1872, p. 247) a story curiously
analogous to the theme of the *Playboy*. Viewed from the
romantic, non-ethical standpoint of ballad-poetry or minstrelsy,
the play loses its criminal aspect, which so many people
objected to.

poetic, creative souls in general, but also as an ironical vision of the dramatist's own personal attitude throughout his " comedy " ? Is not the Playboy the playwright himself, to wit, J. M. Synge, who, like so many Irish humorists —Oscar Wilde and Mr. George Bernard Shaw in particular—chooses as his subject the crudest possible paradox, wherewith he, by a sort of perpetual *double entendre*, authorizes contradictory interpretations of his play and, as Christy did the Mayo countryfolk, constantly and consistently mystifies his public, who apparently have not yet been able to decide whether his " comedy " is a work of serious portraiture or of fanciful tomfoolery ?

The play, as one must own, and as that consummate Irish humorist, Mr. " George A. Birmingham," has justly pointed out,[1] is exceedingly difficult to understand—is, in fact, quite as puzzling as a play by Ibsen was at first to an average English audience.[2] The very length of our commentary is the best proof

---

[1] " The Literary Movement in Ireland," *Fortnightly Review,* Dec., 1907, p. 947.

[2] " Consider, for instance, Synge's masterpiece, *The Playboy of the Western World.* There is *flower of author !* What is it for mankind at large ? An attack on the Irish character. A pretty piece of writing. An amusing farce. Enigmatic cynicism leading nowhere. A *puzzling fellow* wrote it. And mankind at large has little patience with *puzzling fellows.*" (John Galsworthy, " Meditation on Finality," *English Review,* July, 1912, p. 539; reprinted in *The Inn of Tranquillity,* London : Heinemann, 1912, p. 207.)

of this necessity to explain its obscure meaning. That our double-sided construction of the play is the correct one is, we are bold enough to think, conclusively demonstrated by the very definite statement made by Synge himself, in the following unreprinted letter which he sent to a Dublin newspaper[1] during the historic week :

"*The Playboy of the Western World* is not a play with a 'purpose' in the modern sense of the word, but, although parts of it are or are meant to be extravagant comedy, still a great deal that is in it and a great deal more that is behind it is perfectly serious when looked at in a certain light. This is often the case, I think, with comedy, and no one is quite sure to-day whether Shylock or Alceste should be played seriously or not. There are, it may be hinted, several sides to the *Playboy*."

This letter shews, among other things, that it would be a total mistake to understand the *Playboy* as a perfectly serious piece, as it is a total mistake to act it as a rollicking farce, in the fashion adopted of late years by the Abbey Theatre Company. The latter misconception would be the graver one, for Synge attached greater importance to the serious aspect of the *Playboy* than to its imaginative and poetical side. In a private letter to a friend, which is printed here for the first time, Synge emphasizes and even, we think, humorously exaggerates the

---

[1] *Irish Times,* January 30, 1907.

serious element in his play. (We wish we were at liberty to reproduce the eloquent swearwords in the letter, but really they are not publishable. A good many of Synge's letters are in this strain—earnestness of thought mocking itself in grotesque virulence of form.)

"Wednesday morning [no other date].

" Dear * * *,—I can't let * * *'s . . . rot fester in your mind. Of course Playboy is serious. Extravaganza theory is partly my fault : an interviewer . . . ran up and down stairs after me for two hours on the Monday night when there was the first *riot* [underlined], and I was in charge as Yeats was away. He, the interviewer, got in my way— . . .—and said, ' Do you really think, Mr. Synge, that if a man did this in Mayo, girls would bring him a poulet ? ' The next time it was, ' Do you think, Mr. Synge, they'd bring him eggs ? ' I lost my poor temper (. . .), and I said, ' Oh well, if you like its improbable, its extravagant, its extravzance (how's it spelt ?) . . .' He hashed up what I said in a great deal worse than I expected, but I wrote next day *politely* backing out of all that was in the interview. That is the whole myth. It isn't quite accurate to say, I think, that the thing is a generalization from a single case. *If* [underlined] the idea had occurred to me I could and would just as readily have written the thing, as it stands, without the Lynchehaun case or the Aran case. My story —*in its essence* [" essence " underlined four times] is probable given the psychic state of the locality, I used the cases afterwards to controvert critics who said it was *impossible*. Amen. Go brat [for " brath," in Gaelic characters].

"Yours, J. M. SYNGE."

That Synge does exaggerate his meaning in this curious letter, and that the *Playboy* is not so " serious " as he would have us believe, is clearly shewn by the fact that he confesses having written the comedy as a study in temperament or as an artistic reconstruction of the *possible* psychology of the people, irrespective of the actual cases by which the play happened to be borne out once written. The truth, as we have seen, is infinitely more subtle and complex, and must not be unduly simplified. On the one hand, the *Playboy* has a serious or objective side which makes it a pessimistic— some call it cynical—representation of Irish character ; but this gloomy " reality " is relieved by an element of purely subjective "joy," a gift of humour and a beauty of language which make the play true not so much to Irish nature as to Synge himself, in the person of the Playboy.

Apart from this vitally personal element, one may, sociologically, regard the so-called " blackening " or " vilification " of Ireland by Synge in the *Playboy* as the direct outcome of the self-critical spirit engendered by the national revival. Leaving aside Synge's own view of life at large, which made him at times so strangely unsympathetic to Irish life in particular, it is natural enough that a literary renascence should bring about, not a complacent admiration of the national qualities, but a searching analysis of the national defects. This applies to the " pessimism " of the new Irish school of drama ; indeed, it is especially true of the literatures of Celtic and Latin countries, which have a curious tendency to mirror the worse, not the better, aspect of national existence. Like the Catoblepas, the self-devouring monster in the Apocalypse, the Gaelic and Latin peoples are peculiarly self-disparaging, suicidal, self-destructive ; they turn out literary works which may lead the foreign student who takes them as social documents to the gross misconception that the national life which they represent is " morbid." The French naval officer in *Fanny's First Play* makes a speech in which he " cracks up the English and runs down the French " ; and we have it on the authority of Mr. Shaw that M. Raymond Lauzerte, the French actor who played the part, said that he believed every word of it.

Whatever may be thought, said, and written for and against Synge's world-famous comedy, no one will seriously contest its high intrinsic literary merits. Mr. George Moore has acclaimed it as " the most significant play of the last two hundred years," and his judgment, dithyrambic though it be, finds ever-increasing adhesion. The *Playboy* is, if not Synge's best play, at least his most important and representative contribution to the modern stage, and will long remain, for reasons literary and otherwise, the Abbey Theatre Company's centrepiece. One may say in conclusion that it is Ireland to the core in about the same degree as *Don Quixote* is Spain to the core ; while, viewed from an autobiographical standpoint, its explosive success only testifies to the overpowering gusto and vehemence of the man who wrote it.

VIII

The *Playboy* riot had a terrible effect on Synge's health,[1] and early in 1908 he entered the Elpis Private Hospital, Lower Mount Street, Dublin. There he worked on and off at his last play, *Deirdre of the Sorrows*, up to his dying day. Shortly before the first production of the *Playboy*, Synge had become engaged to the talented actress with the wonderfully rich voice who was to create his " Pegeen Mike," Miss " Maire O'Neill " [Marie Allgood], a sister of Miss Sara Allgood, the leading lady of the Abbey Theatre Company. He knew that he was dying, though he told no one about it except his betrothed, who would come and act the new play for him in his sick-room, and give him heart to write again. However, *Deirdre* was to remain unfinished and unrevised ; and it was produced

---

[1] "I think the week's rioting helped to break down his health " (Lady Gregory, *art. cit.*). On the contrary, a member of the family is reported in an interview as having declared that " the Synges were strong."

Photograph by Chancellor

MAIRE O'NEILL
in *Deirdre of the Sorrows*

only posthumously at the Abbey Theatre on January 13, 1910.

The legend of Deirdre, the Irish Helen whose lover Naisi is slain by the old King Conchubar, is one of the most beautiful legends in the literature of the world, and has been an inexhaustible source of inspiration to the modern Irish poets and playwrights. Sir Samuel Ferguson,[1] " Æ,"[2] Mr. W. B. Yeats,[3] Miss Eva Gore-Booth,[4] Father Thomas O'Kelly,[5] have all penned dramas on Deirdre ; while Mr. Darrell Figgis and Mr. J. Crawford Neil, two coming Irish writers, have on the stocks plays on the same subject. Indeed, despite Mr. Standish O'Grady, who wrote : [6] " The Red Branch ought not to be staged. . . . Leave the heroic cycles alone, and don't bring them to the crowd . . .", Irish dramatists regularly turn out new *Deirdres* every year ; and a tradition of their " school" will have disappeared when they cease to do so.

[1] A dramatic poem in his *Poems* (Dublin : M'Gee, 1880).

[2] " Æ"'s *Deirdre* was written in three days. It was published by Messrs. Maunsel of Dublin in their " Tower Press Booklets" (2nd Series, No. 4), but is now out of print.

[3] Mr. Yeats has re-cast his play very frequently.

[4] *The Buried Life of Deirdre*, accepted for production by the Theatre of Ireland, Oct., 1911.

[5] *Deirdre*, a four-act play in Gaelic published by Clódhanna for the Gaelic League. " An tAthair Tomás Ó'Ceallaigh " is the Gaelic translator of *Kathleen ni Houlihan*.—Cf. also J. M. Muldoon's *Dreams of Deirdre* and *The Sons of Usna*.

[6] In the *All Ireland Review*. Quoted by " Æ " in *Some Irish Essays* (Dublin : Maunsel ; London : Brimley Johnson, " Tower Press Booklets," No. 1), p. 21 : " The Dramatic Treatment of Heroic Literature."

JOHN MILLINGTON SYNGE

Many critics are inclined to regret *Deirdre of the Sorrows* as a contradiction in Synge's literary career. How is it, they ask, that a playwright whose art creed was essentially naturalistic and so thoroughly opposed to the mythological idealism of his compeers, should at last have yielded to the lure of dreamland in this sixth work of his, which was to be his swansong? An idle question, for Synge was not responsible for the selection of his subject, which had been suggested to him by Mr. Yeats. But even if Synge's choice had been spontaneous—possibly he himself might have felt that he would not be considered an Irish dramatist if he did not in his turn write a *Deirdre*—the contradiction would be only apparent. One might indeed go to the length of saying that his peasant dramas were a preparation to the selection of a prehistoric subject. Synge, as we know, was preoccupied not so much with the Irish countryfolk as they appear nowadays, as with the Irish countryfolk in so far as they represent a survival of the old-time Gael. The two types had become fairly identical ideas in his mind. No wonder, then, that he should finally have turned to the ancient Gael himself.[1]

---

[1] At the same time one may maintain without contradiction that Synge at least gave himself the illusion of satisfying his historical sense in writing a *Deirdre*. He once told his nephew, Mr. E. H. Synge, that Shakespeare's Romans were his contemporary Elizabethans and could not be otherwise, because the historical sense had not yet come into existence at that period.

An analysis of the play is not needed, as the re-tellings of the saga are already very numerous.[1] Whereas Mr. Yeats's poem-play is in one act and deals only with the crisis, Synge, like " Æ," has divided the legend into three dramatic episodes. This technical point, however, is comparatively immaterial : the very treatment of the legend is far more important.[2] Synge made it peculiarly his own. So little was he forsaking his wonted material—rural life—that he handled the ancient story as a peasant folk-tale. In so doing he was probably untrue to the heroic element in the legend ; but what it lost in the heroic sense it gained in the human sense. Synge drew the character of Deirdre not as a queen, but as an untamed, unsophisticated child of Nature, and brought her out of the land of mystical visions, where poets like Mr. Yeats and "Æ " seemed to confine her, into the world of flesh-and-blood reality. He did his best to adapt a more or less supernatural theme to the requirements of his " realistic " art by introducing into it the harsh vigour that was his delight. This he achieved first by inventing the grotesque, undeveloped character of Owen ; then and mainly by adopting as a medium of expression the curious peasant language of his other plays. Take from a single page in the second act the expressions : " Conchubar is a

---

[1] See Appendix C.
[2] For a full comparison of the three *Deirdres*, see an article by Mr. Francis Bickley in the *Irish Review*, July, 1912, p. 252.

wrinkled fool with a swelling belly on him and eyes falling downward from his shining crown "; " Queens get old, Deirdre, with their white and long arms going from them, and their backs hooping. I tell you it's a poor thing to see a queen's nose reaching down to scrape her chin "; or again, " It's a poor thing to be so lonesome, you'd squeeze kisses on a cur dog's nose " : if one left out the names of the personages, such passages might well figure in the *Playboy* or *The Well of the Saints*.

The idea of making kings and queens talk in Irish *patois* may seem at first sight a little odd, yet on closer examination one admits it to be curiously true to the real spirit of the legend. While the atmosphere of the play differs from that of the very virile old Irish heroics, it is related to them much more closely than Mr. Yeats's *Deirdre* for example, and many pages of Synge's dialect might be translated word for word into ancient Irish—a thing quite impossible with the other dramatic treatments of the romance. True, Synge's diction is based on a living peasant idiom, quaintly naïve and archaic both in individual words and in syntactical construction, but it is elevated or sublimated above, though consistent with, this base, and has become (especially in the lyrical parts) an aristocratic dialect akin to the Elizabethan language of the English Bible.

The play as a whole, being unfinished, does not deserve lengthy criticism. Had Synge lived, it might have been his masterpiece. As it stands, it seems to be the best dramatic *Deirdre*, and at the same time one cannot overlook its rich auto-biographical meaning. Like his Deirdre, Synge had begun to realize the sweet tragedy of love; like his Deirdre, he was doomed to die in the heyday of his power. "Death is a poor untidy thing at best, though it's a queen that dies." It is this coming sense of love, this early expectation of death that gives the play its supreme beauty; the author, having obtained full mastery over his medium, is able to comprehend and express the deepest of all truths—the truth of the nature of existence; it is because he bids farewell to life that he grasps it to the full.

IX

We are now in a position to take a bird's-eye view of the plays and to point out in a general way the Irish and un-Irish elements throughout Synge's dramatic work.

Critics in general have no hesitancy in branding as un-Irish Synge's sardonic humour, already touched upon in connection with *The Tinker's Wedding*. To decide whether it was a product of foreign influence—in particular of Synge's lifelong intimacy with mediæval literature, especially farces and fabliaux—or whether it flowed from the very excess of his own ironical brooding, is practically impossible. Anyhow, Synge has invented a new "tang," a kind of defiant sarcasm which is and will always be like vitriol thrown on the Irish people. Personally we are inclined to regard this humour as the tragi-comic expression of his individual outlook ; and, if a literary parallel be sought for, we should feel tempted to compare it with the humour of Heine. Like Heine's, it savours of utter disillusion and of total renouncement ; it has the same note of passionate, exuberant revolt. It is, in a way, ultimately foreign to the typical gentleness of traditional Irish humour. One must, however, carefully distinguish two sorts of humour in Irish and Anglo-Irish literature : on the one hand, the harmless, optimistic humour represented, say, by the amiable, almost saintly Irishman of the Goldsmith order ; on the other hand, the grim, fierce, scorching humour of the Swift-Wilde-Shaw type, with an occasional touch of the *macabre* in it,[1] as in Swift's famous proposal concerning the children of the Irish poor, where humour becomes so horrible that it makes you laugh. Synge's humour is clearly of the second, not of the first species.

A more distinctly un-Irish element in Synge's plays is his non-religious view of life. Doubtless this had an artistic cause : the desire to return to the relentless savagery of ancient Paganism. But Synge's archaic quest of the older Gaelic

---

[1] I can find only two specimens of ghastliness in the whole of Synge's work : the first is the talk about bones at the opening of the third act of the *Playboy* ; the second, the graveyard poem entitled *In Kerry* (ii. 205).

civilization made him blind to the profounder spirit of modern Ireland. In a way the ancient heathendom may be said to survive in the uncontrollable temperament and passionate outbursts of the average Irish peasant of to-day ; but this is only a superficial appearance ; at bottom he is an ardently religious being, whose whole life is coloured by faith and belief—especially Catholic faith. This aspect of Irish mind is simply ignored by Synge ; it has no place in his works ; and on this score his fellow-countrymen are justified in finding fault with his plays.[1]

Then, from a technical or dramaturgic standpoint, we may point out a general process of accumulation which often renders the situations in Synge's Irish plays somewhat unlikely. This he appears to have derived from his love of melodrama. To illustrate by an example. No doubt Irish peasants, with the tradition of centuries of oppression ever lingering in their memories, may have shielded a criminal from the hated English jurisdiction, and on the other hand it is conceivable that a community noticeable for the lack of virility in its men may have been stirred to hero-worship by the appearance of a strong, courageous individual. But we are given more than enough when (as in the *Playboy*) the two incidents are combined and the crime

---

[1] Cf. some excellent comments on this point in " The Irish National Theatre," by Charles Bewley, *Dublin Review*, Jan. 1913, pp. 132–44.

itself is presented as the cause of the peasants' admiration for the law-breaker.

Needless to add, with the possible exception of this cumulative process, the un-Irish elements in Synge's plays possess a marked æsthetic and literary value. His wonderful satirical humour, which makes the peasants in his plays as different from real Ireland as Don Quixote is from real Spain, is in this respect unsurpassable. However, the un-Irish elements must not make us blind to the solid Irish substance of Synge's drama, which we must now briefly analyze.[1]

The first and pre-eminently Irish feature of the plays is the way in which they bring out the Gael's native imaginativeness. The Irish peasant, because of the ardour of his unsatisfied cravings, finds his most joyful moods, his most poignant griefs, in the life beyond actuality, the life of the imagination—which, in an Irish mind, is apt to become the more real life of the two. This is the very bedrock of the Gaelic temperament; and Synge has rendered this trait of the Irish nature with extraordinary felicity. This desire for life, balked by circumstance or cramped by isolation, and its consequent influence on the evolution of the characters, this perpetual antagonism of Dream *versus* Reality, is the theme

---

[1] Our study of the Gaelic element in Synge's drama has been greatly facilitated by Mr. George Roberts's article, " A National Dramatist," in *The Shanachie*, March, 1907, p. 57, and Miss Mary C. Maguire's essay on " John Synge," in *The Irish Review*, March, 1911, p. 39. To these able interpreters of Synge's genius we wish to make the fullest acknowledgment.

of all his dramatic writings. Take, for instance, Nora, the young wife married to an old husband, yet filled with an irresistible aspiration for youth; the ugly beggars in *The Well of the Saints*, brooding on physical beauty ; Christy, persuaded by the villagers' praise into self-confidence. Further, mentally anticipated emotions are more vivid and "real" than actual feelings. Maurya feels more grief in her foreknowledge of Bartley's death than when his body is actually brought in ; the two lovers in the *Playboy* spend their time and passion not in making love, but in describing the delightful way in which they will make love in the future.

Add to this an intense love of Nature, which Celtomaniacs mistakenly regard as the exclusive appanage of Gaelic and even Anglo-Celtic poetry, and which, in the present instance, had its roots deep down in Synge's inmost temperament. From a boy he had felt the haunting beauty of the Irish scenery, ever and always filled with sounds and voices of all kinds—the noise of the wind and wave, the cry of the heron or the curlew, the roaring of the rain. What is especially remarkable in this connection throughout his dramatic work is an exquisite and almost uncanny power of conjuring up natural appearances—a curious process distinctly reminiscent of ancient Irish poetry, of shewing us, without apparent interruption in the dialogue, glimpses of landscapes. This is indeed a kind of word-scenery—what the French call " décor parlé "— :

by a few subtle touches, a phrase here and there, Synge conveys the perception of a moonlit hillside, a road at night, or still more unanalyzable effects. One instance will suffice. Says Mary Doul in *The Well of the Saints*, "There's the sound of one of them twittering yellow birds do be coming in the spring-time from beyond the sea, and there'll be fine warmth now in the sun, and a sweetness in the air, the way it'll be a grand thing to be sitting here quiet and easy smelling the things growing up and budding from the earth." Nor is this mere "literature," for we know what potent influence Nature's moods exercise over the changeful Irish heart, so that their power partly explains the development of the characters in Synge's plays and endows his descriptions of scenery with a peculiar dramatic efficiency.

This love of Nature has for its congenial accompaniment the admiration of physical beauty, which seems as much part and parcel of the Irish peasant's temperament as it was of the Greek consciousness. Nora will not wed Michael Dara because old age will tarnish her beauty ; Mary Doul fancies herself to be the wonder of the Eastern world ; and Deirdre is painfully aware that death is unsightly. This again evidences Synge's close relation to Gaelic literature : is not this feeling for beauty, this dread of uncomely age, but a survival of the idea which suggested the conception of the Tir-na-nOg, the pre-Christian Paradise of unfading youth? Also, we seem to find a recollection of the social status of women in ancient Gaeldom in the superiority of Synge's female characters in contradistinction to his men. Though they are equal in portraiture and characterization, as personages in the plays the men are in a way inferior to the women. Naisi is not so high-hearted as Deirdre, and all the men in the *Playboy* except Christy are Pegeen's inferiors in courage and brilliancy. The initiative in love-making is always taken by the woman, and to realize how Irish this is one has only to compare the marvellous love-scene in the *Playboy* with some of Dr. Douglas Hyde's *Love-Songs of Connacht*.[1]

An exhaustive examination of the language used by Synge in his plays would require an essay. Of course a philological study of the Irish dialect of English would be totally out of place : it has been done, and well done.[2] We

---

[1] Dun Emer Press, 1894. The book was one of Synge's favourites.

[2] On Irish-English generally, cf. *Vulgarities of Speech Corrected : Provincial Irish Vulgarities* [Anon.] (London, 1826) ; James Russell Lowell, *Bigelow Papers*, second series, Introduction (1848) ; David Patterson, *The Provincialisms of Belfast and Surrounding District Pointed out and Corrected* (1860) ; A. Hume, *Remarks on the Irish Dialect of the English Language* (1878) ; W. H. Patterson, *A Glossary of Words in Use in the Counties of Antrim and Down* (1880) ; "Colonel O'Critical," *Don't, Pat* (1885) ; D. A. Simmons, *A List of Peculiar Words and Phrases at one Time in Use in Armagh and South Donegal* (1890) ; "The English in Ireland," a series of six articles in *The Educational Gazette* (Dublin), 1890 ; *Gentleman's Magazine*, November, 1893 ; "Notes on Ulster English Dialect for comparison with English Dialects by the late A. J. Ellis,

JOHN MILLINGTON SYNGE

need only be concerned here with the accuracy
of Synge's dialect as compared with the real
English speech of Ireland, and with the literary
and dramatic value of his vernacular.

Synge, we have seen, would not have achieved
much through the medium of academic English.
He felt that the time had come to reform the
hideous " stage-Irish " jargon generally employed
by the former school of Anglo-Irish writers to
represent the peculiarities of the Hibernian

F.R.S., . . .", by J. H. Staples, in the *Transactions of the
Philological Society* (London) for 1896–7, pp. 357-98 ; "The
Anglo-Irish Dialect," by the Rev. William Burke, in *The Irish
Ecclesiastical Record* (Dublin), 1896, pp. 694, 777 ; *The Irish
Difficulty : Shall and Will,* by Gerald Molloy, D.D., D.Sc.
(London, Glasgow and Dublin : Blackie and Son, Ltd., 1897) ;
The English Dialect Dictionary, edited by Joseph Wright (1898–
1905) ; " The Irish Brogue," in *The Gael,* December, 1901,
pp. 372–3 ; *The People and Language of Ulster,* being a " dis-
coorse " delivered at the Ulster Association of New South
Wales, Sydney, on March 17, 1909, by Chas. Russell ; "The
Irish Dialect of English," by Miss Mary Hayden, M.A., and
Prof. Marcus Hartog, *Fortnightly Review,* April and May,
1909 ; "The Speech of the Irish Peasantry," in the *Nation*
(London), July 31, 1909, p. 635 ; P. W. Joyce, *English as
We Speak it in Ireland* (London : Longmans, Green & Co. ;
Dublin : M. H. Gill, second ed., 1910), on which see an
interesting book notice with notes on the " brogue " and Irish
words used in County Kildare in the *Kildare Archæological
Society Journal,* July, 1911, pp. 524–39 ; "Irish English," in
the *Saturday Review,* Feb. 25, 1911, p. 244 ; " A Survival
of Elizabethan Speech," by James J. Walsh, in *Harper's
Monthly Magazine,* July, 1911, p. 191 ; "Ulster Modes of
Speech," by Rev. William Cowan, *Chambers's Journal,* seventh
series, vol. ii (Dec., 1911 to Nov., 1912), p. 526 ; "On
Anglo-Irish Syntax," by A. G. van Hamel, *Englische Studien,*
45. Bd., 2. Heft (September, 1912), pp. 272–92 [an article
taking its examples from the works of Yeats and Synge].
224

accent.[1] Besides, his philological studies in Paris and his intimacy with such French writers as Maupassant and George Sand had revealed to him, we have seen, the artistic beauty of dialect. In Ireland, the Hon. Emily Lawless and O'Donovan Rossa had already experimented peasant speech as a literary medium ; Lady Gregory had begun to write in " Kiltartanese,"[2] and Dr. Douglas Hyde had translated fragments of Gaelic literature into Irish-English ; while Mr. Yeats and " Æ " maintained that literature was but recordèd speech.[3] Synge, in his turn, in the course of his rambles through Eastern and Western Ireland, had been struck by the flamboyant imaginativeness of the average peasant's language ; he was known to listen at doors ajar, and took down quaint phrases wherever he went. In the preface to the *Playboy* he declares that all the words and idioms used in his plays have actually been heard by him from the lips of the peasantry.

One must not, however, regard his dialect as a mere note-book transcript. The language

---

[1] Representative specimens of this absurd dialect will be found in the series of " Irish plays " issued by the John Dick's Press, London.

[2] " I wrote in it [the English of Gaelic-thinking people] before Synge did. He said he was amazed to find in my *Cuchulain of Muirthemne* his desired dialect " (Lady Gregory, interview, *The Sun* (N.Y.), Dec. 10, 1911). He wrote to me : " Your *Cuchulain* is a part of my daily bread " (Lady Gregory, *English Review*, art. cit.).

[3] Cf. W. B. Yeats, " Literature and the Living Voice," *Contemporary Review*, Oct., 1906.

in his plays is not a mosaic, and none but an
efficient ragman could patch together wild
sayings overheard in out-of-the-way places.
Synge's Anglo-Irish is in the main a bold re-
creation from Gaelic ; and this was bound to
be so, for, whereas Gaelic has had but little
influence on the Scotch dialect of English, the
Irish dialect has been moulded by the native
Erse. The student who knows Gaelic still
thinks in Gaelic as he reads or hears Synge's
plays. This applies not only to the phraseology
used by his characters, but to the syntax of
their sentences. An aorist like " He is after
doing," or co-ordination used instead of sub-
ordination in the Irishism, " And he going to
to the fair " ("When he was going to the
fair "), are pure Gaelic constructions. Ancillary
clauses, enallages, inversions and hyperbata of
all kinds are unusually plentiful. The curious
thing to be noticed about this perpetual translation of Gaelic into English is that Synge
makes Irish peasants who are not Irish-speaking
—such as the Wicklow peasants, whose dialect
is more akin to Elizabethan English—speak in
the Gaelic fashion like the Western peasants.[1]

[1] Inversely, Synge puts in the mouth of his Western
peasants (Pegeen in the present instance) such Elizabethan,
hence Eastern, archaisms as "bedizened," "inveigle,"
"pandied" ; Christy is called with Shakespearean aptness
the "looney" of Mahon's ; and Deirdre speaks of having
been "spancelled" seven years with Naisi. Geographically
speaking, *Deirdre of the Sorrows* ought to be written in Ulster
dialect.

All his characters, despite geographical differences, talk alike. Probably the reason for this close adherence to the native Erse was that Synge felt that an Irish national theatre in English is, as we have said, something of a contradiction in terms ; but, as he wanted to write his plays in English to appeal to a wider audience, he wrote them in an English modelled on the Gaelic of national Ireland. It is the Gaelic influence that gives colour and distinction to his English. For instance, in the *Playboy*, he uses the phrase " star of knowledge," which is the picturesque English equivalent of the common Gaelic phrase *realt eolais :* re-translated into Gaelic, the phrase is as unpoetical as Fitzgerald's *Rubaiyat of Omar Khayyám* probably is when re-translated into Persian.[1]

---

[1] Synge borrowed the phrase "star of knowledge" from Dr. Douglas Hyde's *Love-Songs of Connacht*, in which Courteous Breed says : "If you were to see the star of knowledge and she coming in the mouth of the road, you would say that it was a jewel at a distance from you, who would disperse fog and enchantment." Similarly Christy's speech to Pegeen : "Squeezing kisses on your puckered lips till I'd feel a kind of pity for the Lord God is all ages sitting lonesome in His golden chair," has been inspired by another passage in the *Love-Songs of Connacht*, in which one reads of Una Bhán : "I had rather be beside her on a couch, ever kissing her— Than be sitting in Heaven in the chair of the Trinity." And Pegeen's promise : "I swear to God I'll wed him, and I'll not renege," may be put side by side with the words of our Saviour in Dr. Hyde's *Religious Songs of Connacht :* "Before the cock crows to-night you will reneague me three times." As has been pointed out at the beginning of this essay, the language of the Bible and of the Psalms had greatly influenced Synge's own dialect.

Synge's dialect, therefore, is not the actual Anglo-Irish dialect. It is too Irish. An adequate rendering of Gaelic into English does not make peasant speech. Here again we detect Synge's habitual process of accumulation. "Literariness" creeps in. His language is crammed and supersaturated with fantastical, overwrought "strings of gab" borrowed from Irish. Even when he is not actually translating Gaelic, he seems to exaggerate the coefficient of Hibernicism. His characters bless and curse each other too well. Whatever may be Ireland's genius for full-flavoured, overwhelming abuse, we find it a little difficult to believe in Pegeen's splendid gush of invective when she quarrels with the Widow Quin. Likewise, Christy's answer to the villagers : "With the help of God I did, surely "[1] [kill my father], "and that the Holy Immaculate Mother may intercede for his soul," is somewhat improbable : an Irish peasant would say either the one or the other, but not the two things in the same sentence. Nor are such voluminous, mouth-filling "jaw-breakers" as "potentate," "retribution," to be heard on the lips of the real Irish countryfolk, however great their well-known love of the word for the word's sake may be. The fact is that, when Synge

---

[1] "Surely" occurs a little too frequently in Synge's plays ; and the real Irish peasant, unlike Synge's peasant, uses "shall" and "should" only very rarely, "will" and "would" nearly always.

declares that he was obliged to listen to the speech of the people through a chink in the floor, he implicitly condemns himself : a real peasant-playwright, such as the Abbey Theatre is bound to produce some day, would not have to hunt for local colour ; he would have the peasant speech in himself, and know how to use it.

Whatever may be the unreality of Synge's Anglo-Irish, it remains that his dialect possesses a literary value which it is difficult to over-estimate. Leaving aside its strange aloofness and the sense of distance which it lends to the mind, its principal quality in this connection is its rhythm. The concept of rhythm, which holds so important a place in latter-day philosophy and æsthetics,[1] underlies Synge's whole view of the drama, his technical execution, the antithetic design of all his plays, and, more especially, his literary use of the Irish *patois*. He was bent on reproducing the suave and subtle " synge-song " of peasant speech, and his vernacular has in it that happy coalescence of harmony and meaning which only a born musician can obtain. Doubtless he had read the wonderful essay in which Walter Pater shews that all arts have a tendency to verge towards, and finally merge in, music. We already know the importance he attached to this element of cadence, and how he trained the Abbey actors to recite

---

[1] Cf. A. Chide, *L'Idée de Rythme* (Paris : Alcan : Bibliothèque de Philosophie Contemporaine) ; the review, *Rhythm*, etc.

the words in his plays with the right intonation
and lilt, which are as essential to an Irish pronunciation as the brogue itself. In a day when
the speech of the stage has a tendency to become
mere stenography, Synge wrote in a prose that
sets him high among the poets. His dialect
reads as well as Mr. Yeats's blank verse. If he
did not write his plays in verse, it is simply
because he felt that peasant prose had that
flavour of reality and raciness which was so
dear to him. Yet his prose, without ever being
sustainedly iambic, contains occasional lines of
blank verse—about eighty in the *Playboy* and
ten at least in *Deirdre*; and it should be re-
remembered that towards the end of his life
Synge tried to invent a new blank-verse form
in dialect.

It now becomes evident that the Irishness of
Synge's plays has its limitations. One must
not treat them as absolute social documents;
or if one does so, one must bear in mind
that they require very careful handling. One
must allow for the obvious exaggeration in the
situations and language, which has its reason
and excuse in the necessity for all drama to
produce startling combinations. Above all, one
must take into account the " personal equation "
in the plays : Synge strove to express himself
first, and his drama, if it is, in a way, true
to Ireland, is primarily true to the individual
vision of the playwright.

AND THE IRISH THEATRE

CHAPTER VII

POEMS AND TRANSLATIONS: SYNGE'S DEATH :
SUMMARY AND CONCLUSION

> . . . What year will they write
> For my poor passage to the stall of night ?
> *Poems : On An Anniversary* (ii. 216).

SYNGE's verse is only a by-product. Its autobiographical value has been considered elsewhere
—in connection with his early years and the
formation of his æsthetic views. Indeed, the
greatest merit of these poems is that they are
principally a self-revelation of Synge. "They
are the man speaking," says Mr. John Masefield.[1]
As poetry proper they may be dismissed briefly :
Synge seems to have sought a little too con-
sciously after that "brutality" of which he
speaks in his introduction, and to have forgotten
in verse that melody of language of which his
prose is so full.

Nature is the main source from which he
draws his inspiration. It is to be remembered
that Synge began to write verse in a decidedly
Wordsworthian strain. In his early piece,
Prelude—the very title of which is reminiscent
of Wordsworth—the kinship with wild Nature

[1] *C. R., art. cit.*

rises to an almost extra-human pitch. But in
his unrepublished sonnet, *Glen Cullen* (1893),
Synge perhaps still more distinctly appears as a
kind of Irish Lake poet. The piece, we think,
is worthy of quotation—

> O river, could'st thou make response in words,
> What questions I should ask of olden time !
> What stories hear of daring deeds and crime,
> Of those who dwelt out here among their herds,
> Feasting on plenteous beef, with milk and curds,
> And then beside thy softly mellowed chime,
> Shouting exultingly a martial rhyme
> That rose spontaneous as a charm of birds ;
>
> But changes since have crept o'er all thy glen,
> And now a thrifty nation needs must strive
> To grow rich wheat where nought then lived but game.
> Yet on thy bank still sings the merry wren,
> And in thy stream the frolic ousels dive,
> While old traditions linger in thy name. [1]

The second noticeable feature of the poems is
their folk-inspiration. Synge had been struck
by the popular doggerel rhymes which he had
heard in Aran and by the wild productions of
the Wicklow ballad-singers. His dramatic spirit
led him to experiments in ballad-poetry, which
are the most successful specimens of his poetic
activities. *Danny* and *The 'Mergency Man*—the
subjects of which he had found in real life[2]—are

---

[1] The Cualanni were the ancient inhabitants of Glen Cullen.
[Synge's own note.]

[2] The story of the 'mergency man is told at length in the
Kerry notes (iv. 109–10). Synge first intended to call his book
of poems *Ballads and Outrages* ; and when Mr. Masefield last
met with him they discussed with enthusiasm the re-creation of
ballad poetry.

typical examples of the grim bluntness which he set forth as essential to verse.

Lastly, one finds in the poems the strong, mighty undercurrent of pessimism and melancholy ever present in all Synge's work. Although his native sadness here expresses itself in an epic rather than strictly lyrical manner—for the spirit of the ballads, in particular, is essentially epic or dramatic—it is none the less conspicuous. *On An Anniversary*, *A Question*, *Epitaph*, betray Synge's early sense of mortality. The fact is that Synge actually died while the slender volume containing his poetic compositions was passing through the press.

"To make it a little less thin,"[1] he put into it a few translations made at different periods of his life. They are felicitous attempts at rendering fragments of European literature into a dialect which, as we already know, was itself a translation. Some of them are almost literal, like the translation of Walther von der Vogelweide.[2] Others, almost more original than Synge's original poems, are independent paraphrases, or rather re-creations, like the Villon pieces. It is significant in this connection that he should have selected implacably realistic

---

[1] As Synge himself wrote in a letter printed in Mr. Yeats's preface to the Cuala Press edition of *Poems and Translations*.

[2] The exact passage translated by Synge will be found in *Die Gedichte Walthers von der Vogelweide, siebente Ausgabe von Karl Lachmann, besorgt von Carl v. Kraus*, Berlin: Georg Reimer, 1907, pp. 68–9; ii. 52, 31 to 38; ii. 53, 9 to 12.

passages from the work of the mediæval poet, rather than the familiar *Ballad of Dead Ladies*, which had already been rendered into English by Dante Gabriel Rossetti and John Payne, and to which Synge himself somewhat scornfully refers in his poem *Queens*, where he speaks of—

Bert, the big-foot, sung by Villon.

Many of the poems and translations were written during Synge's last illness. During his first stay at the Elpis Private Hospital the doctors had thought that an operation would relieve him of his internal pain—some sort of tumour, possibly cancer. Preparations were made for the operation, but the doctors saw it was useless, as the disease had taken too great a hold on him, and they closed the wound up again. Poor Synge thought the operation had been successfully performed, and when the wound had healed up he came out of the hospital for a time (May, 1908), telling one of his friends that he felt sorry that the surgeons should take " so much interest in his intestines, and so little in his genius." He looked healthier and said he " felt much better." On October 26, 1908, his mother died at her residence, Glenageary House, Glenageary, and had to be interred during her son's absence in Germany. Synge had always been very devoted to her, and the news gave him a terrible shock. Very soon he had to return to the hospital, never to leave it alive. During his last illness he was as gentle as a child. He was greatly liked by all at the nursing home. The matron used to have long chats with him each day ; he invariably was writing when she came in, and she would say, " There you are tiring yourself again ! " and he replied, " Stay and talk with me and I won't write any more." Sometimes he was full of fun and in good spirits would converse for hours at a time, speaking on woman suffrage and other modern subjects.

The day before he died he destroyed many letters and poems, and then expressed the wish to be moved into another room with the sunshine on it. His wish was granted; the nurses carried him on a stretcher, and he said on entering the room : " This is a nice room, and I already feel better in it. Now I shall be able to see the Dublin mountains." But he could not see them, and wept. The next day (March 24, 1909), at five in the morning, he said to the nurse, " It is no use fighting death any longer," and, turning over, passed away. He was buried on March 26 in a family vault with his aunt Jane Synge at the Protestant Mount Jerome General Cemetery, Harold's Cross, Dublin. As he himself had predicted in his poem *To the Oaks of Glencree*—

> There'll come a season when you'll stretch
>   Black boards to cover me :
> Then in Mount Jerome I'll lie, poor wretch,
>   With worms eternally.

JOHN MILLINGTON SYNGE

There was no performance at the Abbey Theatre during the week following his death.[1]

A delightful Irish poetess, Miss W. M. Letts, herself an ardent Syngeite, has written the following pathetic lament on " Synge's Grave "[2]—

My grief ! that they have laid you in the town
Within the moidher of its thousand wheels
And busy feet that travel up and down.

They had a right to choose a better bed
Far off among the hills where silence steals
In on the soul with comfort-bringing tread.

The curlew would have keened for you all day
The wind across the heather cried Ochone
For sorrow of his brother gone away.

In Glenmalure far off from town-born men
Why would they not have let you sleep alone
At peace there in the shadow of the glen ?

---

[1] Synge was succeeded as co-director of the Abbey Theatre by Mr. Conal O'Riordan (" F. Norreys Connell "), whose play, *The Piper*, had made a very deep impression on Synge, and who wrote an interesting estimate of his predecessor in the *English Review* for June, 1909. Synge in his will had left £80 per annum during her spinsterhood to Miss Marie Allgood (" Maire O'Neill ") or £52 per annum for the remainder of her life in the event of her marriage, and the residue of his personal estate (valued at £2,362) to his nephews, Edward Millington Stephens and Edward Hutchinson Synge, in equal shares. Miss O'Neill has now married Mr. Geo. H. Mair, M.A., of the *Manchester Guardian*, and resides in London ; she has officially severed her connection with the Abbey Theatre, and the part of Pegeen Mike is now filled by Miss Eithne Magee.

[2] *Westminster Gazette*, December 20, 1912 ; republished in *Songs from Leinster* (London : Smith, Elder, 1913), p. 42. The authoress (in a letter) modestly describes her book as " a record of things heard or seen," a phrase not inapplicable to a great deal of Synge's own writings.

AND THE IRISH THEATRE

To tend your grave you should have had the sun,
The fraughan and the moss, the heather brown,
And gorse turned gold for joy of spring begun.

You should have had your brothers wind and rain,
And in the dark the stars all looking down
To ask " When will he take the road again ? "

The herdsmen of the lone back hills that drive
The mountain-ewes to some far-distant fair
Would stand and say, " We knew him well alive,

That God may rest his soul ! "   Then they would pass
Into the silence brooding everywhere,
And leave you to your sleep below the grass.

But now among these alien city graves
What way are you without the wind's harsh breath,
You free-born son of mountains and wild waves ?

Ah ! God knows better—here you've no abode,
So long ago you had the laugh at death,
And rose, and took the wind-swept mountain road.

Thus was brought to an early close a life
that had been fairly uneventful, yet picturesque
enough in its earlier portion, if on the whole
sad and unhappy.   The untimeliness of Synge's
death is certainly to be deplored—he was not
yet thirty-eight.   It was felt as a heavy loss to
Irish letters.   At the same time, it seems
unlikely that his writings, which form such a
complete, self-consistent body of work, would
have admitted of such further developments as
might have brought out fresh aspects in his art.
Had he lived longer he might have repeated
himself and wearied his admirers.

Synge was fully conscious of this, and towards the end of his life was trying to work in a new vein. On the one hand, he had formed projects that were anything but dramatic—for example, he was planning translations of fragments from the great literatures into the Anglo-Irish dialect, notably a complete rendering of the *Imitation of Christ*.[1] But even in playwriting he was changing his *manière*. Though he had once said in hospital that " it was a pity that he should die, for he had still more than one playboy in his belly," the remark simply evidenced his buoyant fondness for life, not his intention of persevering in peasant drama, the interest of which he felt he had exhausted. At that period he was thinking of a play on slum life (of which he had made a close study in Patrick Street, Dublin), but had not yet conceived the plot. Also, he was contemplating the creation of a new form : blank verse in dialect—or at least blank verse containing as many dialect words as possible, for the long cadences of Anglo-Irish dialect cannot easily go into ordinary blank verse. He had experimented this medium in a three-act play (which was well advanced when he died) on the same subject as Shakespeare's *Cymbeline*. In it a sea-captain boasted to a companion of his wife's fidelity, and in resisting the seducer, the lady idealized her husband so much that she could no longer put up with him when he actually came back. One of the most characteristic lines of

---

[1] W. B. Yeats, *op. cit.*, p. 31.

the play was that in which the sailor complained
of life on board, where one has to eat

. . . So much salt food that our shins itch.

However interesting these new attempts might
have become, one can judge Synge only on his
actual published *opus*. Three elements may be
distinguished in his work : the foreign element,
the Irish element, the personal element. The
foreign element europeanized or universalized
Synge's Irish subjects and his treatment of them.
The Irish element, in return, defined and concen-
trated his international culture, which otherwise
might have blurred his vision. The personal
element gave richness, depth and intensity to his
blending of Continental art with Irish observation. It is by far the most important element
of the three, and if sometimes at odds with the
Irish objectivity of Synge's writings, it has given
them their true artistic quality and their human
appeal. Synge has put in his drama the essence
of his whole being, and this primordial truthfulness to Self makes him peculiarly representative
of that spirit of " sincerity " which is so marked
a characteristic of the contemporary theatre.[1]

Of his place in literature it is much too soon
to speak with certainty. We cannot yet gauge
the comparative significance or insignificance
of his work, nor foresee its ultimate upshot.
Rarely, however, has a writer become a classic

---

[1] Cf. John Galsworthy, "The New Spirit in the Drama,"
Hibbert Journal, April, 1913.

in so short a time as Synge. Almost alone of all the Irish authors, he has achieved a world-wide reputation. His plays, in text or in translation, have won the currency of half the globe. There is a veritable " Synge cult " in Oxford and Cambridge ; and transatlantic Universities[1] have gone so far as to take Synge's plays as text-books of English literature. Some critics, indeed, compare him with Shakespeare, which is an obvious exaggeration : his literary production is too slender and his range too exiguous. Dithyrambic encomium is as absurd and deadly as wholesale depreciation ; and Synge, whose fortunes have undergone strange vicissitudes, has suffered equally from both.

The causes of his popularity are manifold. There is, to begin with, the *succès de scandale*. Next, the political and sectarian exploitation. Then, the exotic and conventional love of Irish local colour. Lastly, the unbiassed artistic recognition. Only the fourth cause is important and lasting. Whatever may be thought of the riots occasioned by Synge's plays, one cannot deny

---

[1] Yale, Harvard and Pennsylvania. Prof. Baker of Harvard has done much to make Synge's plays known and studied in America. It is noteworthy that Synge's work was appreciated in America long before it was appreciated either in England or in Ireland, but only by a few clear-sighted experts such as Mr. John Quinn, Mr. James Gregg, Mr. James Huneker, Mr. Chas. A. Bennett, Mr. W. B. Blake and Mr. Cornelius Weygandt. Synge's recognition by the American public at large dates back only to the comparatively recent first *tournée* of the Irish Players (1911), with the memorable arrest in Philadelphia which gave them a place in the one-cent dailies.

him the true literary gift. His was a *conscience
d'artiste*, and as such he will endure.

He has as yet exercised but little influence.
An individual genius seldom finds followers.
In his native country, admiration for him has
often been the result of faddism and of a certain
tendency in Dublin to ape the London literary
coteries; criticism has long judged him with
wrong standards, Nationalist or Catholic, which
vitiated the true artistic estimation; but at last
Synge is coming into his own. In the first
place, his mark is recognizable in the work of
writers of Irish travel-notes[1] and recorders of
folk-tales.[2] As regards Abbey Theatre drama,
Synge seems to have strangely reacted on
Mr. Yeats himself. Anyone who compares
Mr. Yeats's earlier *genre* with his latter-day
theories will be able to ascertain the point.
There is "a great gap" between *The Countess*

[1] William Bulfin, *Rambles in Eirinn* (Dublin : Gill, 1907);
Joseph Campbell, *Mearing Stones* (Dublin : Maunsel, 1911);
cf. in the same connection Mr. Pádraic Colum's *My Irish
Year* (London : Mills & Boon, 1912), and Mr. Jack B.
Yeats's extremely Syngesque drawings in *Life in the West of
Ireland* (Dublin : Maunsel, 1912). (*e.g.* the sketch entitled
"The man with a broken head" is obviously Old Mahon.)

[2] *e.g.* Miss B. Hunt, *Folk-Tales of Breffny* (London : Macmillan, 1912). In "The Seven Soldiers of the North : a
legend of Ulster," by A[nthony] T. M[ahaffy] ("An Lor-
gaire," President, Gaelic League), published in the *Irish
Review*, January, 1913, I find (p. 600) the words, "Whity
mud and red mud, and turf on them, and the fine sands of
the sea," which are the very same as those applied by Sara to
Christy's boots in the second act of the *Playboy*; but of course
the article is a skit.

JOHN MILLINGTON SYNGE

Cathleen and *The Green Helmet,* styled by its author a " heroic farce," a title which Synge might have applied to certain portions of his *Deirdre of the Sorrows.* The fact is Mr. Yeats has in a way rebelled against himself. Formerly he was avowedly writing for " a little company of studious persons," and described the theatre as " the preparation of a priesthood " ; now he requires " intensity of personal life in art," which " bids us touch and taste and hear and see the world " ; and is distinctly reminiscent of Synge's creed of " reality and joy " when he declares that " all true arts, as distinguished from their commercial and mechanical imitation, are a festival where it is the fiddler who calls the tune." [1]

As to the younger playwrights, it seems plausible to assert that the pessimistic, almost distracting realism which expresses itself in the powerful and ably constructed plays of Mr. S. Lennox Robinson,[2] Mr. T. C. Murray,[3] Mr. Joseph Campbell[4] and Mr. St. John G. Ervine[5]

---

[1] Quoted by Mr. Francis Bickley, " Synge and the Drama," *New Quarterly*, Feb., 1910. The last-quoted sentence was written earlier than the Preface to the *Playboy*.

[2] (At present manager of the Abbey Theatre). *Harvest ; The Cross-Roads ; The Clancy Name ; Patriots.*

[3] *Birthright ; The Village Schoolmaster ; Maurice Harte.*

[4] *Judgment*—a play also exhibiting curious traces of Russian influence.

[5] *Mixed Marriage ; The Magnanimous Lover* (1913), a play which, by its use of the word " bastard," provoked a hullabaloo reminiscent of the heroic days of Synge's *Playboy* and Norreys Connell's *Piper.*

is more or less in the line of Synge's naturalism. The fate-ridden peasant evolved by him is a fairly frequent type in the works of these dramatists ; however, they seem to lack Synge's humour, and it is a moot point among Irish judges themselves to decide whether their gloomy and occasionally sensational characters are, after all, more true to Gaelic nature than the rollicking stage Irishman of old.

Synge, we have seen, holds a very high place in the already lengthy list of dialect writers,[1] and appears to be responsible for the creation and generalization of an " Abbey " *patois,* widely different from the real vernacular of Anglo-Ireland. While some of the Irish play-wrights, such as Mr. George Fitzmaurice,[2] Miss W. M. Letts,[3] Mr. " Rutherford Mayne," [4] Mr. John D. Guinan,[5] and even at times Lady Gregory herself,[6] actually write in " Syngese," one feels that Synge's influence in point of language has been more subtle and far-reaching. Somehow or other he has launched dialect as a dramatic medium of expression. By his own achievement, he has initiated the younger men

[1] Cf. *English Dialects from the Seventh Century to the Present Day,* by the late Prof. W. W. Skeat (Cambridge University Press), pp. 110–1.

[2] *The Piedish ; The Country Dressmaker ; The Magic Glasses.*

[3] *The Eyes of the Blind ; The Challenge.*

[4] *Red Turf* (1911), written in the speech of Connacht, though the author is an Ulster dramatist.

[5] *The Cuckoo's Nest* (produced Abbey Theatre, March 13, 1913), a play containing a love-scene *à la Synge.*

[6] *New Comedies* (Putnams, 1913).

to the unsuspected beauties of Irish peasant idiom, and at the same time encouraged the older writers to persevere in their experiments.

It would not be very difficult to link up Synge's drama with more or less analogous developments in the recent British theatre. Some critics have expressed the wish that the Irish playwrights may exercise a regenerating influence on the ailing English drama. This influence has hardly begun to make itself felt. However, the Wessex novels of Mr. Thomas Hardy seem to have reintroduced a vein of rural drama into English literature. On the other hand, England at present possesses a playwright whose genius is not unlike Synge's : we refer to Mr. John Masefield. Although we are in a position to state that Mr. Masefield never felt the literary influence of Synge, whom he personally knew, nor shewed him his plays when they were still in manuscript, his village tragedies such as the beautiful *Nan* bear a distinct resemblance to Synge's dramatic works.[1] Like Synge, Mr. Masefield has written his plays in prose ; like him, he has written verse. Yet his plays, no less than his verse, possess a poetical quality, like Synge's own prose. This, again, is but a literary parallel ; all we mean to suggest is that Mr.

---

[1] Although Synge did not influence Mr. Masefield, the Irish movement has more or less done so ; and without Mr. Yeats he would not have written his own country plays. Curiously enough, the Antrim peasants in chap. v of Mr. Masefield's novel, *Multitude and Solitude* (London : Grant Richards, 1909), speak exactly the dialect of Synge's own peasants.

Masefield is the only living English dramatist who may be put in the same class with Synge.

There is at present a keen appreciation of Synge in the English literary world. It is significant to learn, on the testimony of Miss M. Betham-Edwards,[1] that " one of the last literary subjects " which engaged the late William Hale White's attention " was Synge, whose plays he had been reading and re-reading." It would be simply ludicrous to ascribe to Synge the revival of English dialect drama as exemplified, say, by Mr. Stanley Houghton's *Hindle Wakes*; yet his impulse is clearly beginning to bear fruit. " My two plays, *Miles Dixon* and *Mary's Wedding*,"[2] says (in a letter) Mr. Gilbert Cannan, " were written under the influence of Synge, an influence which I count the healthiest in the English theatre." In the first of these plays we are confronted with the vicissitudes of a new Christy Mahon warning the unknown son whom he has discovered in his old age against the danger of becoming another Playboy. *Mary's Wedding* is described as an attempt—very much on Synge's own lines—" not to reproduce exactly the Westmorland dialect, which would be unintelligible to ears coming new to it, but only to catch the rough music of it and the slow inflection of

---

[1] "Some Reminiscences of the Author of 'Mark Rutherford'" (II), by Miss Betham-Edwards, *British Weekly*, March 20, 1913, p. 714.
[2] In *Four Plays* (London : Sidgwick and Jackson, 1913).

northern voices." Together with these two very successful experiments, there are in the work of quite young and unknown English dramatists many immature and hitherto unpublished plays bearing traces of Synge's idiom. None of them can catch his real flavour and inner spirit, of course, only the little tricks of him—the external " Syngeisms."

It may therefore be confidently urged that Synge's name is one of the chosen few that are bound to survive. Of course his body of work is a little slim ; of course Synge, after all, may be grudged the palm given to the unique, meteoric geniuses that do mankind honour ; and quite possibly one might discover in the range of European literature rural writers almost equivalent to Synge, or at least comparable with him. Yet no one will seriously contest that his writings bear the hallmark of a signal literary ability and of an almost unprecedented temperament. In this age of manufactured shibboleths, ready-made art creeds and literary industrialism, it has been Synge's merit to go back to the fresh, intuitive, live perception of a primitive and gruesome reality that alone could satisfy the craving of his imagination for some vivid, pungent stuff to work on. He has had the honour of belonging to an admirable regional school without endorsing its somewhat rigorous parochialism, but, on the contrary, introducing into it a wider outlook, a sense of human perspective due to a sound and comprehensive

European learning. He did not, however, allow himself to be absorbed in his movement, or in any movement ; always keeping himself free from influence proper—indigenous or outlandish—he asserted silently in his life and perhaps a little noisily in some of his writings his artistic independence. Like all who truly express themselves, he expressed his country, he expressed mankind ; but being a certain type of Irishman, and a certain type of man, he expressed Ireland and mankind only as he saw them, or saw himself in them. His plays are Ireland ; they are mankind ; above all, they are Synge.

Whether he is to have actual literary disciples in English-speaking countries and elsewhere, the future will decide. As his case stands, however, with his strong, all-pervading personal note, he is not likely to find many imitators. One can imitate a style—one may even, without any great difficulty, parody Synge's dialect—but one cannot imitate an organic individuality. Synge's mental and artistic idiosyncrasy was almost exclusively his own when he lived : now he is dead, it will not, in all probability, become anyone else's. At all events, the present writer's intention has been, not to make disputable prophecies on Synge's literary future, but simply to clear away " the mists that do be gathering " around his name and work ; a task rendered all the more difficult by the peculiar opacity of Irish mists.

APPENDICES

APPENDIX A

GENERAL BIBLIOGRAPHY

(1) SYNGE'S WORKS

(*a*) DESCRIPTIVE LIST OF EDITIONS

1. *Irish and English.*

[The following were published in Synge's lifetime]—

1. RIDERS TO THE SEA was published earlier than IN THE SHADOW OF THE GLEN (although it is later in date of composition) in SAMHAIN, October, 1903 (No. 3), pp. 25–33.

2. IN THE SHADOW OF THE GLEN originally appeared in SAMHAIN, December, 1904 (No. 4), pp. 34–44.

   THE SHADOW OF THE GLEN and RIDERS TO THE SEA were issued together in one volume. Royal 16mo. 1*s.* London : Elkin Mathews, Vigo Street, W., (May 8), 1905. Now in its second edition (December, 1907) and sixth thousand as No. 24 of the Vigo Cabinet Series. Paper, 1*s.*, cloth, 1*s.* 6*d.*

   [The first edition contains the curious misprint *F. M. Synge.*]

3. THE WELL OF THE SAINTS. The Abbey Theatre Series of Plays. Vol. I. Published at the Abbey Theatre. Crown 8vo. Paper, 1*s.*, cloth, 2*s.* 1905.

   The same, with an introduction by W. B. Yeats (dated " Abbey Theatre, January, 1905 "), being volume four of Plays for an Irish Theatre. Crown 8vo, 7¾ × 5, pp. 110. 3*s.* 6*d.* net. London : A. H. Bullen, 47 Great Russell Street, W.C., (December), 1905.

   The same, with introduction by W. B. Yeats. Crown 8vo, 8 × 5, pp. 96. 2*s.* net. Dublin : Maunsel (December), 1907.

251

APPENDIX A

4. The Playboy of the Western World. A Comedy in three acts. Dublin : Maunsel & Co., Ltd., (March), 1907. Crown 8vo, 8 × 5¼, pp. 96. Paper, 1s., cloth, 2s. [An unexpurgated version of the play, with Synge's preface dated "January 21, 1907." Only a few copies of this edition remain.]

 The same, Theatre Edition. Dublin : Maunsel & Co., Ltd., 1907. Paper cover, 1s. [A "bowdlerized" edition of the play, without Synge's preface.]

 The same, reissue. Crown 8vo, pp. 94. 1s. net. Dublin : Maunsel, (November), 1909.

5. The Aran Islands. Large paper edition, with twelve drawings by Jack B. Yeats. Coloured by hand. Crown 4to, hand-made paper. 21s. net. Issued jointly by Elkin Mathews, London, and Maunsel, Dublin, (April), 1907. [150 copies were printed, some of them signed by author and illustrator ; a few remain.]

 The same, ordinary edition, with the drawings in black and white. Demy 8vo, 9¼ × 5¾, pp. 202. Antique paper, 5s. net. [A few copies remain.]

6. The Tinker's Wedding. A Comedy in Two Acts (also : "Scenes"). Dublin : Maunsel (January), 1908. (With Synge's preface dated "December 2, 1907.") Crown 8vo, 7¾ × 5, pp. 58. 2s. net. (Originally issued uniform with the Playboy, but now out of print in this form.)

[The following were published posthumously]—

7. Poems[1] and Translations. Cuala Press,[2] Churchtown, Dundrum, Co. Dublin (June 5), 1909. [With a preface by W. B. Yeats dated "April 4, 1909." 250 copies were issued, price 10s. 6d. net each.]

---

[1] Synge's poem, *Beg-Innish*, is also to be found in *The Dublin Book of Irish Verse*, edited by John Cooke (Dublin : Hodges and Figgis ; Oxford : Henry Frowde, Oxford University Press, 1909), No. 514, pp. 721–2.

[2] Late Dun Emer Press, managed by Miss Elizabeth Corbet Yeats (the poet's sister), who endeavours to revive the ancient Irish art of fine printing. An eighteenth-century type has been cast for the purpose, and paper is made of linen rags without bleaching materials at the Saggart Mills, Co. Dublin. The pages are printed on a hand-press, and the books are chosen and edited by Mr. W. B. Yeats. This most interesting enterprise is not unlike William Morris's Kelmscott Press, and justifies Mr. G. B. Shaw's dictum that the Irish art movement seems to be "a quaint little offshoot of English pre-Raphaelitism." (*John Bull's Other Island :* "Preface for Politicians," p. xxv).

APPENDIX A

8. Deirdre of the Sorrows. Cuala Press (July 5), 1910. [With a preface by W. B. Yeats dated "April 1910." 250 copies were issued, price, 10s. 6d. net each.]

9. The Works of John M. Synge. A Collected Edition in four volumes. Demy 8vo. Printed on antique laid paper, bound in buckram, gilt top, with four portraits from drawings by Mr. John B. Yeats, R.H.A., and Mr. James Paterson, and from photographs. Maunsel & Co., Ltd., 96 Middle Abbey Street, Dublin (November 22), 1910. 24s. net. [1,250 sets were issued. The edition has now been sold out, and at a premium (cf. The New Age, August 3, 1911, p. 328, and The Glasgow Evening News, July, 1911); sets, when they can be had, already fetch a high price. The demand was particularly great at Oxford and Cambridge (cf. The Sphere, April 22, 1911). Mr. George Roberts, the managing editor of the publishing firm, informs us that the rapid sale is ascribable to the influence of the Press, notably of such articles as "The Work of John M. Synge" in The Spectator, April 1, 1911, p. 482.]
[This edition is as follows:
Vol. I. Plays: The Shadow of the Glen, Riders to the Sea, The Well of the Saints, The Tinker's Wedding.
Vol. II. Plays, Poems and Translations: The Playboy of the Western World, Deirdre of the Sorrows, Poems, Translations from Petrarch, Translations from Villon and others.
[The Cuala Press edition (*supra*, No. 7) did not contain the following poems and translations included in Vol. II of the Collected Edition:
Poems: In Kerry—The 'Mergency Man—Danny —To the Oaks of Glencree—Dread—The Curse.
Translations: (1) From Petrarch: Laura is Ever Present to Him—He Ceases to Speak of Her Graces and Her Virtues Which are No More— He Sends His Rhymes to the Tomb of Laura to Pray Her to Call Him to Her—Only He who Mourns Her and Heaven that Possesses Her knew Her while She Lived. [Moreover

253

these titles have been rendered not by Synge himself, but by another translator.]

   (2) Walter von der Vogelweide.
   (3) Leopardi : SILVIA].

Vol. III. THE ARAN ISLANDS.

Synge had previously published :

   (1) *A Story from Inishmaan*, in the NEW IRELAND REVIEW (Dublin), November, 1898, p. 153.

   (2) *The Last Fortress of the Celt*, in THE GAEL (a magazine formerly published in New York), April, 1901, p. 109, some of which is incorporated in the book—is really part of Synge's material. This article was illustrated with photographs taken by Synge in the Islands and signed "Synge, Paris."

   [THE GAEL for July, 1901, p. 231, contained the following note : "The *Pilot* last week printed a most interesting article entitled 'The Last Fortress of the Celt,' which it found in one of the lesser known Irish papers. We now learn that it appeared originally in *The Gael*, of New York. . . .—*Boston Pilot*."]

   (3) *A Dream of Inishmaan*, in THE GAEL, March, 1904, revised and incorporated in the present volume, pp. 97–8.

   (4) *An Impression of Aran*, in the MANCHESTER GUARDIAN, January 24, 1905, p. 12, reprinted in Part I of the book, pp. 1–9 (line 10) of the present volume.

Vol. IV. IN WICKLOW—IN WEST KERRY—IN THE CONGESTED DISTRICTS—UNDER ETHER.

   [The essays in this volume originally appeared as journalistic contributions. The following is a concordance which may prove of use for a comparative study of the successive versions and an examination of Synge's curious work of re-writing :

   (1) IN WICKLOW.

(a) *The Vagrants of Wicklow* (vol. iv, pp. 1–12) :
  re-written (but not improved) from THE SHANACHIE, No. 2, pp. 93–8.

(b) *The Oppression of the Hills* (pp. 13–19) :
  MANCHESTER GUARDIAN, February 15, 1905, p. 12.

(c) *On the Road* (pp. 20–6) :
MANCHESTER GUARDIAN, December 10, 1908,
p. 14 (title : *In Wicklow. On the Road*).
(d) *The People of the Glens* (pp. 27–41) :
THE SHANACHIE, March 1907, pp. 39–47.
(e) *At a Wicklow Fair. The Place and the People* (pp. 42–50) :
MANCHESTER GUARDIAN, May 9, 1907, p. 12
(title : *At a Wicklow Fair* ; end quite different).
(f) *A Landlord's Garden in County Wicklow* (pp. 51–7) :
MANCHESTER GUARDIAN, July 1, 1907, p. 12.
(g) *Glencree* (pp. 58–62), had not been published before.

(2) IN WEST KERRY.

(a) Vol. iv, pp. 65–83 (line 9) :
THE SHANACHIE, vol. ii, No. 4 (Summer, 1907),
pp. 61–70 (title : *In West Kerry*).
(b) pp. 83 (line 10) –119 :
THE SHANACHIE, vol. ii, No. 6 (Autumn, 1907), pp.
138–50 (title: *In West Kerry. The Blasket Islands*).
(c) pp. 120 (line 1) –154 :
THE SHANACHIE, vol. ii, No. 6 (Winter, 1907), pp.
233–43 (title : *In West Kerry. To Puck Fair*).

(3) IN THE CONGESTED DISTRICTS.

Originally appeared in serial form in the MANCHESTER
GUARDIAN.[1] The general title, IN THE CONGESTED
DISTRICTS, was repeated in each instalment, which
contained sketches by Mr. Jack B. Yeats :
(a) *From Galway to Gorumna* (vol. iv, pp. 157–65) :
M. G., June 10, 1905, p. 7 (one sketch).
(b) *Between the Bays of Carraroe* (pp. 166–73) :
M. G., June 14, 1905, p. 3 (two sketches).
(c) *Among the Relief Works* (pp. 174–80) :
M. G., June 17, 1905, p. 7 (two sketches).
(d) *The Ferryman of Dinish Island* (pp. 181–8).
M. G., June 21, 1905, p. 5 (one sketch).
(e) *The Kelp Makers* (pp. 189–95).
M. G., June 24, 1905, p. 7 (one sketch).
(f) *The Boat Builders* (pp. 196–202).
M. G., June 28, 1905, p. 5 (one sketch).

---

[1] Synge mentions the name of the paper in one of the essays : *Erris*, vol. iv,
p. 223 : (i) in above list. He was paid £25 4s. for the whole series of articles.

(g) *The Homes of the Harvestmen* (pp. 203–9).
 M. G., July 1, 1905, p. 7 (one sketch).
(h) *The Smaller Peasant Proprietors* (pp. 210–17).
 M. G., July 5, 1905, p. 5 (one sketch).
(i) *Erris* (pp. 218–24).
 M. G., July 8, 1905, p. 7 (one sketch).
(j) *The Inner Lands of Mayo. The Village Shop* (pp. 225–31).
 M. G., July 19, 1905, p. 5 (one sketch).
(k) *The Small Town* (pp. 232–8).
 M. G., July 22, 1905, p. 7 (one sketch).
(l) *Possible Remedies* (pp. 239–45).
 M. G., July 26, 1905, p. 5.]

10. A Pocket Edition of the Plays (Dublin : Maunsel, 1911), printed on antique paper, foolscap 12mo, quarter parchment and boards, gilt top ; in four volumes [sold separately], 2*s.* 6*d.* net each.
 Vol. I. THE PLAYBOY OF THE WESTERN WORLD. 7 × 4½, pp. 140 (June).
 Vol. II. DEIRDRE OF THE SORROWS. 7¼ × 4¼, pp. 106 (July).
 Vol. III. THE WELL OF THE SAINTS. 7 × 4¼, pp. 102 (July).
 Vol. IV. THE TINKER'S WEDDING, RIDERS TO THE SEA, THE SHADOW OF THE GLEN. 7 × 4¼, pp. i–24 (October).
 Note.—Messrs. Maunsel have lately opened a branch in London (Oakley House, Bloomsbury Street, W.C.), where this edition can also be had.

11. A Uniform Library Edition of J. M. Synge's Works in five volumes, large crown 8vo, printed on antique wove paper, bound in dark blue cloth, gilt top. [The volumes are sold separately ; complete sets are supplied in buckram binding.] Dublin : Maunsel, 1911 :
 POEMS AND TRANSLATIONS. 8½ × 5½, pp. 62. 3*s.* 6*d.* net (November).
 IN WICKLOW, WEST KERRY AND CONNEMARA. Illustrated by Jack B. Yeats. 8½ × 5½, pp. 256. 5*s.* net (November).
 THE ARAN ISLANDS. With the illustrations which

APPENDIX A

appeared in the first edition of the book (cf. *supra*, **No.** 5). 8½ × 5½, pp. 272. 6*s*. net (November).

FOUR PLAYS: RIDERS TO THE SEA, THE SHADOW OF THE GLEN, THE TINKER'S WEDDING, THE WELL OF THE SAINTS. 8¼ × 5¼, pp. 190. 5*s*. net (December).

TWO PLAYS: THE PLAYBOY OF THE WESTERN WORLD, DEIRDRE OF THE SORROWS. 8¼ × 5¼, pp. 208. 5*s*. net (December).

[This edition is also procurable at Messrs. Maunsel's London office.]

2. *American.*

Mr. Francis Hackett, in the CHICAGO EVENING POST, July 2, 1909, p. 1, stated that "his [Synge's] plays are not published in America." Yet in the Spring of 1905,

(1.) POET-LORE, a Boston monthly (vol. xvi, pp. 1–22: "Two Irish Plays from the Gaelic Originals") published RIDERS TO THE SEA—which was still uncopyrighted— together with Dr. Douglas Hyde's THE TWISTING OF THE ROPE, and (*ibid.*, pp. 40–53) a prefatory note on "The Irish Literary Drama" by Miss Vida D. Scudder, later issued in book form at $1·25. THE BOSTON EVENING TRANSCRIPT, March 25, 1911, said that "the Yale University Press has arranged with Maunsel to publish in America the complete works of Synge. Meanwhile John W. Luce, of Boston, will have ready four reprints: THE ARAN ISLANDS, KERRY AND WICKLOW, THE TINKER'S WEDDING, RIDERS TO THE SEA". This announcement of a Yale University Press edition of Synge's works was premature, the manager having failed to agree as to terms with Messrs. Maunsel. Accordingly

(2.) Messrs. John W. Luce & Co., 143 Federal Street, Boston, Mass.—Boston, as is well known, is the great Irish-American centre—by arrangement made with Synge's Executors through Messrs. Maunsel, are the sole authorized publishers of his works in America. Their issue (bound uniformly in green paper and boards with vellum back and gold stamping) is as follows:

THE PLAYBOY OF THE WESTERN WORLD. 1911. Net $1·00.

IN THE SHADOW OF THE GLEN. 1911. Net $·60.

257

APPENDIX A

RIDERS TO THE SEA. With an introduction by Edward J. O'Brien. 1911. Net $ ·60.

THE TINKER'S WEDDING. Net $ ·75.

THE ARAN ISLANDS. Sketches of travel and a note-book to the plays. With an introduction by Edward J. O'Brien, 12 illustrations by Jack B. Yeats, and a sketch map of the islands. 1911. Net $1·25.

DEIRDRE OF THE SORROWS. 1911. Net $1·00.

KERRY AND WICKLOW. Sketches in rural Ireland. With frontispiece portrait of the author. 1912. Net $1·25.

CONNEMARA and POEMS AND TRANSLATIONS ready shortly.

[All the above copyrighted by L. E. Bassett.]

(3.) Mr. John Quinn, the well-known Irish-American attorney and counsellor-at-law who defended the Abbey Theatre Players when they were arrested and prosecuted in Philadelphia, an ardent admirer of Synge and a constant patron of things Irish in America, has privately printed from time to time limited editions of several of Synge's works. It is an interesting fact that these editions were designed by Mr. E. Byrne Hackett, of the Yale University Press, New Haven, Conn. Mr. Quinn copyrighted THE WELL OF THE SAINTS in 1904, in an edition limited to fifty copies, printed by himself; THE PLAYBOY OF THE WESTERN WORLD in 1907 (simultaneously with its publication in Ireland); he also had privately printed for himself an edition limited to fifty copies on hand-made paper of POEMS AND TRANSLATIONS in 1909 (simultaneously with the Cuala Press edition), this being printed in New York in order to preserve the copyright from type set there; and lastly (after Synge's death) an edition limited to fifty copies on hand-made paper, uniform with POEMS AND TRANSLATIONS, of DEIRDRE OF THE SORROWS, (1910, pp. 90, Library of Congress, No. 10—15091), published simultaneously with the Cuala Press edition. Mr. E. Byrne Hackett did not have those editions printed for Mr. Quinn, but simply gave him the name of a printer who did part of the work.

258

APPENDIX A

1. *Czech.*

Pan Karel Mušek, of the Royal Bohemian National Theatre, Prague, has excellently translated THE SHADOW OF THE GLEN into Czech under the title *Ve Stínu Doliny* for a cycle of "Literary Dramas" arranged by the "Circle of Bohemian Writers" and produced at the Theatre, Smíchov (a suburb of Prague). The translation, which was done at the instance of Mr. Richard J. Kelly, a Dublin lawyer and journalist, remains unpublished.

Pan Karel Mušek's versions of *The Well of the Saints* (*Studeň Světců*) and *Riders to the Sea* (*Mořeplavci*) have been neither published nor produced. Synge (in a letter) also gave Pan Karel Mušek permission to translate the *Playboy* into Czech, but the translation has not yet been written.

2. *Dutch.*

The Well of the Saints has been translated by Heer Leo Simons and published under the title *De Heiligenbron: Tooneelspel in drie Bedrijven, alleen-geautoriseerde Vertaling van L. Simons* in the "Tooneelbibliotheek onder Leiding van L. Simons uitgegeven door de maatschappij voor Goede en Goedkoope Lectuur," Amsterdam, 1912. The translation, which contains a portrait of Synge and an introduction on the state of Irish Drama at the time of Synge's death, was done for the Dutch actor Willem Royaards, who saw the original play at the Abbey Theatre when Mr. Conal O'Riordan ["F. Norreys Connell"], a personal friend of Heer Leo Simons, had become co-director of it. Heer W. Royaards will probably enact the translation, which was reviewed by Mr. Conal O'Riordan in the *Irish Review*, December, 1912, p. 557 ("Synge in Dutch").

3. *French.*

M. Louis Pennequin of Douai has translated *The Shadow of the Glen* and *Riders to the Sea* under the respective titles *La Brume du Vallon* and *La Chevauchée à la Mer*. These versions have been neither published nor produced.

[Signora N. Esposito also wrote (during Synge's lifetime)

a French translation of *Riders to the Sea*, the title of which remained undecided. See *infra : 6. Russian.*]

M. P. H. Raymond-Duval has translated *The Tinker's Wedding* into Berrichon dialect under the title *Les Noces du Rétameur*. Neither published nor produced.

The present writer possesses the exclusive rights of translation and performance of *The Playboy of the Western World* and *The Well of the Saints*. *Le Baladin du Monde Occidental* will be published in serial form in the *Grande Revue* (Paris) before July 1, 1914, and in book form before January 1, 1915. The translation has now been accepted for production by the Théâtre Subventionné de l'Œuvre, and the desirability of its being staged at the Théâtre des Arts has also been considered. *La Fontaine aux Saints* will be published in magazine form before January 1, 1915 and in book form before January 1, 1916, and produced before January 1, 1917.

The rights of *Deirdre of the Sorrows* and Synge's other works have been provisionally reserved for the present writer.

4. German.

Der Heilige Brunnen (*The Well of the Saints*), by Dr. Max Meyerfeld, has been published by the firm S. Fischer, Verlag, Berlin, 1906, and produced in Berlin in 1906 and in Munich in 1908.

The Playboy of the Western World has been translated under the title *Der Held des Westerlands*, by Mr. Chas. H. Fisher and Herr G. Sil-Vara, a Viennese author, journalist and playwright who resides in London. Herr Sil-Vara has succeeded in placing the *Playboy* at Prof. Max Reinhardt's Kammerspiele, Berlin, at the Neue Wiener Bühne, Vienna and at the Stadttheater in Münster. The German version, published by Georg Müller in Munich, has appeared in book form (1912) with a preface on the Irish school.

Arrangements have been made with Dr. Fred. B. Hardt of Munich for the translation into German of *Riders to the Sea*, *The Shadow of the Glen* and *The Tinker's Wedding*, but the translations have not yet been produced. They will be published by Georg Müller in Munich only when they have been accepted for production.

APPENDIX A

5. *Irish Gaelic.*

Mr. W. P. Ryan (Uilliam P. O'Riain), in his article "A Singer o' the Green" (DAILY CHRONICLE, February 4,1911, p. 6) refers to RIDERS TO THE SEA as "the only one of his [Synge's] plays as yet translated into Irish." The translation, which is the work of Mr. Thomas MacDonnell (Tomás MacDomhnaill), of Leinster College, Dublin, has not been printed, but only typewritten for private circulation. The author has not apparently decided definitely on the title of the translation. The English title of Synge's play is more or less picturesque, and its literal rendering, *Marcaigh chun na Fairrge,* or *Cinniri chun na Mara,* would seem somewhat odd in Irish. So would the more alliterative title, *Marcaigh chun na Mara,* apart from the further fact that "Mara" (genitive) and "Muir" (nominative) are not much used for "sea" in modern Irish, except in place-names and a few traditional phrases. So it has been felt that a more expressive, in fact, some independent, title must be given. One of the foregoing would do only as a tentative title. There was some delay over the copyright question, and the translation was about to be played at the Dublin Oireachtas, when Messrs. Maunsel raised points about acting rights ; so the idea was dropped. Arrangements are being made for the publication of the translation by the Gaelic League.

6. *Russian.*

Signora Esposito of Dublin [Nathalie Pétrovna Klebnikoff] wrote (during Synge's lifetime) a Russian version of *Riders to the Sea* entitled Жертвы Моря [*i. e. The Victims of the Sea*]. Synge refers to her translations (which have never been published) in a letter to a friend dated "Ireland, Sunday, June '04."

(*c*) UNPUBLISHED AND UNREPRINTED WORKS.

For the sake of easier reference we here reproduce in a connected form the various items of information that will be found scattered in our text concerning Synge's unpublished and unreprinted writings.

261

APPENDIX A

1. *Unpublished MSS.*

The majority of these remain in the hands of Synge's Executors, Messrs. Edward Synge and Francis Edmund Stephens, Mrs. Stephens, his sister, and Mr. W. B. Yeats. Some are not publishable, while others are purely of biographical interest. Synge was very anxious about the fate of his manuscripts and scattered writings (cf. W. B. Yeats, *Synge and the Ireland of his Time*, Preface, and Synge's letter in Mr. Yeats's introduction to the Cuala Press edition of *Poems and Translations*). Among his most interesting unpublished MSS. are the plays and poems which he wrote when a boy, the impressionistic essays of his Paris period, his story of a fiddler (see p. 27), his play on monastic life (p. 42), his scenario of a play on the Rebellion of '98 (p. 87, n. 5), his projected translations of great foreign works into Anglo-Irish, notably a rendering of the *Imitation of Christ* (p. 238), his plays on Dublin slum life and on the Cymbeline story (p. 238). Early versions of the Wicklow papers and a few rejected drafts of the published plays have also been preserved.

2. *Unreprinted Writings.*

Mainly contributions to the Press—

ACADEMY AND LITERATURE (London) :

June 11, 1904, p. 630 (under heading : "Literary Notes ") : a most interesting unsigned paragraph [identified on the authority of Mr. F. J. Fay : cf. an article on " John Millington Synge as Critic of Boucicaultian Irish Drama," by Mr. Joseph Holloway, in the *EVENING HERALD* (Dublin), July 10, 1913, p. 2] on performances of *The Shaughraun* at the Queen's Theatre, Dublin—valuable as a document on Synge's fond study of melodrama and on his view of the Irish National Theatre's relation to the " Stage Irishman " school. Presumably the three subsequent paragraphs (on Fr. P. S. Dineen's *Irish-English Dictionary*, Miss Agnes O'Farrelly's *O'Growney Memorial Volume*, and Mr. Frank Hugh O'Donnell's *The Stage Irishman of the Pseudo-Celtic Drama*) were also by Synge.

November 12, 1904, p. 455 : signed review of " Fiona MacLeod " 's *The Winged Destiny*.

APPENDIX A

DUBLIN DAILY EXPRESS:
   December 17, 1898, p. 3 : " La Sagesse et la Destinée."
Signed " J. M. S."
   January 28, 1899, p. 3 : " Anatole le Braz. A Breton
Writer." Signed " J. M. Synge."
   Together with these two reviews, written in a style
curiously influenced by Walter Pater, Synge also con-
tributed an account of a Socialist meeting in Paris at
which Sébastian Faure spoke—mere reporting, and not
very good.

L'EUROPÉEN (24 rue Dauphine, Paris vi^e) :
   March 15, 1902, pp. 11–2 : *La Vieille Littérature
Irlandaise.* Signed " J. M. Synge, Dublin."
   May 31, 1902, pp. 12–3 : *Le Mouvement Intellectuel
Irlandais.* Signed " J. M. Synge, Dublin."

FREEMAN'S JOURNAL (Dublin) :
   Short paragraphs not now identifiable. March 22, 1900,
p. 4 : unsigned leading article on " A Celtic Theatre"
[in Brittany] for which Synge was paid on April 13, 1900.

GAEL (AN GAODHAL) (New York) :
   April, 1903, p. 117 : *An Autumn Night on the Hills*
(signed). Illustrated by Mo. Flaherty.

IRISH TIMES (Dublin) :
   Miscellaneous paragraphs and book-reviews not now
identifiable. Anonymous notice of *The Story of the World,*
by Miss M. B. Synge (Synge's cousin), published by
Messrs. Blackwood on June 20, 1903.

KOTTABOS (Trinity College, Dublin) (New Series). Hilary
Term, 1893, p. 103 : *Glen Cullen.* [A Sonnet.] Signed
" J. M. Synge."

MANCHESTER GUARDIAN :
   March 6, 1906, p. 5, Review of A. H. Leahy's transla-
tion of " Heroic Romances of Ireland," vol. ii (signed).
   November 16, 1906, p. 5, Review of Mr. Stephen
Gwynn's " Fair Hills of Ireland " (unsigned).
   January 24, 1908, p. 12, Article entitled : *Good Pictures
in Dublin. The New Municipal Gallery* (signed).

APPENDIX A

Speaker (London) : list of signed articles.
[+ Out of print.]

+ Vol. iii, p. 245 (December 8, 1900) : Review of "Danta Amhrain is Caointe, Sheathruin Ceitinn," edited by the Rev. J. C. MacErlean, S.J. Title of Review, *The Poems of Geoffrey Keating*.

Vol. vi, p. 284 (June 7, 1902) : Review of "Cuchulain of Muirthemne," by Lady Gregory. Title of Review, *An Epic of Ulster*.

Vol. vi, p. 340 (June 21, 1902) : Review of "Donegal Fairy Stories," collected and told by Seumas MacManus. Title of Review, *Irish Fairy Stories*.

Vol. vi, p. 605 (September 6, 1902) : Review of Geoffrey Keating's "History of Ireland" (Foras Feasa ar Eirinn), edited by David Comyn. Title of Review, *An Irish Historian*.

+ Vol. viii, p. 57 (April 18, 1903) : Article under heading *Loti and Huysmans*. (Review of "L'Inde (sans les Anglais)," "L'Oblat," and also Anatole France's " Monsieur Bergeret à Paris.")

Vol. x, p. 17 (April 2, 1904) : Review of "The Irish Mythological Cycle and Celtic Mythology," by H. d'Arbois de Jubainville. Title of Review, *Celtic Mythology*.

Dr. C.-A. Picquenard of Quimper informs me that Synge also wrote an article in French on the Bigoudens, the natives of the Pont-l'Abbé district in Brittany, whose origin, manners and customs have excited the curiosity of many ethnographers and anthropologists ; but the date of the article and the name of the paper in which it was published are apparently undiscoverable.

Note.—Synge's correspondence is scanty and of little value. I am indebted to Mr. John Masefield, Mr. W. B. Yeats, Miss E. C. Yeats, Mr. A. Synge Owen, Mr. Stephen Mackenna, Pan Karel Mušek, Mr. Stephen Gwynn, M.P., Mr. R. I. Best, M.R.I.A., Mr. A. Francis Steuart, of Edinburgh, and others, for shewing me some of his letters. They were as a rule short and of no great interest. Synge had a spiky and sometimes illegible handwriting. Some of his letters have been reproduced in Mr. W. B. Yeats's prefaces to the Cuala Press editions.

APPENDIX A

The substance of Synge's private diaries—which he never kept—is embodied in his prose observations. He refers to his diary in IN WEST KERRY (Collected Edition, vol. iv, p. 119). Mr. Jack B. Yeats kept diaries of the Connemara tour which have not seen the light of publicity.

(ii) SOURCES OF INFORMATION.

The following is a selection of the best books, essays, appreciations, special articles, reviews, paragraphs, etc., dealing directly or indirectly with Synge and the Irish Theatre. The Author will be obliged for further references sent to him care of his publishers.

(a) BOOKS AND PAMPHLETS (INCLUDING FORTHCOMING WORKS).

Archer, William: *Playmaking : A Manual of Craftmanship* (London : Chapman & Hall, 1912). Synge : pp. 298, 304.

[Armstrong, Cecil Ferard] : *The Dramatic Author's Companion*, by " A Theatrical Manager's Reader," with an Introduction by Arthur Bourchier, M.A. (London : Mills & Boon, 1910). Synge, p. 42.

Baker, G. P., Professor of Drama at Harvard University, who is at present studying the developments of the art at Stratford, Dublin and Manchester, will embody his observations in a forthcoming critical study.

Bickley, Francis: *J. M. Synge and the Irish Dramatic Movement* (London : Constable, " Modern Biographies " ; Boston and New York : Houghton Mifflin, 1912).

Bithell, Jethro (translated by Franz Hellens) : *W. B. Yeats* (Editions du Masque : Paris : Librairie Générale des Sciences, Arts et Lettres ; Brussels : H. Lamertin, 1913). Synge : p. 15 n. 1, pp. 18, 20, 35, 43.

Borsa, Mario : *The English Stage of To-day* (translated from the original Italian and edited by Selwyn Brinton), (London and New York : John Lane, 1908) : chap. viii (pp. 286–314) : " The Irish National Theatre."

Brown, Stephen J., S.J. (edited by) : *A Guide to Books on Ireland*. Part I : Prose Literature, Music and Plays. (The Plays section compiled by Mr. Joseph Holloway, architect of the Abbey Theatre.) (Dublin : Hodges & Figgis ; London : Longmans, Green & Co., 1912.)

APPENDIX A

Cannan, Gilbert: *The Joy of the Theatre* (London:
B. T. Batsford: "The Fellowship Books," 1913):
pp. 32-3: reference to Synge.

Carter, Huntly: *The New Spirit in Drama and Art*
(London: Palmer, 1912). The Irish Literary Theatre: p.33.

Chambers's *Biographical Dictionary* (London and Edinburgh: W. & R. Chambers): Synge will appear on
page 897 of the next reprint, also in the next revised
issue of Chambers's *Encyclopædia*.

Colum, Pádraic: *My Irish Year* (London: Mills &
Boon, 1912). Synge: pp. 93, 94.

Compton-Rickett, Arthur: *English Literature* (London
and Edinburgh: Jack, 1912). Synge: p. 111.

Cousin, John W.: *A Short Biographical Dictionary of
English Literature* (London: Dent; New York: Dutton,
1910). Article, "Synge, John Millington": p. 370.

Dukes, Ashley: *Modern Dramatists* (London: Palmer,
1911). Synge: pp. 95, 97, 275.

"Eglinton, John" [Magee, W. K.]: *Literary Ideals
in Ireland* (London: Unwin; Dublin: *Daily Express*
Office, 1899).

Elton, Oliver: *Modern Studies* (London: Edward
Arnold, 1907). Final chapter ("Living Irish Literature"), vi. ("Synge").

Ervine, St. John G., the well-known Ulster playwright,
has in preparation a work entitled *Five Irish Dramatists*
(Wilde, Shaw, Yeats, Synge, Lady Gregory).

Figgis, Darrell: *Studies and Appreciations* (London:
Dent; New York: Dutton, 1912): p. 23: "J. M.
Synge" [reprinted from the London *Bookman*, *q. v.*];
p. 34: "The Art of J. M. Synge" [reprinted from
the *Fortnightly Review*, also the *Forum*, *q. v.*].

Galsworthy, John: *The Inn of Tranquillity* (London:
Heinemann, 1912). Reference to the *Playboy*, p. 202;
Synge: p. 207 [from the *English Review*, *q. v.*].

Gregory, Lady Augusta, is publishing with Putnams
(London and New York) in the Autumn of 1913 a book
entitled *Our Irish Theatre: A Chapter of Autobiography.*
It gives an account of the beginning and growth of the
theatre in Ireland, and contains a chapter on Synge,
which has already appeared in the *English Review, q. v.*

APPENDIX A

Gunnell, [Miss] Doris, Assistant Lecturer in French Language and Romance Philology at Leeds University, according to the "Courrier Littéraire" of *Paris-Journal*, December 23, 1911, was to publish in Paris a book on the Irish theatre. Miss Gunnell denies the fact; however, she published an article on "Le Nouveau Théâtre Irlandais" in the *Revue, q. v.*, and has written two other articles: one on the Irish theatre, accepted for publication in the *Mercure de France*, and another (in collaboration with M. Nayral de Puybusque) on J. M. Synge, the publication of which by the *Nouvelle Revue Française* is still undecided.

Gwynn, Stephen: *To-day and To-Morrow in Ireland* (Dublin: Hodges & Figgis; London: Macmillan, 1903), p. 87: "The Gaelic League and the Irish Theatre."

Gwynn, Stephen: see *infra*: MacCarthy, Justin.

Henderson, W. A.: *The Playboy of the Western World, by J. M. Synge. A Play that shocked. A Compendium of Comments, Criticisms, Calumnies, Carpings, Caricatures, Cavillings, Clamours, Congratulations*, Compiled by. (Private.)

Henderson, W. A.: *1909. The Irish National Theatre Movement. A Year's Work at the Abbey Theatre. Events: Death of J. M. Synge, March 24th; London Season, June 7th; Revival of the Playboy, May 27th; Production of Blanco Posnet, August 25th*; told in Press-cuttings by. (Private.) [These and other valuable collections of press-cuttings will be bequeathed by the compiler to the National Library of Ireland.]

Howe, P. P.: *The Repertory Theatre, A Record. A Criticism.* (London: Martin Secker, 1910). Chapter ii (pp. 42–51): "Experiments in Repertory."

Howe, P. P.: *J. M. Synge: A Critical Study.* Demy 8vo, 7s. 6d. net. (London: Martin Secker; New York: Mitchell Kennerley, 1912.)

[Mr. Howe says in his Prefatory Note that "a book is shortly to make its appearance that will tell from direct reminiscence all that the world is entitled to hear, written by those who knew Synge well." It was indeed suggested that a brief biography, with some personal details and memories, should be put together in a cheap form as

267

a memento, to be sold at the Abbey Theatre. However, the scheme has not yet materialized, and very likely never will.]

Hueffer, Ford Madox : *The Critical Attitude* (London : Duckworth, 1911). Synge [the *Playboy*] referred to on pp. 82, 83, 84.

Huneker, James : *The Pathos of Distance : A Book of A Thousand and One Moments* (London : T. Werner Laurie, 1913), containing studies on Mr. George Moore and the Celtic Awakening (pp. 228–35 : " John M. Synge "). Curiously enough, an essay on M. Henri Bergson, the French thinker, bears the Syngesque title " The Playboy of Western Philosophy."

Jackson, Holbrook : *All Manner of Folk* (London : Grant Richards ; New York : Mitchell Kennerley, 1912), " John M. Synge " : pp. 61–77.

Kennedy, J. M. : *English Literature : 1880–1905* (London : Stephen Swift, 1912). Synge : pp. 281, 309.

Lebeau, Henry, intends to write a volume of personal recollections about Synge and other Irish men of letters.

Letts, Miss W. M. : *Songs from Leinster* (London : Smith, Elder, 1913), p. 42 : " Synge's Grave " [a poem reprinted from the *Westminster Gazette, q.v.*] ; see also p. 40 : " For Sixpence " [a poem written from the point of view of the sixpenny audience at the Abbey Theatre when W. G. Fay was acting there in the *Playboy*].

Lynd, Robert : *Home Life in Ireland* (London : Mills & Boon, 1906), p. 304 *et seq.* : " Literature and Music " (a paragraph on Synge).

MacCarthy, Justin (edited by) : *Irish Literature*, 10 vols. (John D. Morris—The de Bower Elliot Co., Chicago, 1904) : a chapter on " The Irish Theatre " by Mr. Stephen Gwynn, M.P.

Mair, G. H., M.A., *English Literature : Modern* (London : Williams & Norgate, " Home University Library," 1911). Synge : pp. 247 *et seq.* [reprinted from the *Manchester Guardian, q.v.*].

Malye, Jean : *La Littérature Irlandaise Contemporaine* (Paris : E. Sansot, 1913). Synge : pp. 41, 50, 51.

Marriott, Ernest : *Jack B. Yeats, being a true impartial view of his pictorial and dramatic art*, etc., *with a portrait*

APPENDIX A

of the artist when a child, by his father, and a chart of Pirate Island [a monograph read at a meeting of the Manchester Literary Club, and re-written from the *Manchester Quarterly*, July 1911] (London: Elkin Matthews (December), 1911, 1s.). Cf. p. 10.

Masefield, John: *Dictionary of National Biography* (London: Smith, Elder, 1912), Second Supplement, vol. iii, pp. 468–71, article "Synge, John Millington." [The most reliable statement of fact.]

Montague, C. E.: *Dramatic Values* (London: Methuen, 1911). Cf. pp. 1–15, 54, 91, 154, 201 *et seq.*, 212.

Montague, C. E.: *Essays and Studies by Members of the English Association*, vol. ii, collected by H. C. Beeching (Oxford: Clarendon Press, 1911): "The Literary Play," (pp. 71 *et seq.*): Synge, pp. 81, 85.

Moore, George: *Hail and Farewell* (London: Heinemann): I. *Ave* (1911; also in the Tauchnitz Collection, Leipzig, No. 4314). II. *Salve* (Heinemann, 1912, p. 197: a passing reference to the *Play Boy* [*sic*]. III. *Vale* (to be published in the Autumn of 1913) will deal with Synge and his relation to Yeats.

More, Paul Elmer: *The Drift of Romanticism* (*Shelburne Essays*, 8th Series) (Boston and New York: Houghton Mifflin Co., 1913), pp. 135–6: reference to Synge (in essay on 'Fiona MacLeod).'

Nevinson, H. W.: *Books and Personalities* (London and N.Y.: John Lane, 1905). "Irish Plays of 1904": pp. 248–9, *Riders to the Sea*; p. 250, *In the Shadow of the Glen.*

O'Donoghue, D. J.: *The Poets of Ireland: a biographical and bibliographical dictionary of Irish writers of English verse* (Dublin: Hodges Figgis & Co.; London: Henry Frowde, Oxford University Press, 1912), p. 448: article "Synge, John Millington."

Oliver, D. E.: *The English Stage: Its Origins and Modern Developments* (London: John Ouseley, second edition, 1912). The Irish Literary Theatre, Yeats, Synge, etc., pp. 118 *et seq.*

Paul-Dubois, L.: *L'Irlande Contemporaine et la Question Irlandaise* (Paris: Librairie Académique Perrin, 1907), pp. 407–10: "Le théâtre irlandais"; English translation by

APPENDIX A

T. M. Kettle (Dublin : Maunsel, 1911), pp. 423–6 : "The Irish Theatre."

Quinn, John : see Shaw, G. B.

Randall, [Miss] Ethel Claire, of Chicago University, wrote in 1906 for her A.M. degree a thesis on the Irish Literary and Dramatic Revival, entitled, *The Celtic Movement : The Awakening of the Fires*, which remains unpublished in the University Library.

Ransome, Arthur : *Oscar Wilde : A Critical Study* (London : Martin Secker, 1912), p. 137 ; (London : Methuen, 1913), p. 148.

Roberts, George, is said to be projecting a book on Synge.

Roosevelt, Th. : see Shaw, G. B.

Ryan, W. P. : *The Irish Literary Revival : its history, pioneers and possibilities* (London : published by the author at 1 Constance Road, East Dulwich, S.E., and by Ward & Downey, 12 York Buildings, Adelphi, W.C. ; also on sale at Dobell's, 77 Charing Cross Road, 1894).

Ryan, W. P. : *The Pope's Green Island* (London : Nisbet, 1912), ch. xxiv, p. 299 : "Ireland at the Play."

Sharp, R. Farquharson : *A Short History of the English Stage* (London, Felling-on-Tyne and New York : The Walter Scott Publishing Co., 1909), ch. xx, p. 317 : "The Dublin Theatres."

Shaw, G. B. : *A Note on the Irish Theatre by Theodore Roosevelt and an "interview" on the Irish Players in America by George Bernard Shaw* (New York : Mitchell Kennerley, 1912). [Mr. Roosevelt's contribution to this booklet is a reprint of his "Introduction" to "The Irish Players" in the OUTLOOK (N.Y.), December 16, 1911, p. 915, *q.v.*]. Introductory note by John Quinn.

Walbrook, H. M. : *Nights at the Play* (London : Ham-Smith, 1911), a selection in book form of Mr. Walbrook's theatrical notices in the PALL MALL GAZETTE (*q.v.*) between 1907 and 1910. One of them (pp. 107–9) deals with Synge and the *Playboy*.

Walkley, A. B. : *Drama and Life* (London : Methuen, 1907), p. 309 : "The Irish National Theatre" [reprinted from the TIMES, May 8, 1903].

Weygandt, Cornelius : *Irish Plays and Playwrights*

APPENDIX A

(London : Constable ; Boston and New York : Houghton Mifflin, 1913).

Yeats, William Butler and Jack B. : *Synge and the Ireland of His Time*, by William Butler Yeats, *with a note concerning a walk through Connemara with him* by Jack B. Yeats (Cuala Press, July 26, 1911). 350 copies, 10*s*. 6*d*. each. Copyrighted in America by Mitchell Kennerley. (Now out of print.)

[The book, which is very short (pp. 43), was first intended to contain other biographical contributions by writers who had known Synge personally. For instance, a contribution by Mr. John Masefield (probably a reprint of his reminiscence of Synge in the CONTEMPORARY REVIEW, April 1911, p. 470) had been announced in the prospectus of the Cuala Press for January, 1911 ; the intention, however, was not adhered to. *Synge and the Ireland of His Time* (cf. Preface) would have been prefixed as an introduction to the Collected Edition of Synge's works, had it not been withdrawn owing to ninety pages being published in the Edition without Mr. W. B. Yeats's consent. Mr. Yeats also published his essay in the FORUM (New York), August 1911, p. 179, under the title " John M. Synge and the Ireland of His Time " (it was the principal article in the issue and was specially advertised on the cover), with the omission of a somewhat unfelicitous sentence (pp. 2–3 of the Cuala Press edition) which we need not quote here. Reference to this characteristic omission will be found in the IRISH REVIEW (Dublin), September 1911, pp. 326–7 (" Dramatic Values," by Walter Mennloch).—Mr. Jack B. Yeats's *With Synge in Connemara* originally appeared in the NEW YORK EVENING SUN *about* July 18, 1909,[1] and in the IRISH NATION (Dublin), August 14, 1909, under the title " Memories of Synge."].

Yeats, W. B. : *Collected Works* (Stratford-on-Avon : A. H. Bullen, The Shakespeare Head Press, 1908). Cf. vol. iv, pp. 79–247 (" The Irish Dramatic Movement "), especially pp. 112, 120, 192 *n*., 227, 228–30, 231 [reprints from SAMHAIN and the ARROW] ; vol. viii, p. 173 (" Mr.

---

[1] Repeated inquiry has failed to ascertain the date. Mr. Jack B. Yeats says the middle of the month.

APPENDIX A

Synge and his Plays " = Mr. Yeats's Introduction to *The Well of the Saints*), and pp. 197 ff. (Bibliography by Allan Wade).

Yeats, W. B.: Prefaces to the Cuala Press editions of *Poems and Translations* and *Deirdre of the Sorrows*.

Yeats, W. B.: *Ideas of Good and Evil* (London: Bullen, 1903) : p. 257 : " The Theatre."

Yeats, W. B. : *Where there is Nothing :* Dedication of Plays for an Irish Theatre.

Yeats, W. B. : *The Cutting of an Agate* (New York : the Macmillan Co., 1913). [In this are gathered Mr. Yeats's essays on Synge, Lady Gregory, John Shaw-Taylor, Spenser, and miscellaneous thoughts on poetry and the drama.]

(*b*) *NEWSPAPERS AND PERIODICALS.*

ABERDEEN FREE PRESS.
February 6, 1911.

ACADEMY AND LITERATURE (London).
May 9, 1903, p. 465, " The Experiments of Mr. Yeats."
May 16, 1903, p. 495, " Irish Plays and Players " (a letter by W. B. Yeats).
June 10, 1911, p. 723.
October 14, 1911, p. 485, Review of Yeats's *Synge and the Ireland of His Time.*
February 15, 1913, p. 212, Charles Bewley's article on " The Irish National Theatre," in the *Dublin Review, q. v.*

ADVERTISER (London).
May 8, 1909.

AMERICA (New York).
September to December, 1911, especially October 28, p. 64 ; November 4, pp. 78–79 (" The Plays of the ' Irish ' Players," by Fr. M. Kenny, S.J.) ; December 30, p. 267.

AMERICAN CATHOLIC QUARTERLY (Philadelphia).
July, 1912 : " Irish Drama and Irish Views," by Fr. George O'Neill, S.J. [reprinted in IRISH CATHOLIC, *q.v.*].

AMERICAN MAGAZINE (New York).
February, 1912, p. 491 : " The Theatre. Some Plays Worth While," by Walter Pritchard Eaton.

March 1912, p. 550, "Lady Gregory" (portrait on p. 549), by Dana Gatlin; p. 625, "The Theatre. The Literary Drama," by Walter Pritchard Eaton.

AMERICAN REVIEW OF REVIEWS.

December 1912, p. 750, Review of P. P. Howe's *J. M. Synge : A Critical Study.*

ARROW (Dublin), edited by W. B. Yeats.[1]

No. 1, October 20, 1906 : *passim.*

ATHENÆUM (London).

August 14, 1909 (on Synge as a poet).

February 18, 1911, p. 182, "The Works of J. M. Synge."

June 24, 1911, p. 727.

August 26, 1911, p. 240, Review of Yeats's *Synge and the Ireland of His Time.*

December 16, 1911.

June 8, 1912, p. 663 (the *Playboy* at the Court Theatre).

June 22, 1912, p. 715 (*The Well of the Saints* at the Court Theatre).

June 29, 1912, p. 726, "Synge and the Theatre" (Review of P. P. Howe's *J. M. Synge : A Critical Study*) ; p. 741, "The Irish Drama."

July 16, 1912, p. 24 (*Riders to the Sea* at the Court Theatre).

July 20, 1912, pp. 71–2 : "The Close of the Irish Season."

October 5, 1912, p. 387 : Review of Francis Bickley's *J. M. Synge and the Irish Dramatic Movement.*

March 1, 1913, p. 260 : Review of Cornelius Weygandt's *Irish Plays and Playwrights.*

BELFAST EVENING TELEGRAPH.

August 4, 1909.

BELFAST NEWS-LETTER.

March 25, 1909.

August 4, 1909.

BELTAINE, the organ of the Irish Literary Theatre (an occasional publication. No. 1 : May 1899, London : at the Sign of the Unicorn ; Dublin : at the DAILY EXPRESS office. 3*d.*) (Preceded SAMHAIN, *q. v.*)

Passim.

---

[1] Took the place of *Samhain* for a couple of years (between No. 6 and No. 7) : cf. *Samhain*, No. 7, p. 1.

APPENDIX A

BIRMINGHAM POST.
> February 1, 1911.

BOOKMAN (London).
> August, 1909 : "Earth to Earth" (a review of *Poems and Translations*), by Francis Bickley.
> April, 1911, p. 30 : "J. M. Synge," by Darrell Figgis.
> August, 1912, Review of John Masefield's *The Widow in the Bye-Street*, by Francis Bickley (short but suggestive parallel with Synge).

BOOKMAN (N.Y.).
> October, 1910, p. 145 : Review of the *Playboy*, by C. Hamilton.
> January, 1912 : "The Irish National Theatre."

BOOK-NEWS MONTHLY (Philadelphia).
> February, 1912, p. 379 : "The Art of the Irish Players and a Comment on their Plays," by Cornelius Weygandt (University of Pennsylvania) ; p. 409 : "Dramatists without a Country," by Montrose J. Moses, author of *The American Dramatist*.

BOSTON EVENING TRANSCRIPT.
> March 25, 1911.
> During the months of October and November, 1911, this paper had almost daily articles dealing with the Irish Plays.

BOSTON GLOBE.
> October 17, 1911, p. 9 : "Representative Boston men criticize the 'Playboy of the Western World.'"

(A) BROADSIDE (Cuala Press) (a double sheet issued monthly at the price of 1s. No. 1 : June, 1908).
> July, 1909 : "The Stage Irishman," by Jack B. Yeats.
> September, 1909 : "The Playboy," by Jack B. Yeats.

(A) BROADSHEET, published by Elkin Mathews, Vigo Street, London, W., preceded A BROADSIDE, and ran for 24 numbers, with contributions by W. B. Yeats, Lady Gregory, Prof. York Powell, "Æ" John Masefield, Wilfrid Gibson, and drawings by Miss Pamela Coleman Smith and Jack Yeats. (Cf. Ernest Marriott's *Jack B. Yeats*, pp. 13–4.)

THE) BROADSIDE (Boston).
> March, 1911 : "A Note on J. M. Synge."

APPENDIX A

CHICAGO DAILY TRIBUNE.
> November 1, 1910 : " An Irish Fantasy. A New Comedy Farce," by Burns Mantle.
> January 21, 1911.
> February 7, 1912.

CHICAGO EVENING POST.
> July 2, 1909 : "Synge. Poems and Translations," by Francis Hackett; partial reprint of Max Beerbohm's article : "Irish Players" (SATURDAY REVIEW, June 12, 1909).

CHURCH QUARTERLY (London).
> July, 1911, p. 406 : " The Poetry of Ireland."

CLAIDHEAMH SOLUIS (Dublin).
> April 30, 1910.

CONTEMPORARY REVIEW (London).
> October, 1906, p. 472 : " Literature and the Living Voice," by W. B. Yeats.
> September, 1910 : "Some Irish Poetry," by Geraldine E. Hodgson, Litt.D.
> April, 1911, p. 470 : " John M. Synge," by John Masefield.
> August, 1911, p. 240 : " The Rise of the Irish Theatre," by Charles Tennyson.

CORK CONSTITUTION.
> September 2, 1910, and following issues.
> October 16, 1912 : Review of Francis Bickley's *J. M. Synge and the Irish Dramatic Movement*.

CORK EXAMINER.
> November 11, 1910.

CORK FREE PRESS.
> November 11, 1910 : Report of D. Corkery's lecture on " The Drama of J. M. Synge," in the Lecture Hall of the School of Art, Cork, November 10, 1910.

COSMOPOLIS (London).
> June, 1898 : " The Celtic Element in Literature," by W. B. Yeats (republished in *Ideas of Good and Evil*).

COUNTRY LIFE (London).
> January 21, 1911.

APPENDIX A

COURT JOURNAL (London).
   June 16, 1909.
CRAFTSMAN (N.Y.).
   January 1912, p. 352 : " The Irish Players in America :
Their Purpose and Their Art," by Ann Watkins.
CURRENT LITERATURE (N.Y.).
   December 1911, p. 675 : " The Stormy Début of the
Irish Players."
DAILY CHRONICLE (London).
   January 30, 1899, p. 3 : " Mr. Moore, Mr. Archer
and the Literary Theatre," by W. B. Yeats.
   March 25, 1909, p. 1.
   June 10, 1909.
   June 12, 1909.
   July 26, 1909 (on " Synge as a poet ").
   February 4, 1911, p. 6 : " A Singer o' the Green," by
W. P. Ryan.
DAILY GRAPHIC (London).
   May 8, 1909.
DAILY MAIL (London).
   June 8, 1909.
   July 12, 1912, p. 2 : " A Drifting, Silent Man. The
genius of J. M. Synge" [review of Mr. P. P. Howe's
J. M. Synge : A Critical Study].
DAILY NEWS (London and Manchester) (now DAILY NEWS
   AND LEADER).
   March 26, 1909.
   June 8, 1909.
   February 1, 1911, p. 3 : " The Dramatist of Ireland,"
by R. A. Scott-James.
   July 18, 1911.
   January 19, 1912, p. 1.
   January 20, 1912, p. 5.
   February 2, 1912, p. 2.
   May 31, 1912, p. 8 : Lady Gregory's " Irish Folk-
History Plays."
   June 4, 1912, p. 2 : " Dublin Players in London. ' The
Playboy ' at the Court Theatre."
   June 14, 1912, p. 8 : " Syngolatry " by Robert Lynd
[a review of P. P. Howe's J. M. Synge : A Critical Study].

APPENDIX A

DAILY TELEGRAPH (London).
June 8, 1909.

DANA, a magazine of independent thought (Dublin : Hodges
and Figgis ; London : Nutt) (edited by " John Eglinton "
[W. K. Magee:] and Fred. Ryan).
Vol. i (May, 1904–April, 1905), p. 319 : "The Irish
National Theatre," by Thomas Keohler.
p. 351 : "The Irish National Theatre" (second performance of " The Well of the Saints ").
p. 364 : "The Well of the Saints" (an article in
French), by "A Lover of the West" [Henry Lebeau].
Also published in the REVUE D'ART DRAMATIQUE ET
MUSICAL, *q.v.*
p. 313: "A Literary Causerie," by F. M. Atkinson
(announcement of "The Well of the Saints" as vol. i.
of the Abbey Theatre Series).

DIAL (Chicago).
Vol. li (July 1–December 16, 1911), p. 521 : " The
Irish Theatre Society," by E. K. D.
January 16, 1911, p. 37 : a very comprehensive essay
on " John Synge and his Plays," by Warren Barton Blake.

DIVADELNI'LIST MÁJE (Prague).
Ročník iii, Číslo 2 (2. Listopadu 1906) : " Irské
Literární Divadlo," by Karel Mušek.

DOME (London).
April, 1899 ; January, 1900 : " The Irish Literary
Theatre," by W. B. Yeats (republished as " The Theatre "
in *Ideas of Good and Evil*).

DUBLIN DAILY EXPRESS.
May 1899 : see *supra*, Books : " Eglinton, John."
May 28, 1909.
April 20, 1911.

DUBLIN EVENING MAIL.
October 30, 1908.

DUBLIN REVIEW.
January, 1913, pp. 132–44 : " The Irish National
Theatre," by Charles Bewley.

APPENDIX A

ENGLISH REVIEW (London).

June, 1909, pp. 609–13 : " John Millington Synge," by Norreys Connell.

July, 1912 : " Meditation on Finality," by John Galsworthy (Synge, p. 539).

September, 1912, Review of P. P. Howe's *J. M. Synge: A Critical Study.*

December, 1912, " Strindberg's Plays," by Austin Harrison (comparison between Strindberg's *The Crown Bride* and Synge's *Riders to the Sea*).

March, 1913 : " Synge," by Lady Gregory.

EVENING BULLETIN (Philadelphia).

January 17, 1912, p. 1.

EVENING HERALD (Dublin).

March 24, 1909 : " Death of Synge."

May 28, 1909.

February 14, 1913 : " The Playboy and its reception in Montreal," by Joseph Holloway (quotes letter by " B." objecting to " Repertoire of Irish Players " in MONTREAL DAILY HERALD, January 28, 1913).

EVENING POST (New York).

August 13, 1909 : Review of *Poems and Translations.*

November 24, 1911 : " Music and Drama. The Irish Players," by Towse.

January 11, 1913, p. 6 : " John Synge," by Stuart P. Sherman.

EVENING STANDARD AND ST. JAMES'S GAZETTE (London).

June 12, 1909.

January 24, 1911 (by " A. P.").

October 3, 1912 : Review of Francis Bickley's *J. M. Synge and the Irish Dramatic Movement.*

October 12, 1912 :   (Ditto).

February 23, 1913 : Review of Cornelius Weygandt's *Irish Plays and Playwrights.*

EVENING SUN (N.Y.).

April 2, 1909.

April 3, 1909 : " Some Recollections by an Irish Painter " (J. B. Yeats).

April 24, 1909.

APPENDIX A

About July 18, 1909 : "Memories of Synge," by Jack B. Yeats. See *supra*, Books : Yeats, William Butler and Jack B., and the note.

April 1, 1911 (by John Quinn).

November 21, 1911 : "News of the Theatre. The Irish Players make their first appearance in New York."

EVENING TELEGRAPH (Dublin).

May 19, 1909 (by W. J. Lawrence).

May 13, 1911 : "The Abbey Theatre. The Playboy of the West and the Abbey Peasant," by F. R. [Fred. Ryan].

May 20, 1911 : "The Irish Peasant in Abbey Theatre Plays" : reply by Pádraic Colum to Fred Ryan's article.

June 3, 1911 : "The Irish Peasant and the Abbey Dramatists" : reply to Pádraic Colum by Fred. Ryan.

EVERYBODY'S MAGAZINE (N.Y.).

February, 1912, p. 231 : "The Players."

EVERYMAN (London : J. M. Dent).

October 18, 1912 (Vol. i, No. 1), p. 8 : "J. M. Synge and the Revival of the Irish Drama," by G. M. Brophy.

EYE-WITNESS (London) (now NEW WITNESS).

February 1, 1912 : a letter to the Editor by Conal O'Riordan on "The Cult of the Play Boy."

FORTNIGHTLY REVIEW (London).

1901, p. 1,050 : "The Irish Theatre," by Stephen Gwynn.

December, 1902, p. 1,044 : "An Uncommercial Theatre," by Stephen Gwynn.

December, 1907, p. 947 : "The Literary Movement in Ireland," by "George A. Birmingham" [Rev. J. O. Hannay].

September, 1911, p. 545 : " Some Writers of the Celtic Renaissance," by K. L. Montgomery.

December, 1911, p. 1,056 : "The Art of J. M. Synge," by Darrell Figgis [also in the FORUM, *q.v.*].

FORUM (N.Y.).

August, 1911, p. 179 : "John M. Synge and the Ireland of His Time," by W. B. Yeats. See *supra*, Books : Yeats, William Butler and Jack B.

January, 1912, p. 55 : "The Art of John M. Synge,"

APPENDIX A

by Darrell Figgis (practically the same article as in
FORTNIGHTLY REVIEW, December, 1911, p. 1,056, but
for a few unimportant "cuts"); p. 120 : editorial note.

FREEMAN'S JOURNAL (Dublin).

April 8, 1902 : "Irish Influence on English Literature,"
by Prof. York Powell.

January 30, 1907.

March 25, 1909.

May 28, 1909.

July 19, 1909 : "J. M. Synge. His Art and Message,"
a lecture delivered in Dublin, July 17, 1909, by "Seumas
O'Cuisin" [James Cousins], W. J. Lawrence in the chair.

January 23, 1912, p. 3 [an almost verbatim report of
the present writer's lecture on "J. M. Synge's Life in
France and his Relations to French Literature" (National
Literary Society, Dublin, January 22, 1912, Dr. George
Sigerson in the chair), and of the debate in which Mr.
Pádraic Colum, Mr. Stephen MacKenna, Rev. Prof.
O'Neill, Mr. D. J. O'Donoghue and Dr. Sigerson took
part]; "The Playboy": a letter by "Observer."

GLASGOW HERALD.

February 16, 1911.

GLASGOW NEWS.

July 7, 1910.

February, 2, 1911.

GLOBE (London).

June 8, 1909.

GLOBE AND COMMERCIAL ADVERTISER (N.Y.).

November 28, 1911, "The Playboy of the Western
World is delightful comedy," by Louis Sherwin.

HARPER'S WEEKLY (N.Y.).

March 9, 1907, p. 344 : "The Irish Peasant as a
Dramatic Issue," by Sydney Brooks.

November 11, 1911, p. 11 : "The Theater of Beauty,"
by W. B. Yeats (an address delivered before the Dramatic
Club of Harvard University).

November 25, 1911, p. 17 : "Synge and the Irish.
Random Reflections on a much-discussed dramatist from
the standpoint of a fellow-countryman," by J[ohn] B.
Yeats.

APPENDIX A

December 9, 1911, p. 19 : "A New Thing in the Theatre. Some Impressions of the much-discussed Irish Players."

HARVARD MONTHLY (Cambridge, Mass., U.S.A.).

November, 1911, p. 44 : "The Irish Dramatic Movement," by J. Donald Adams.

HEARTH AND HOME (London).

December 15, 1912 : Review of Francis Bickley's *J. M. Synge and the Irish Dramatic Movement.*

Christmas No., 1912 : An interview with Mr. W. B. Yeats.

HIBBERT JOURNAL (London).

April, 1913, p. 508 *et seq.* : "The New Spirit in the Drama," by John Galsworthy (refers to Synge's "sincerity" and "lyric satire").

HOLBORN REVIEW (London).

July, 1913 : "John Millington Synge," by Ernest H. Pittwood.

ILLUSTRATED LONDON NEWS.

June 12, 1909, p. 870 : "Irish Theatre Society at the Court" (The *Playboy* at the Court Theatre).

June 4, 1910, p. 854 : Production of *Deirdre of the Sorrows* at the Court Theatre.

INDEPENDENT (N.Y.).

April 13, 1911, pp. 792–3 : "An Irish Playwright" [by Warren Barton Blake].

November 7, 1912 : "John Synge and his Critics" (review of Francis Bickley's *J. M. Synge and the Irish Dramatic Movement* and of P. P. Howe's *J. M. Synge : A Critical Study*).

March 6, 1913, p. 515 : "Irish Plays and Players," by Warren Barton Blake (review of Cornelius Weygandt's *Irish Plays and Playwrights*).

IRISH BOOK-LOVER (London and Dublin).

October, 1909, p. 33.

December, 1910, p. 79 : report of Miss Ethel Rolt Wheeler's lecture on "Ideals in Irish Poetry and Drama" (Irish Literary Society, London, November 5, 1910, Mr. Herbert Trench in the chair).

March, 1911,

APPENDIX A

May, 1911, p. 155.
July, 1911, p. 197.
August, 1911, pp. 8, 14, 16.
September, 1911, pp. 24, 31–32.
October, 1911, pp. 38, 45.
November, 1911, p. 65 (cover): "I. L. S., London, April 20, 1912, Lecture: The Irish Drama, by Mr. Joseph Campbell."
December, 1911, pp. 74, 83.
January, 1912, p. 97 and cover: "I. L. S., London, January 6, 1912, meeting of social circle, subject for discussion: 'The Playboy.'"
March, 1912, pp. 132–3: report of the present writer's lecture on "J. M. Synge's Life in France and his Relations to French Literature" (National Literary Society, Dublin, January 22, 1912).
August, 1912, pp. 7, 8: "Yeats, Synge and the 'Playboy'" (from J. M. Hone in the *Saturday Review*).
February, 1913, pp. 127, 128.
April, 1913; cover, pp. 156, 157: review of Cornelius Weygandt's *Irish Plays and Playwrights*.

IRISH CATHOLIC (Dublin).
August 31 and September 7, 1912: "Abbey Theatre Libels: Rev. George O'Neill, S.J., on 'Irish' Drama" [reprinted from AMERICAN CATHOLIC QUARTERLY, *q.v.*].

IRISH HOMESTEAD (Dublin).
Christmas No., 1897.
December 1, 1906: "The Tinker's Curse," an art plate by Jack B. Yeats.

IRISH INDEPENDENT (Dublin).
January 28, 1907.
August 16, 1907.
March 25, 1909.
March 26, 1909: "John M. Synge. A Personal Appreciation," by D. J. O'Donoghue.
May 28, 1909.
August 21, 1911: "The Synge Boom. Foreign Influences," by D. J. O'Donoghue. (The article occasioned a correspondence in the next few issues of the paper.)
November 29, 1911.

APPENDIX A

January 19, 1912.

February 12, 1912 : "Stage Irishman," by D. J. O'Donoghue.

October 10, 1912 : review of Francis Bickley's *J. M. Synge and the Irish Dramatic Movement*.

Irish Literary Society Gazette (London).

June, 1899 (Vol. i, No. 4), p. 5 : report of Mr. W. B. Yeats's lecture on "The Irish Literary Theatre" (I. L. S., London, April 23, 1899, Mr. Edmund Gosse in the chair).

Irish Nation (Dublin).

April 3, 1909.

May 1, 1909.

August 14, 1909 : "Memories of Synge," by Jack B. Yeats : see *supra*, Books : Yeats, William Butler and Jack B.

Irish News and Belfast Morning News.

August 4, 1909.

October 5, 1912 : Review of Fras. Bickley's *J. M. Synge and the Irish Dramatic Movement*.

Irish Review (Dublin).

March, 1911, p. 39 : "John Synge," by Mary C. Maguire.

May, 1911, p. 107 : a short paragraph on a lecture by Miss Agnes O'Farrelly, M.A., on "The Irishman on and off the Stage" (National Literary Society, Dublin, April 10, 1911).

July, 1911, frontispiece : "Abbey Players," by Grace Gifford (an amusing sketch of Sara Allgood and J. M. Kerrigan in an Irish-American *rôle*).

September, 1911, p. 325 : "Dramatic Values," by Walter Mennloch (a review of W. B. Yeats's *Synge and the Ireland of his Time* and of C. E. Montague's *Dramatic Values*).

October, 1911 : "The Tinker's Curse," an art plate by Jack B. Yeats.

December, 1911, p. 476 : "On those who dislike the Playboy," by W. B. Yeats.

February, 1912, p. 606 : "The Decline of Abbey Theatre Drama," by G. Hamilton Gunning.

APPENDIX A

July, 1912, p. 252 : "Deirdre," by Francis Bickley.

December, 1912, p. 505 : "At the Abbey Theatre" (a poem), by W. B. Yeats. Imitated from Ronsard.

p. 557 : "Synge in Dutch," by Conal O'Riordan.

February, 1913, p. 628 : "The Abbey Theatre," by Ernest A. Boyd.

May, 1913, pp. 140–3 : "The Drama in Ireland," by Bryan Cooper.

IRISH TIMES (Dublin).

January 29, 1907.

March 25, 1909 : (1) Editorial on Synge.
(2) Obituary notice of Synge.
(3) "Synge's Will."

May 28, 1909.

January 23, 1911 : "J. M. Synge ; His Work and Genius."

February 8, 1912, p. 7 : "The Stage Irishman, Origin and Development." Lecture by the Rev. J. O. Hannay ["George A. Birmingham"], at the Royal Dublin Society, February 7, 1912 (full report). Also Editorial on p. 4.

December 27, 1912 : "The Irish National Theatre," by Ernest Boyd.

December 28, 1912 : (a letter to the Editor in reply to the above), by Ellen Duncan.

IRISLEABHAR MUIGHE NUADHAD ar n-a chur amach do Connradh Chuilm Naomhtha (Dublin : Gill).

An Cnáisg, 1909 (Leabhar i. Uimhir 2), pp. 22–9 : "National Drama in Ireland," by Eoghan ua Fuaráin.

An Cnáisg, 1910 (Leabhar i. Uimhir 3), p. 6 : "The Anglo-Irish Dramatic Movement," by Eoghan ua Fuaráin.

JOURNAL DES DÉBATS (Paris).

April 19, 1905 : "Le Réveil de l'Ame Celtique," by Aug. Filon.

KOREA DAILY NEWS.

March 16, 1907.

LADIES' FIELD (London).

March 25, 1911.

LIFE (N.Y.).

December 14, 1911 (vol. lviii, No. 1520), p. 1090 : "Drama," by Metcalfe.

APPENDIX A

LITERARY DIGEST (N.Y.).
April 17, 1909: "Ireland's Greatest Dramatist" (Synge: portrait).

LITERARY WORLD (London).
June 5, 1913, pp. 182–3 : "The Irish Theatre" (review of Cornelius Weygandt's *Irish Plays and Playwrights*).

LITERATURE (London).
May 6, 1899, p. 474 : "The Irish Literary Theatre," by W. B. Yeats.

LIVERPOOL DAILY POST AND MERCURY.
April 12, 1911.

LIVERPOOL ECHO.
July 2, 1910.
April 22, 1911.

LLOYD'S NEWSPAPER (London).
June 10, 1909.

LUMÍR (Prague).
Ročník xxxv, Číslo 8, p. 383 : an article on *The Aran Islands*, by Karel Mušek.

MAIL (Dublin).
January 30, 1907.
March 24, 1909.
March 26, 1909 : "Synge's funeral."

MANCHESTER DISPATCH.
February 20, 1911.
October 7, 1912 : review of Fras. Bickley's *J. M. Synge and the Irish Dramatic Movement*.

MANCHESTER GUARDIAN.
January 2, 1905 : "The Irish National Theatre" [by John Masefield].
March 25, 1909, p. 6 : editorial.
p. 7 : obituary notice of Synge.
January 19, 1911.
February 27, 1911.
June 24, 1912 : "The Workmanship of Synge," by C. E. Montague (review of P. P. Howe's *J. M. Synge : A Critical Study*).
October 8, 1912 : review of Fras. Bickley's *J. M. Synge and the Irish Dramatic Movement*.

APPENDIX A

March 14, 1913: review of Cornelius Weygandt's *Irish Plays and Playwrights*.

MAYNOOTH JOURNAL: see IRISLEABHAR MUIGHE NUADHAD.

MERCURE DE FRANCE (Paris).

May 16, 1912, p. 228: a paragraph on the Irish Theatre *ap.* Archibald Henderson (*tr.* Henry D. Davray), "Le Nouveau Drame en Angleterre: H. Granville Barker."

METROPOLITAN MAGAZINE (N.Y.).

January 1912, p. 23: "W. B. Yeats and the Irish Players," by Montrose J. Moses.

MILWAUKEE NEWS.

February, 1911, to March 21, 1912: "Notes on the Celtic Renaissance," by J. Crawford Neil.

MORNING LEADER (London).

May 8, 1909.

May 15, 1909: "Three Poets Departed," by William Archer.

MORNING POST (London).

June 10, 1909.

January 26, 1911: "The Playwright of the Western Wild," by Edmund Gosse.

NATION (London).

April 3, 1909: "The Art of J. M. Synge," by Fras. Bickley.

July 17, 1909: "John Synge's Art."

June 4, 1910: "The Art of the Artless," by William Archer.

June 17, 1911 (by H. W. M.).

September 11, 1909, p. 857.

June 18, 1910, p. 425: "The Irish Theatre," by W. B. Yeats and A. Gregory.

March 25, 1911: "Astringent Joy."

August 26, 1911, p. 767: "The Virile Poet."

NATION (N.Y.).

October 12, 1911: "Drama" (review of the John W. Luce edition of *The Aran Islands, Riders to the Sea,* and *The Tinker's Wedding*).

November 30, 1911: "The Drama" (a critique of the Irish plays presented in America, largely devoted to Synge's works).

APPENDIX A

December 26, 1902, p. 608 : "John Synge," by Stuart P. Sherman [also in the EVENING POST (N.Y.), *q.v.*].

NATIONAL REVIEW (London).
July, 1911, p. 834 : "Romance and the Modern Stage," by Lord Dunsany.

NEW AGE (London).
June 17, 1909.
June 16, 1910 (by Ashley Dukes).
October 6, 1910 (by Ashley Dukes).
April 13, 1911 (by Herbert Hughes).
July 13, 1911, p. 256.
July 20, 1911, p. 271.
See also :
August 17, 1911, p. 374 : "The Abbey Theatre," by "Jacob Tonson" [Arnold Bennett].
August 24, 1911 : "The Abbey Theatre," by "Jacob Tonson."
August 31, 1911, p. 416 : "The Adoration of the Peasant," by Edward MacNulty.
p. 431 : "The Abbey Theatre" (a reply to "Jacob Tonson," by "An Irish Playgoer").
September 7, 1911, p. 454 : a reply by Sidheog ní Annain.

NEW DRAMA (Boston : Richard G. Badger & Co.).
April, 1912 (No. 1), pp. 15–6 : "The Irish Players in Philadelphia," by C. P.

NEW IRELAND REVIEW (Dublin).
May, 1907 : "Neo-Paganism and the Stage," by Michael J. Gill.

NEW QUARTERLY (edited by Desmond MacCarthy. London : Dent).
February, 1910, p. 73 : "Synge and the Drama," by Francis Bickley.

NEW WITNESS (London).
January 2, 1913, pp. 282–3 : "Synge and His Critics."
February 20, 1913, p. 504 : "Poetry and the Peasant," (review of Synge's *In Wicklow and West Kerry*).

NEW YORK DRAMATIC MIRROR.
Passim—especially December 27, 1911, p. 5 : "Lady

APPENDIX A

Gregory, guiding genius of the Irish Players," by Chauncey L. Parsons.

NEW YORK PRESS.
> November 27, 1911 : " Seumas MacManus raps the ' Playboy.' "
> November 28, 1911, p. 1.
> December 4, 1911 : " League disowns the Irish Players."

NEW YORK TIMES.
> April 14, 1909 : " Saturday review of books," by Louis Untermayer.
> November 26, 1911 : " Acting of the Irish Players."

NORTH AMERICAN REVIEW (N.Y.).
> October, 1906, p. 771 : " Is the Celtic Revival Distinctly Irish ? " by Mary K. Ford.
> October 1911, p. 566 : " Ireland's National Drama," by John Edward Hoare.
> October 1912, p. 571 : review of P. P. Howe's *J. M. Synge : A Critical Study*.

NORTHERN WHIG (Belfast).
> December 1, 1908.
> March 25, 1909.

OBSERVER (London).
> June 6, 1909 : " A People's Drama," by A. Harrison.
> June 13, 1909.

OUTLOOK (London).
> June 12, 1909.
> April 12, 1913, p. 513 : " The ' Abbey ' Movement " (review of Cornelius Weygandt's *Irish Plays and Playwrights*).

OUTLOOK (N.Y.).
> December 16, 1911, p. 915 ff. : " The Irish Players " : " Introduction " by Theodore Roosevelt ; " Lady Gregory and the Abbey Theatre," by John Quinn ; " MacDarragh's Wife : A Play in one act," by Lady Gregory. See *supra*, Books : Shaw, G. B.

OXFORD AND CAMBRIDGE REVIEW (London) (now BRITISH REVIEW).
> July, 1912 : " The Playboy in the Theatre," by P. P. Howe.

APPENDIX A

November, 1912 : Current Topics : The Abbey Theatre : " J. M. Synge and the Irish Revival," by George Lowther.

Oxford Chronicle.
July 5, 1912 : " The Genius of J. M. Synge" (review of P. P. Howe's *J. M. Synge : A Critical Study*).

Pall Mall Gazette (London) : cf. *supra*, Books : Walbrook, H. M.
June 8, 1909.
June 9, 1909.
June 18, 1909.
June 23, 1909.
January 16, 1911 : " A Playboy of the Western World."

Papyrus (A Magazine of Individuality, edited by Michael Monahan, N.Y.).
February, 1912, p. 18 : "The Matter with the Playboy " ; also paragraph on p. 30.

Peasant (Dublin).
January 4, 1908.

Phalange (Paris).
January 20, 1911, p. 52 : " Le Théâtre Irlandais (J. M. Synge, Lady Gregory)," by "Jean Florence " [Prof. Blum].

Philadelphia Record.
October 22, 1912 : "In the Public View : The Irish Players."

(De) Ploeg (a Dutch periodical).
Tweede Jaargang, No. 2 (Augustus, 1909) [by L. Simons].

Poet-Lore (Boston).
1905, vol. xvi, p. 40 : " The Irish Literary Drama," by Vida D. Scudder (an address delivered at the opening of the Twentieth Century Club series of plays).

Public Ledger (Philadelphia).
January 20, 1912, p. 1.

Quarterly Review (London).
July 1911 (No. 428), p. 219 : " Irish Plays and Playwrights," by Charles Tennyson.

APPENDIX A

RECORD-HERALD (Chicago).

April 11, 1909: "The Playboy of the Western World for the first time in America," by James O'Donnell Bennett.

April 14, 1909 : "The Playboy of the Western World" and "Die Meistersinger," by James O'Donnell Bennett.

November 1, 1910 : "Mrs. Fiske Presents two Plays" [one of which was *The Shadow of the Glen*] by James O'Donnell Bennett.

March 3, 1912 : "Lessons of the Abbey Theatre Engagement," by James O'Donnell Bennett.

REFEREE (London).

June 13, 1909.

REVUE (late REVUE DES REVUES) (Paris).

January 1, 1912, p. 91 : "Le Nouveau Théâtre Irlandais," by Miss Doris Gunnell.

REVUE D'ART DRAMATIQUE ET MUSICAL (Paris).

April 15, 1905, pp. 56–60 : "Les Spectacles du Mois-Mars 1905—Étranger : Irlande : Dublin : *The Well of the Saints*," by Henry Lebeau. [Also in DANA, *q. v.*]

REVUE DU MOIS (Paris).

October 10, 1911, p. 456 : "Le Théâtre de J. M. Synge," by Madame Madeleine Cazamian.

REVUE GERMANIQUE (Paris).

January–February, 1909, p. 123, and January–February, 1911 : "Le Théâtre Irlandais," by Henri Ruyssen.

May–June, 1912, p. 290.

RHYTHM.

March, 1913 : review of Fras. Bickley's *J. M. Synge and the Irish Dramatic Movement*.

SAINT LOUIS GLOBE DEMOCRAT.

February 12, 1911.

SAMHAIN, the organ of the Irish National Theatre Society (an occasional review edited by W. B. Yeats, published by Sealy, Bryers and Walker in Dublin, and by T. Fisher Unwin in London, and sold at sixpence). No. 1 : October 1901. No. 2 is out of print. (A continuation of BELTAINE, *q.v.*)

APPENDIX A

No. 3, pp. 7, 25–33 ; No. 4, pp. 13, 34–44 ; No. 5, p. 4 ; No. 6 ; No. 7, pp. 2, 7–8, 35.

(Many of the paragraphs have been reprinted in Mr. W. B. Yeats's Collected Works : see *supra*, Books.)

SATURDAY REVIEW (London).

June 12, 1909 : "Irish Players," by Max Beerbohm.

January 28, 1910.

June 4, 1910 : "The Irish Players in *Deirdre of the Sorrows*," by Lord Dunsany.

February 25, 1911 : "The Extra-Occidental Theatre," by "P. J." (John Palmer).

May 6, 1911, p. 540 : a paragraph on Shakespeare and Synge at Stratford-on-Avon.

May 20, 1911, p. 616 : a letter by G. E. Morrison about Synge's dialect.

June 10, 1911, p. 705 : "The Irish Players," by "P. J."

June 17, 1911, p. 746 : "The Irish Players" (a letter by Leonard Inkster).

June 24, 1911, p. 770 : "The Acting of the Irish Players," by "P. J."

June 24, 1911, p. 777 : a letter by Edward MacNulty.

July 1, 1911, p. 17 : letters by F. J. Fay and Leonard Inkster.

July 8, 1911, pp. 48–9 : letters on the "Playboy" by St. John G. Ervine and Edward MacNulty.

July 13, 1912 : "The Success of the Irish Players," by John Palmer (review of P. P. Howe's *J. M. Synge : A Critical Study*).

SEWANEE REVIEW (Am.).

October, 1904, p. 420 : "The Irish Literary Revival," by Cornelius Weygandt (University of Pennsylvania, Philadelphia).

SHANACHIE (an Irish miscellany, illustrated, published quarterly at 1*s.*, by Maunsel, Dublin : No. 1, 1906).

March, 1907, p. 57 : "A National Dramatist," by George Roberts.

SINN FÉIN (Dublin) (late UNITED IRISHMAN, *q. v.*).

July 17, 1909 : "J. M. Synge : His Art and Message" by "Seumas O'Cuisin" (James H. Cousins). (From a lecture.)

APPENDIX A

April 2, 1910, by "Che Buono" (William Bulfin).

February 10, 1912 : "The Playboy in France," by H. MacDonald (refers to art. in TEMPS, January 23, 1912, *q.v.*).

March 15, 1913 : "The Future of the Peasant Play," by Maurice Fitzgerald.

SMART SET (N.Y., London and Paris).

October, 1912, pp. 147–52 : "Synge and Others," by H. L. Mencken.

SOUTHPORT GUARDIAN.

October 23, 1912 : review of Fras. Bickley's *J. M. Synge and the Irish Dramatic Movement.*

SPECTATOR (London).

April 1, 1911, p. 482 : "The Work of J. M. Synge."

SPHERE (London).

April 22, 1911.

STANDARD (London).

June 8, 1909.

June 10, 1909.

STAR (London).

June 8, 1909.

July 24, 1909 (on Synge as a poet, by James Douglas).

February 11, 1911 (by James Douglas).

February 18, 1911 (by James Douglas).

SUN (N.Y.).

November 26, 1911 : "The Irish Players and their Audiences."

November 28, 1911, p. 1 : "Playboy mobbed."

November 30, 1911 : "The Consputation of Synge."

December 10, 1911, p. 2.

January 28, 1912, p. 7 : "'The Playboy of the Western World' and the trouble it made."

SUNDAY RECORD-HERALD (Chicago).

December 17, 1911 : "Viewing the Irish Players in the Light of Reason," by Walter Pritchard Eaton.

February 4, 1912 : "The Story of the Irish Players" (by George Moore, Sara Allgood, T. W. Rolleston, Augusta Gregory, W. B. Yeats).

APPENDIX A

SUNDAY TIMES (London).
June 13, 1909.

TABLET (London).
November 2, 1912 : review of Fras. Bickley's *J. M. Synge and the Irish Dramatic Movement.*

TEMPS (Paris).
July 25, 1904. Feuilleton du Temps. Chronique Théâtrale. "L'année Théâtrale en Angleterre," by A. B. Walkley.
January 23, 1912 : "Un Théâtre Irlandais," by Philippe Millet.

THEATRE (N.Y.).
June, 1911, p. 204 : "Synge," by Warren Barton Blake (portrait).

TIMES (London).
May 8, 1903 : "The Irish National Theatre," by A. B. Walkley (see *supra*, Books : Walkley).
June 28, 1907 : Literary Supplement, p. 202 (review of *The Aran Islands*).
March 25, 1909, p. 13.
June 12, 1909.
February 23, 1911 (Literary Supplement).
August 29, 1912 (Literary Supplement : "J. M. Synge" (review of P. P. Howe's *J. M. Synge : A Critical Study*).
March 17, 1913 : Irish Number, p. 15 : "The Abbey Theatre : its origins and accomplishments."

T.P.'s WEEKLY (London).
April 9, 1909, p. 469 : "J. M. Synge : Irish Dramatist, Writer, Poet," by T. M. [Thomas MacDonagh].
June 16, 1911, p. 744 : "The Irish Players," by "B."
August 18, 1911, p. 201 : review of Yeats's *Synge and the Ireland of his Time* by "Bernard Lintot."
September 22, 1911, p. 361.
April 4, 1913 : "Mr. W. B. Yeats : Poet and Mystic," an interview by Sybil Bristowe.
April 18, 1913 : "The Irish National Theatre," a letter to the Editor by Raymond Crompton Rhodes.
May 2, 1913, p. 566 : "The Irish National Theatre," a letter to the editor by F. Sheehy Skeffington.

APPENDIX A

TRANSVAAL LEADER.
December 17, 1912 : review of Fras. Bickley's *J. M. Synge and the Irish Dramatic Movement*.

ULSTER ECHO (Belfast).
August 4, 1909.

UNITED IRELAND (Dublin).
July 11, 1891 : " Plays by an Irish Poet " (Dr. John Todhunter), by W. B. Yeats.
January 16, 1892, p. 5 : " The New Speranza," by W. B. Yeats.
January 30, 1892 : " Clovis Hugues on Ireland," by W. B. Yeats.
May 27, 1893, p. 1 : Mr. W. B. Yeats's lecture on " Nationality and Literature " at the Molesworth Hall, Dublin (National Literary Society), Mr. George Coffey in the chair.
May 27, 1893, p. 2 : " Miss Gonne in France."

UNITED IRISHMAN (Dublin) (a continuation of the NATION newspaper, now SINN FÉIN).
August 31, 1901 : " Ireland and the Arts," by W. B. Yeats (republished in *Ideas of Good and Evil*).
October 24, 1903 : " The Irish National Theatre and Three Sorts of Ignorance," by W. B. Yeats.
January 7, 1905, p. 5 (reference to SAMHAIN about *The Shadow of the Glen*).
January 28, 1905, p. 1 (Mr. W. B. Yeats's answer to the Editor and the Editor's reply).
February 4, 1905 (Mr. W. B. Yeats's answer to the Editor and the Editor's reply).
February 11, 1905 : (1) analysis and criticism of *The Well of the Saints* ; (2) Synge's letter to the Editor concerning *The Shadow of the Glen*.
February 17, 1906 : report of Dr. George Sigerson's lecture on the Abbey Theatre (National Literary Society, Dublin, February 5, 1906).

UNIVERSITY MAGAZINE (Montreal).
February, 1911, pp. 91–109 : " Synge," by J. E. Hoare.

APPENDIX A

WEEKLY FREEMAN (Dublin).
March 20, 1909 : "Sara Allgood's Autobiography."
December 7, 1912 (Xmas No.) : "The Abbey Theatre: Its History and Mystery," by W. J. Lawrence.

WEEKLY IRISH TIMES.
March 30, 1912 : "Return of Abbey Players" [from America].

WESTMINSTER GAZETTE (London).
June 8, 1909.
June 10, 1909.
February 4, 1911.
December 20, 1912 : "Synge's Grave," a poem by Miss W. M. Letts.

WESTMINSTER REVIEW (London).
July, 1911 : "W. B. Yeats and Ireland," by John MacGrath.
May, 1913 : "Synge and Loti," by Maurice Bourgeois.

YALE REVIEW (Yale Publishing Association, Inc., New Haven, Conn., U.S.A.).
January, 1912 (New Series, vol. i, No. 2), p. 188 : "The Irish Theatre and the People," by Lady Gregory ; p. 193 : "The Plays of John M. Synge," by Charles A. Bennett.

YORKSHIRE TELEGRAPH (Sheffield).
May 23, 1911.

(c) *Unreported Lectures.*

January 28, 1905. Irish Literary Society, London. Mr. F. Norreys Connell on "Some Irish Dramatists," Mr. Max Beerbohm in the chair.

March 26, 1905. Playgoers' Club at Hotel Cecil, London. Mr. F. Norreys Connell on "The Stage Irishman," Mrs. Alice Meynell in the chair.

November 13, 1910. Keble College Essay Club, Oxford. Mr. Arthur Synge Owen on "J. M. Synge."

April 10, 1911. National Literary Society, Dublin. Miss Agnes O'Farrelly on "The Irishman on and off the Stage."

February 18, 1913. South London T.P.'s Literary and Social Circle. Mr. Oswald Harland on "The Drama of J. M. Synge."

APPENDIX A

March 8, 1913. Irish Literary Society, London. Miss Ethel Rolt-Wheeler on "Romance in Irish Poetry and Drama," Mr. W. B. Yeats in the chair.

March 16, 1913. Playgoers' Club, London. Mr. H. M. Walbrook on "Ireland on the Stage and off," Mr. F. Norreys Connell in the chair.

March 18, 1913. Newport Literary Society, Monmouthshire. Maurice Bourgeois on "John M. Synge," Mr. T. E. Watson in the chair.

April 12, 1913. Irish Literary Society, London. Maurice Bourgeois on "Synge and France," Mr. Cloudesley Brereton in the chair.

ADDENDA TO APPENDIX A

Page 258. After last line insert : "(4) RIDERS TO THE SEA and IN THE SHADOW OF THE GLEN were reprinted in the BIBELOT (Portland, Maine, U.S.A. : Thomas B. Mosher) for July [with a biographical and bibliographical foreword on J. M. Synge] and August, 1913."

Page 265. Before last line insert : "Bryant, [Dr.] Sophie : *The Genius of the Gael: A Study in Celtic Psychology and its Manifestations* (London : T. Fisher Unwin, 1913). Chapter VI : 'The Gael in Literature.'"

Page 274. After line 2 insert : "BLUE REVIEW (London : Martin Secker), July, 1913 : review of Cornelius Weygandt's *Irish Plays and Playwrights,* and of Lady Gregory's *New Comedies,* by Frank Swinnerton."

Page 276. After last line (DAILY NEWS AND LEADER) insert : "July 14, 1913, p. 6 : 'The Irish Players,' by E. A. Baughan."

Page 279. After line 20 (EVERYMAN) insert : "August 15, 1913, p. 555 : 'J. M. Synge,' by J. M. Hone. Portrait by W. H. Caffyn [from a photograph by James Paterson, R.S.A.] on front outside page."

Page 287. After line 23 (NEW AGE) insert : "August 7, 1913, p. 425 : references to articles on 'The Irish Theatre,' by Marianne Trebitsch-Stein in the NEUE FREIE PRESSE, and on 'the Irish Renaissance and George Moore,' by Beda Prilipp in the GRENZBOTEN (Berlin)."

Page 295. After line 22 (YALE REVIEW) insert : "July, 1913 : 'John M. Synge,' by Prof. Henry S. Canby."

APPENDIX B

A LIST OF THE BEST-KNOWN PORTRAITS OF SYNGE

1. An oil painting by Mr. John B. Yeats, R.H.A., on view in the staircase of the Municipal Art Gallery, Harcourt Street, Dublin, to which it was bequeathed by Sir Hugh P. Lane.

   Reproduced as the frontispiece to Mr. P. P. Howe's *J. M. Synge: A Critical Study* and in the *Independent* (N.Y.), November 7, 1912, p. 1072.

   Exhibited under No. 26 at the Whitechapel Art Gallery Exhibition of Irish Art, May and June, 1913, to which two sketches of Synge by Mr. John B. Yeats, the one in the possession of Miss Lily Yeats (No. 34), and the other the property of the Abbey Theatre (No. 45), were also lent.

2. An (unsigned) drawing by Mr. John B. Yeats, published in No. 4 of *Samhain* (December, 1904), facing p. 34.

   Mr. John Masefield concludes his reminiscences of Synge (*Contemporary Review*, April, 1911), with the words: "It is difficult to believe that there can be any portrait more like him," and writes in the *Dictionary of National Biography* (article "Synge, John Millington"): "The best likeness."

   T. M. [Thos. MacDonagh], in his article "J. M. Synge: Irish Dramatist, Writer, Poet" (*T.P.'s Weekly*, April 9, 1909, p. 469), quotes the following entry from his diary: "Very like paintings and sketches of him by J. B. Yeats."

3. A full-face pencil sketch by Mr. George W. Russell ("Æ") (1904), in the possession of Mr. "Seumas O'Sullivan."

   Mr. Russell also did an oil-painting of Synge which has been lost.

APPENDIX B

4. A drawing (1906) by Mr. James Paterson, R.S.A., the frontispiece to vol. iv of the Collected Edition.

Reproduced in the *Pall Mall Gazette*, January 16, 1911, and in the London *Bookman*, April 1911, p. 30.

5. A photograph (May 17, 1906) by Chancellor, the frontispiece to vol. iii of the Collected Edition.

6. A pencil sketch by Mr. J. B. Yeats (May, 1907), reproduced in *Harper's Weekly* (N.Y.), November 25, 1911, p. 17; in the *Independent* (N.Y.), April 13, 1911, p. 792; also in Mr. Cornelius Weygandt's *Irish Plays and Playwrights*, facing p. 160.

7. A pencil sketch of "Synge at Rehearsal" (January 25, 1907), by Mr. John B. Yeats, the frontispiece to the separate edition of *The Playboy of the Western World* and to vol. ii of the Collected Edition.

Reproduced in the *Manchester Guardian*, March 25, 1909, and in *The Broadside*, March, 1911, p. 1; also as the frontispiece to Mr. H. M. Walbrook's *Nights at the Play*, and in Mr. Holbrook Jackson's *All Manner of Folk*, facing p. 62.

8. A photograph [1908] by Mr. James Paterson, the frontispiece to vol. i. of the Collected Edition.

Reproduced as the frontispiece to Mr. Francis Bickley's *J. M. Synge and the Irish Dramatic Movement*, and to Heer Leo Simon's *De Heiligenbron*, the Dutch version of *The Well of the Saints*.

9. A painting (1913) by Mr. James Paterson, done from photographs and from personal reminiscence, on view at the Paterson Gallery, Old Bond Street, London, March 1913. It was to be exhibited at the Royal Academy, but unaccountably was not.

Besides these, there are other portraits of Synge by Mr. Robert Gregory, Mr. John B. Yeats, and Mr. Jack B. Yeats.

Of this last Mr. R. A. Scott-James ("The Dramatist of Ireland," *Daily News*, February 1, 1911, p. 3), remarks : "Mr. Jack Yeats, in a drawing usually much admired, has preposterously transformed Synge . . . into . . . 'a fine, fiery fellow' of the tradition" [an allusion to Pegeen's definition of poets in the *Playboy* : "Fine, fiery fellows when their temper's roused."]

We do not know of any published full-length portrait of Synge.

APPENDIX C

A BIBLIOGRAPHICAL NOTE ON THE EXEGESIS AND NON-DRAMATIC VERSIONS OF THE DEIRDRE SAGA

A thorough study of the dramatic treatment of a legend must always be based on, or supplemented by, a full knowledge of the legend itself, a critical examination of its several recensions, variants and renderings other than dramatic. A bibliography of the Deirdre saga having never been compiled, it has been thought of use to subjoin a list of all the authorities that have been consulted for the study of Synge's tragedy. The very enumeration of the works published on the Deirdre legend both in Ireland and in Scotland will furthermore convey some idea of the enormous bulk of literature to which it has given birth ; indeed it has with reason been compared in this respect with the legends of Helen and Isolde.

1. Irish re-tellings.

Deirdri, or the lamentable fate of the sons of Usnech, etc. (text and translation, with historic account of the facts), by Theophilus O'Flanagan, A.B., Secretary of the Gaelic Society, in the solitary volume containing the *Transactions of the Gaelic Society of Dublin* (Dublin : John Barlow, 1808).

Thomas Stott, *Ancient Irish Poetry : The Songs of Deardra translated from the Irish with other poems* (London : 1825).

John Hawkins Simpson, *Poems of Oisin, Bard of Erin* (Dublin : MacGlashan & Gill, 1857) : " Deardra."

Prof. Eugene O'Curry, *Atlantis* (a register of literature and science conducted by members of the Catholic University of Ireland. Dublin : [printed] 1858–70), vol. iii, p. 377 (Yellow Book of Lecan version).

Prof. Eugene O'Curry, *Lectures on the Manuscript Materials of Ancient Irish History* (delivered at the Catholic University of Ireland during the sessions of 1855 and 1856). Dublin : 1861. Cf. pp. 14, 96, 294 ; Appendix, p. 589 n.

APPENDIX C

Prof. Eugene O'Curry, *On the Manners and Customs of the Ancient Irish . . .* edited, with an introduction . . . by W. K. Sullivan (London, Dublin : [printed] 1873), vol. ii, p. 325.

Deirdrè, in the "No Name Series" (Boston, U.S.A. : Robert Bros., 1876) : a romantic narrative poem in English verse, published anonymously by Dr. Robert Dwyer Joyce.

Irische Texte (Leipzig, 1887) : two renderings of the original text, one by E. Windisch (t. i, pp. 67–82), and another by Whitley Stokes (t. ii, 2, pp. 109–78).

Sir Samuel Ferguson, *Hibernian Nights' Entertainments* (Dublin : Sealy, Bryers & Walker, 1887) : contains a prose version of the story.

H. d'Arbois de Jubainville, *L'Epopée Celtique en Irlande* (*Cours de Littérature Celtique*, t. v, pp. 217 *et seq.*) ; *Cours de Littérature Celtique, passim* (Paris, 1892).

Standish O'Grady, *The Coming of Cuculain* (London : Methuen, 1894).

Dr. Douglas Hyde, *Three Sorrows of Story-telling and Ballads of St. Columkille* (London : T. Fisher Unwin, 1895). Deirdre (a poem), pp. 1–39.

Dr. John Todhunter, *Three Irish Bardic Tales, being metrical versions of the three tales known as the three sorrows of story-telling* (London : Dent, 1896) : " The Fate of the Sons of Usna," pp. 47–147.

Dr. George Sigerson, *Bards of the Gael and Gall* (London : T. Fisher Unwin, first edition, 1897 ; second edition, revised and enlarged, 1907) : cf. second edition, Introduction, pp. 26–7, " The Fate of the Sons of Usnach," pp. 124–8, and Appendix, p. 383–8.

Mr. T. W. Rolleston made *Deirdre* the subject of the Prize Cantata at the Dublin Féis Céoil in 1897 ; music by Signor Michele Esposito (Dublin : M. H. Gill & Son ; E. Ponsonby ; Edinburgh : Patrick Geddes & Colleagues, Outlook Tower, Castle Hill, 1897).

Eleanor Hull, *The Cuchullin Saga in Irish Literature* (London : Nutt, Grimm Library, No. 8, 1898). Deirdre : pp. xlvii, 22, 24, 25, 31–7, 45–8, 50, 53.

Dr. Douglas Hyde, *A Literary History of Ireland* (London : T. Fisher Unwin, 1899), pp. 26, 94 *n.* ;

chap. xxv (critical study of the legend and prose translation of the Belfast MS.; cf. especially pp. 303–4 *n.*).

Herbert Trench, *Deirdre Wed and Nineteen Other Poems* (London: Methuen, 1901), partially reprinted in *The Dublin Book of Irish Verse* (No. 515, pp. 722–7), ed. by John Cooke (Dublin: Hodges & Figgis; London: Henry Frowde, Oxford University Press, 1909).

Sagen aus dem alten Irland, übersetzt von Rudolf Thurneysen (Berlin: Wiegandt & Grieben, 1901), pp. 13 ff.: "Derdriu."

Lady Gregory, *Cuchulain of Muirthemne: The story of the men of Ulster arranged and put into English* [prose], with a preface by W. B. Yeats (London: John Murray, 1902): The Fate of the Sons of Usnech, pp. 104–43.

C. L. Thomson, *The Celtic Wonder World* (Horace Marshall: 1902, No. 2 of the Romance Readers): "Deirdre."

Eleanor Hull, *The Story of Deirdre in its bearing on the social development of the folk-tale*, in FOLKLORE, vol. xv, pp. 24–39 (read at meeting, November 18, 1903).

"Deirdre," by Maire ni Siudlaig, Inginide na Heireann, in *The Gael* (N. Y.), March, 1904, pp. 85–6.

A. H. Leahy, *Ancient Heroic Romances of Ireland* (London: Nutt, 2 vols., 1905): cf. "The Death of the Sons of Usnach" (Leinster version) in vol. i.

More, Paul Elmer: *Shelburne Essays*, 1st series (N.Y. and London: Putnams, 1905), p. 147: "The Epic of Ireland."

Charles Squire, *The Mythology of the British Isles: an introduction to Celtic myth, legend, poetry and romance* (London: Blackie, 1905; new edition, 1910); or *Celtic Myth and Legend, Poetry and Romance* (London: Gresham Publishing Co., 1912): Deirdre, pp. 190–200.

Eleanor Hull, *A Text-Book of Irish Literature* (Dublin: Gill; London: Nutt, 2 vols., 1906), vol. i, pp. 24, 87–9; cf. Bibliographical Appendix in vol. ii.

Dr. Kuno Meyer, *The Death-Tales of the Ulster Heroes* (Royal Irish Academy, Todd Lecture Series. Dublin: Hodges & Figgis, 1906).

Dr. P. W. Joyce, *Old Celtic Romances* (London: Longmans, third edition, revised and enlarged, 1907): "The Fate of the Children of Lir, Tuireann and Usnach."

APPENDIX C

T. W. Rolleston, *Myths and Legends of the Celtic Race* (London : Harrap, 1911) : pp. 196–201) : "Deirdre and the Sons of Usna"; pp. 296 ff. : "The Tales of Deirdre and Grania."

Dr. Kuno Meyer, *Selections from Ancient Irish Poetry* (London : Constable, 1911) : two laments of Deirdre when sailing with Naisi from Scotland to die in Ireland.

Eleanor Hull (selected and edited by), *The Poem-Book of the Gael* (London : Chatto & Windus, 1912), pp. 74–7 : "The Lamentation of Deirdre for the Sons of Usna" (from the Book of Leinster : original text *ap. Irische Texte*, vol. i, pp. 77 *et seq.*). Revised from the same writer's *The Cuchullin Saga in Irish Literature* (*q. v.*), pp. 23–53 ("The Tragical Death of the Sons of Usnach").

Mr. Alfred Perceval Graves has made three translations into English verse of "The Death of the Children of Usnech" : (i) "Deirdre's Farewell to Scotland" (*Contemporary Review*, March, 1912: "Celtic Nature Poetry"); (ii) "Deirdre's Lament," from the same source as the first and, like it, founded on *Irische Texte* ii (Leipzig, 1884), pp. 127, 145, and on Prof. Kuno Meyer's English prose rendering; (iii) "The Great Lamentation of Deirdre for the Sons of Usna," based on Miss E. Hull's prose translation of *Irische Texte* ii, 77–81. The three translations will appear in *The Harpstrings of the Irish Gael*, an anthology of English verse translations of Gaelic poems, edited by Mr. Graves for the Devin-Adair Publishing Co., N.Y. Finally, Mr. Graves has written a lyric to an early air entitled "Lamentation of Deirdre for the Sons of Usnach" (on which see *Journal of the Irish Folksong Society*, vol. viii), to be shortly published by Stainer & Bell, London, in a setting by Charles Wood, Mus.Doc., to Mr. Graves's words.

A meeting of the Social Circle of the Irish Literary Society, London (February 15, 1913), was devoted to the subject of Deirdre.

W. Lorcan O'Byrne, *A Land of Heroes* (London : Blackie, n. d.) : "Sons of Tuircan, Lir, Usna."

"Cathbad's Prophecy," a poem by Ruth Duffin in *Everyman* (London : Dent), April 18, 1913, p. 4.

APPENDIX C

2. *Scotch re-tellings.*

The Deirdre saga is recognizable in James Macpherson's *Fingall,* under the heading " Darthula."

Loch Etive and the Sons of Uisnech, anonymously published (Macmillan, 1879) by Dr. Angus Smith.

William Graham, *Deirdire and the Sons of Uisneach. A Scoto-Irish Romance of the first century, A.D. Compiled from various sources. Illustrated.* (Edinburgh : Norman MacLeod, n.d.)

Alexander Cameron, *Reliquiæ Celticæ* (Inverness : *Northern Chronicle* Office, 1892–4), i. 119–20, 151–2 ; ii. 421.

" Fiona MacLeod " [William Sharp], *The Laughter of Peterkin* (London : Constable, 1897), " Darthool and the Sons of Usnach."

The Literature of the Celts : its History and Romance, by Magnus Maclean (Blackie & Son : London, Glasgow and Dublin, 1902) : " Deirdre " (pp. 146–52).

" Fiona Macleod," *Deirdrê and the Sons of Usna* (Portland, Maine, U.S.A. : Thos. B. Mosher, 1903).

" Fiona Macleod," *The House of Usna* (Portland, Maine, U.S.A. : Thos. B. Mosher, 1903).

Deirdire and the Lay of the Children of Uisne, orally collected in the Island of Barra (from the recital of Ian MacNeill, *alias* " Ian Donn," aged 83) *and literally translated by Alexander Carmichael* (Edinburgh : Norman MacLeod ; London : David Nutt ; Dublin : Gill & Son, 1905).

Dr. Carmichael—the compiler of *Carmina Gadelica* (for twenty-three years an excise officer in the Hebrides) first published the Gaelic recital in the *Transactions of the Gaelic Society of Inverness,* vol. xiii, pp. 241–57 ; the English translation, *ibid.,* vol. xiv, pp. 370–87 (1887), also in the *Celtic Magazine* (edited by Alexander MacBain), vol. xiii, pp. 69–85 (December, 1887) and pp. 129–38 (January, 1888)—the first instalment of this translation being in its turn re-translated into French by M. Georges Dottin *ap.* H. d'Arbois de Jubainville, *Cours de Littèrature Celtique,* t. v, pp. 235–52. An interesting review of this important version and its comparison with former recensions of the legend will be found in the REVUE CELTIQUE, t. xxvi, pp. 268–70; also in the CELTIC REVIEW, January 15, 1906 (Vol. ii, No. 7), pp. 287–9 (by Mr. Alfred Nutt).

Donald Mackinnon, *A Descriptive Catalogue of Gaelic Manuscripts in the Advocates' Library, Edinburgh, and elsewhere in Scotland* (Edinburgh : William Brown, 1912), Deirdre : pp. 169–71.

Mrs. Kennedy-Fraser (the daughter of the celebrated Edinburgh vocalist, and the compiler of the well-known "Kennedy-Fraser" volume of Scotch folk-songs) has recently collected in the Outer Hebrides a number of very impressive Gaelic melodies relating to the legend of Deirdre, which she has now edited with Mr. Kenneth MacLeod under the title *Sea Tangle* (London and N. Y. : Boosey & Co., 1913). Mrs. Kennedy-Fraser and her sisters, Miss Margaret Kennedy and Mrs. Tobias Matthay, gave a recital of "Ossianic Lays and Labour Lilts" at the Æolian Hall, London, on February 12, 1913.

Celtic Review, May, 1913, p. 289 : "The House of the Dwarfs," by David MacRitchie ; *ibid.*, p. 347 : "Deirdre—The Highest Type of Celtic Womanhood," by Miss A. C. MacDonell (in progress).

APPENDIX D

FIRST PERFORMANCES OF SYNGE'S PLAYS IN VARIOUS COUNTRIES AND PLACES [1]
(TO MAY, 1913)

1. *In the Shadow of the Glen.*

First Produced at the Molesworth Hall, Dublin, on Thursday, October 8, 1903, at 8.15.

[Original Cast—

Dan Burke	. . .	George Roberts.
Nora Burke	. . .	Maire Nic Shiubhlaigh.
Michael Dara	. . .	P. J. Kelly.
A Tramp	. . .	W. G. Fay.]

Royalty Theatre, London, Saturday, March 26, 1904.

Abbey Theatre, Dublin, Tuesday, December 27, 1904.

[Michael Dara . . . P. MacShiubhlaigh].

Corn Exchange, Oxford, Thursday, November 23, 1905.

Victoria Assembly Rooms, Cambridge, Friday, November 24, 1905.

St. George's Hall, Langham Place, London, Tuesday, November 28, 1905.

The Theatre, Smíchov, near Prague, Bohemia, March, 1906.

[Dan Burke	. . . .	Mr. Vojta.
Nora Burke	. . . .	Mrs. Táborská.
Michael Dara .	. . .	Mr. Kaŭkofský.
A Tramp	. . . .	Mr. Jiřikovský.]

Midland Hall, Manchester, Monday, April 23, 1906.

St. George's Hall, Liverpool, Wednesday, April 25, 1906.

Theatre Royal, Cardiff, Monday, June 25, 1906.

Tyne Theatre, Newcastle-on-Tyne, June 20, 1906.

Lyceum Theatre, Edinburgh, June 27, 1906.

Theatre Royal, Hull, July 4, 1906.

Theatre Royal, Aberdeen, July, 1906.

---

[1] Mr. W. A. Henderson, formerly Secretary of the Abbey Theatre, has kindly given much help in the preparation of this Appendix.

APPENDIX D

Abbey Theatre, Dublin, Saturday, January 19, 1907.
[Dan Burke . . . . F. J. Fay.
Nora Burke . . . . Maire O'Neill.
Michael Dara . . . . Arthur Sinclair.
A Tramp . . . . . W. G. Fay.]
Royal Bohemian National Theatre, Prague, August 22, 1907.
[Dan Burke . . . . Alois Sedláček.
Nora Burke . . . . Marie Hübnerová.
Michael Dara . . . . Eugen Viesner.
A Tramp . . . . . Karel Mušek.]
Abbey Theatre, Dublin, Thursday, October 17, 1907.
[Dan Burke . . . . . Arthur Sinclair.
Michael Dara . . . . F. J. Fay.]
Abbey Theatre, Dublin, Thursday, March 7, 1908.
[Michael Dara . . . . J. A. O'Rourke.
A Tramp . . . . . J. M. Kerrigan.]
Theatre Royal, Belfast, November 30, 1908.
Gaiety Theatre, Manchester, February 15, 1909.
Opera House, Cork, April 22, 1909.
Court Theatre, London, June 9, 1909.
New Theatre, Oxford, June 16, 1909.
Opera House, Belfast, August 4, 1909.
Albert Hall, Leeds, April 16, 1910.
New Theatre, Cambridge, May 25, 1910.
Masonic Hall, Oxford, May 28, 1910.
Presented for the first time on the American stage by Mrs.
Fiske (Minnie Maddern Fiske) on Monday, October 31, 1910,
at the Grand Opera House, Chicago.
[Dan Burke . . . . Harold Russell.
Nora Burke . . . . . Alice John.
Michael Dara . . . . Redmond Flood.
A Tramp . . . . . Holbrook Blinn.]
Memorial Theatre, Stratford-on-Avon, May 3, 1911.
Argyle Theatre, Birkenhead, July 10, 1911.
The Manchester Hippodrome, August 14, 1911.
Plymouth Theatre, Eliot Street, Boston, September 23, 1911.
Hyperion Theatre, New Haven, November 6, 1911.
Abbey Theatre, Dublin (School of Acting), Nov. 16, 1911.
[Dan Burke . . . . George St. John.
Nora Burke . . . . Mary Roberts.
Michael Dara . . . . Farrell Pelly.
A Tramp . . . . . Jack Martin.]

APPENDIX D

Maxine Elliot's Theatre, New York, December 15, 1911.
[Nora Burke . . . . Sara Allgood.]
Opera House, Chicago, February 21, 1912.
Coliseum, London, Monday, July 29, 1912.
[Dan Burke . . . . Arthur Sinclair.
Nora Burke . . . . Sara Allgood.
Michael Dara . . . . H. E. Hutchinson.
A Tramp . . . . . Fred. O'Donovan.]
The Fine Arts Theatre, Chicago, January 20, 1913.
His Majesty's Theatre, Montreal, January 29, 1913.
The Nixon Theatre, Pittsburg, February 5, 1913.
Chestnut Street Opera House, Philadelphia, March 19, 1913.
Abbey Theatre, Dublin, Thursday, April 24, 1913.
[Nora Burke . . . . Ann Coppinger.]
Repertory Theatre, Liverpool, Monday, April 28, 1913.
[Dan Burke . . . . Wilfred E. Shine.
Nora Burke . . . . . Maire O'Neill.
A Tramp . . . . . Shiel Barry.
Michael Dara . . . . J. A. Dodd.]

2. *Riders to the Sea.*

First produced under the direction of W. G. Fay by the Irish National Theatre Society, at the Molesworth Hall, Dublin, on Thursday, February 25, 1904, at 8.15.
[Original Cast—
Maurya . . . . . Honor Lavelle.
Bartley . . . . . W. G. Fay.
Cathleen . . . . . Sara Allgood.
Nora . . . . . . Emma Vernon.
Men and Women : P. J. Kelly, Seumas O'Sullivan, George Roberts, Maire Nic Shiubhlaigh, Maire Ni Gharbhaigh, Doreen Gunning.]
Royalty Theatre, London, March 26, 1904, at 2.
Jordan Hall, Boston, December 13, 1905 (performed by the Committee on Drama and Music of the XXth Century Club, staged by Mr. Clayton Gilbert of the "Emerson School of Oratory").
Abbey Theatre, Dublin, Saturday, January 20, 1906, at 8.15.
[Maurya . . . . . Sara Allgood.
Bartley . . . . . W. G. Fay.
Cathleen . . . . . Maire O'Neill.
Nora . . . . . . Brigid O'Dempsey.]

APPENDIX D

Theatre Royal, Wexford, Monday, February 26, 1906.
Midland Hotel, Manchester, Tuesday, April 24, 1906.
St. George's Hall, Liverpool, Thursday, April 26, 1906.
Theatre Royal, Cardiff, Tuesday, June 12, 1906.
Tyne Theatre, Newcastle, Monday, June 18, 1906.
Lyceum Theatre, Edinburgh, Monday, June 25, 1906.
Theatre Royal, Hull, Monday, July 2, 1906.
Theatre Royal, Aberdeen, Monday, July 2, 1906.
New Theatre, Oxford, Tuesday, June 4, 1907.
Royalty Theatre, Glasgow, Monday, May 13, 1907.
Victoria Assembly Hall, Cambridge, Monday, May 20, 1907.
Midland Institute, Birmingham, Tuesday, May 28, 1907.
Great Queen Street Theatre, London, Tuesday, June 11, 1907.
Theatre Royal, Waterford, Monday, August 12, 1907.
The Theatre, Kilkenny, Monday August 19, 1907.
Opera House, Cork, Wednesday, August 21, 1907.
Midland Theatre, Manchester, November 27, 1907.
Repertory Theatre, Melbourne, 1908.
Court Theatre, Galway, Monday, January 6, 1908.
Abbey Theatre, Dublin, Monday, August 3, 1908.
    [Bartley   .   .   .   Arthur Sinclair.
    Nora   .   .   .   Eileen O'Doherty.]
Theatre Royal, Belfast, Thursday, December 3, 1908.
Gaiety Theatre, Manchester, Wednesday, February 17, 1909.
Court Theatre, London, Wednesday, June 9, 1909.
Gilooley Hall, Sligo, Thursday, December 30, 1909.
Opera House, Belfast, Monday, April 4, 1910.
Albert Hall, Leeds, Friday, April 15, 1910.
New Theatre, Cambridge, Wednesday, May 25, 1910.
    [Bartley   .   .   .   J. M. Kerrigan.]
Kelly's Theatre, Liverpool, Monday, April 3, 1911.
Grand Opera House, Scarborough, Saturday, May 6, 1911.
Albert Hall, Leeds, Monday, May 8, 1911.
Victoria Hall, Bradford, Wednesday, May 17, 1911.
Grand Opera House, Harrogate, Saturday, May 20, 1911.
Temperance Hall, Sheffield, Wednesday, May 24, 1911.
Athenæum, Bury, Saturday, May 27, 1911.
Plymouth Theatre, Eliot Street, Boston, October 4, 1911.
    [Cathleen   .   .   Maire Nic Shiubhlaigh.]
Opera House, Providence, Monday, October 30, 1911.
Maxine Elliot's Theatre, New York, December 4, 1911.

APPENDIX D

Opera House, Indianapolis, January 25, 1912.
Opera House, Chicago, February 13, 1912.
Adelaide Literary Theatre, October 5, 1912.
Abbey Theatre, Dublin (School of Acting), March 7, 1912.

[Maurya . . . . Helen Moloney.
Bartley . . . . George St. John.
Cathleen . . . . Nell Gallagher.
Nora . . . . Violet McCarthy.]

The Fine Arts Theatre, Chicago, January 13, 1913.
Abbey Theatre, Dublin (2nd Abbey Co.), March 13, 1913.

[Maurya . . . . Nora Desmond.
Bartley . . . . George St. John.
Cathleen . . . . Nell Byrne.
Nora. . . . . Helen Moloney.]

Chestnut Street Opera House, Philadelphia, March 20, 1913.

3. *The Tinker's Wedding.*

First produced by the Afternoon Theatre at His Majesty's Theatre, London, on Thursday, November 11, 1909, at 2.15.

[Michael Byrne . . . Jules Shaw.
Mary Byrne . . . Clare Greet.
Sarah Casey . . . Mona Limerick.
A Priest . . . . Edmund Gurney.]

Note.—The New York NATION (October 12, 1911 : Vol. 93, No. 2,415, p. 347) states that *The Tinker's Wedding* has also been acted in America. We have failed to obtain particulars of the production. The only American notice of *The Tinker's Wedding* is a review in the BOSTON TRANSCRIPT for October 18, 1911 : it contains no reference to any American production of the play.

Performed in connection with the "Flitch of Dunmow," Essex, May 23 and 24, 1913 (together with Sir J. M. Barrie's *The Twelve Pound Look*) with the following cast—

Michael Byrne . . . Tom Gibbons.
Mary Byrne . . . Mrs. Robertson-Scott.
Sarah Casey . . . Miss Elizabeth Keith.
A Priest . . . . H. Cranmer-Byng.

4. *The Well of the Saints.*

First produced by the Irish National Theatre Society, under the direction of W. G. Fay, at the Abbey Theatre, Dublin, Saturday, February 4, 1905.

309

APPENDIX D

Martin Doul	.	.	. W. G. Fay.
Mary Doul.	.	.	. Emma Vernon.
Timmy	.	.	. George Roberts.
Molly Byrne	.	.	. Sara Allgood.
Bride	.	.	. Maire Nic Shiubhlaigh.
Mat Simon.	.	.	. P. MacShiubhlaigh.
The Saint	.	.	. F. J. Fay.]

Corn Exchange, Oxford, Thursday, November 23, 1905.
Victoria Assembly Rooms, Cambridge, Saturday, November 25, 1905.
St. George's Hall, London, Monday, November 27, 1905.
Max Reinhardt's Theatre, Berlin, 1906.
Abbey Theatre, Dublin, Thursday, May 14, 1908.

[Martin Doul	.	.	. Arthur Sinclair.
Mary Doul.	.	.	. Sara Allgood.
Timmy	.	.	. Ambrose Power.
Molly Byrne	.	.	. Maire O'Neill.
Bride.	.	.	. Eileen O'Doherty.
Mat Simon.	.	.	. J. M. Kerrigan.
The Saint.	.	.	. J. A. O'Rourke.]

Played in Munich in August, 1908.
Gaiety Theatre, Manchester, Tuesday, February 16, 1909.
Court Theatre, London, Tuesday, June 8, 1909.

[Timmy . . . Sydney J. Morgan.]

New Theatre, Oxford, Tuesday, June 15, 1909.
Opera House, Belfast, Tuesday, April 5, 1910.
Plymouth Theatre, Eliot Street, Boston, Saturday, September 23, 1911.

[Molly Byrne	.	.	. Cathleen Nesbitt.
Mat Simon.	.	.	. J. A. O'Rourke.
The Saint	.	.	. J. M. Kerrigan.]

Opera House, Providence, Wednesday, November 1, 1911.
Academy of Music, Northampton, Mass., Wednesday, November 8, 1911.
Hermanus Blacker Hall, Albany, November 11, 1911.
Belasco's Theatre, Washington, November 13, 1911.
Maxine Elliot's Theatre, New York, December 15, 1911.
Adelphi Theatre, Philadelphia, January 18, 1912.
Opera House, Chicago, February 28, 1912.
Opera House, Chicago, May 21, 1912.
Royalty Theatre, Glasgow.
Wallack's Theatre, New York, March 12, 1913.

APPENDIX D

5. *The Playboy of the Western World.*

First produced by the National Theatre Society at the Abbey Theatre, Dublin, under the direction of W. G. Fay, on Saturday, January 26, 1907, at 9.

[Original Cast—

Christopher Mahon . .	W. G. Fay.
Old Mahon . . .	Ambrose Power.
Michael James Flaherty .	Arthur Sinclair.
Margaret Flaherty . .	Maire O'Neill.
Shawn Keogh . . .	F. J. Fay.
Philly Cullen . . .	J. A. O'Rourke.
Jimmy Farrell . . .	J. M. Kerrigan.
Widow Quin . . .	Sara Allgood.
Sara Tansey . . .	Brigid O'Dempsey.
Susan Brady . . .	Alice O'Sullivan.
Honor Blake . . .	Mary Craig.
Peasants	U. Wright, Harry Young.]

New Theatre, Oxford, Wednesday, June 5, 1907.

[Susan Brady . . .	Cathleen Mullamphy.
Honor Blake . . .	Anne Allgood.]

Great Queen Street Theatre, London, Monday, June 10, 1907.

[Old Mahon	J. M. Kerrigan.
Jimmy Farrell	Ernest Vaughan.]

First produced in America, at the Illinois Theatre, Chicago, by Hart Conway and his students of the School of Acting of the Chicago Musical College, on Tuesday, April 14, 1909.

Abbey Theatre, Dublin (under the direction of Norreys Connell), Thursday, May 27, 1909.

[Christopher Mahon . . .	Fred O'Donovan.
Old Mahon	Sydney J. Morgan.
Shawn Keogh	J. M. Kerrigan.
Jimmy Farrell	Norreys Connell.
Sara Tansey	Eileen O'Doherty.
Honor Blake	Anne Hynes.
Peasant	Eric Gorman.]

Royal Court Theatre, London, Monday, June 7, 1909.
Grand Opera House, Belfast, Tuesday, August 3, 1909.
Gaiety Theatre, Manchester, Monday, November 22, 1909.

311

APPENDIX D

[Jimmy Farrell . . . . U. Wright.
Susan Brady . . . . Mary Nairn.
Honor Blake . . . . Sheila O'Sullivan.]

The members of the Philomathian Society, University of Pennsylvania, apply for permission to produce the *Playboy* per letter dated February 24, 1910, and signed 'John Dolman, Jr., Moderator.'

Albert Hall, Leeds, Thursday, April 14, 1910.
    [Honor Blake . . . . Eithne Magee.]

New Theatre, Cambridge, Monday, May 23, 1910.
Masonic Buildings, Oxford, Thursday, May 26, 1910.
Opera House, Cork, Monday, August 29, 1910.
Memorial Theatre, Stratford-on-Avon, Monday, May 1, 1911.
Grand Opera House, Scarborough, Saturday, May 6, 1911.
Albert Hall, Leeds, Wednesday, May 10, 1911.
Victoria Hall, Bradford, Monday, May 15, 1911.
Grand Opera House, Harrogate, Thursday, May 18, 1911.
Temperance Hall, Sheffield, Monday, May 22, 1911.
Athenæum, Bury, Thursday, May 25, 1911.

Plymouth Theatre, Eliot Street, Boston, Monday, October 16, 1911.
    [Pegeen Mike . . . Eithne Magee.
    Susan Brady . . . Maire Nic Shiubhlaigh.
    Honor Blake . . . Cathleen Nesbitt.]

Opera House, Providence, Tuesday, October 31, 1911.
Hyperion Theatre, New Haven, Tuesday, November 7, 1911.
Belasco Theatre, Washington, Wednesday, November 15, 1911.
Maxine Elliot's Theatre, New York, Monday, November 27, 1911.
Music Hall, Reading, Wednesday, January 3, 1912.
Lyric Theatre, Allentown, Pa., Thursday, January 4, 1912.
Adelphi Theatre, Philadelphia, Monday, January 15, 1912.
Opera House, Indianapolis, Thursday, January 25, 1912.
Opera House, Chicago, Tuesday, February 6, 1912.

Mr. Martin Harvey has acquired from Synge's Executors in August, 1912, the right to give twelve performances of the *Playboy*, with the proviso that none of these shall take place in Ireland or in London.

APPENDIX D

Abbey Theatre, Dublin, Wednesday, August 28, 1912.

[Widow Quin . . . Eileen O'Doherty.
Sara Tansey . . . Shiela O'Sullivan.
Susan Brady . . . Una O'Connor.
Honor Blake . . . Kathleen Drago.]

The Fine Arts Theatre, Chicago, Wednesday, January 1, 1913.

[Widow Quin . . . Mona O'Beirne.
Sara Tansey . . . Kathleen Drago.
Honor Blake . . . Nora Clancy.]

His Majesty's Theatre, Montreal, Monday, January 27, 1913.
The Nixon Theatre, Pittsburg, Monday, February 3, 1913.
Wallack's Theatre, New York, Wednesday, February 12, 1913.
Chestnut Street Opera House, Philadelphia, Wednesday, March 19, 1913.

6. *Deirdre of the Sorrows.*

First produced at the Abbey Theatre, Dublin, on Thursday, January 13, 1910.

[Lavarcham . . . Sara Allgood.
Old Woman . . . Eileen O'Doherty.
Owen . . . J. A. O'Rourke.
Conchubor . . . Arthur Sinclair.
Fergus . . . Sydney J. Morgan.
Deirdre . . . Maire O'Neill.
Naisi . . . Fred O'Donovan.
Ainnle . . . J. M. Kerrigan.
Ardan . . . John Carrick.
Two Soldiers . . . Ambrose Power, Harry Young.]

[Incidental Music composed by Mr. John F. Larchet, R.I.A.M., Conductor of the Abbey Theatre Orchestra—
Prelude (played before Act I) : Emain Macha.
Interlude No. 1 (played before Act II) : Alban.
Interlude No. 2 (played before Act III) : Funeral March (The Return to Emain Macha).]

Gaiety Theatre, Manchester, April 20, 1910.
Abbey Theatre, Dublin, April 28, 1910.
Court Theatre, London, May 30, 1910.

Deirdre of the Sorrows will be produced at Mr. Maurice Browne's Little [Repertory] Theatre, Chicago, during the season commencing October, 1913.

313

ADDENDA

Page 6. Line 13. "episcopal ancestors" : to whom see references in *The Correspondence of Jonathan Swift*, ed. Elrington Ball (London : Geo. Bell & Sons), vol. i. (1910), p. 53 ; vol. v. (1913), p. 16.

Page 9. Note 1. Add : "Curiously enough the mill was the property of the late Mr. E. M. Synge, J. M. Synge's cousin."

Page 134. Line 20. After "Rosicrucians" insert "Le Sâr Péladan and Villiers de l'Isle-Adam."

Page 162. Last line. After "fate" insert footnote : "(1) *Vide* E. J. Gwynn, 'On the Idea of Fate in Irish Literature,' *Journal of the Ivernian Society* (Cork), April, 1910 ; and W. Y. Evans-Wentz, *The Fairy-Faith in Celtic Countries* (Oxford University Press, 1910), p. 278."

Page 193. Note 1. An Irish speaker, in whose dialect of English "West" is synonymous with "back" (cf. P. W. Joyce, *English as we speak it in Ireland*, second edition, p. 168), might not unnaturally construe the phrase "the Western World" as having, besides its purely geographical signification, the somewhat deprecatory by-meaning "the *backward* world."

Page 236. Note 2, line 2 (see also page 268, line 22) : "Synge's Grave" was also reprinted in the *Bibelot* (Portland, Maine, U.S.A. : Thos. B. Mosher) for July, 1913, p. [244].

INDEX

INDEX

INDEX

317

INDEX

318

INDEX

INDEX

INDEX

INDEX

INDEX

Gunning, Doreen, 307
Gunning, G. Hamilton, 283
Gurney, Edmund, 309
Gwynn, E. J., 314
Gwynn, Stephen, M.P., 118, 167, 263, 264, 267, 268
Gypsies, 12, 181

Hackett, E. Byrne, 258
Hackett, Francis, 257, 275
Haffigan, Tim (in *John Bull's Other Island*), 108
Hail and Farewell, 50, 116, 117, 121, 136, 269
Hamel, A. G. van, 224
Hamilton, Alexander, K.C., family-tree.
Hamilton, C., 274
Hamilton, Bp. Hugh (1729-1805), family-tree.
Hamilton, Isabella, family-tree.
Hammond, J. L., 49
Hamon, Augustin, 46
Hamon, Count Louis, 46
Handel Street, Bloomsbury, London, 48, 76
Handy Andy, 108
Hannay, Rev. James O. [" George A. Birmingham "], 115, 279, 284
Hanrahan, 122
Harcourt, 23
Harcourt Street, Dublin, 7
Hardt, Dr. Fred. B., 260
Hardy, Thomas, 244
Harland, Oswald, 295
Harleian MSS., 4
Harold's Cross, Dublin, 235
Harper's Monthly Magazine, 75, 224
Harper's Weekly, 37, 132, 196, 280, 298
The Harpstrings of the Irish Gael, 302
Harrington Street, Dublin, family-tree.
Harris, Walter, 3
Harrison, Austin, 278, 288
Harrogate, 122
Harry Lorrequer, 108
Hart, Father (in *The Land of Heart's Desire*), 192
Hartog, Prof. Marcus, 194, 224
Harvard Monthly, 281
Harvard University, 240, 265, 280
Harvest, 242
Harvey, Martin, 312
Harvey, Wm., 109
Harz, 18
Hatch, Elizabeth, family-tree.
Hatch, John, family-tree.
Hauptmann, Gerhardt, 17
Haverty, Geraldine M., 105
Hayden, Miss Mary, 194, 224
Hayes, Annie (Mrs. Robert Traill), family-tree.
Hayes, Sir Samuel, Bart., family-tree.
Hazlitt, William, 102
Healy, Chris, 21
Hearn, Charles, 13
Hearn, Lafcadio, 13
Hearth and Home (London), 281
The Heather Field, 120, 121
Hebrew, 11, 12
Hebrides, 303, 304
Hedda Gabler, 149
Heidelberg, 75
Heijermans, Hermann, 169

Der Heilige Brunnen, 182, 260
De Heiligenbron, etc., 259, 298
Heine, Heinrich, 17, 218
Der Held des Westerlands, 260
Helen, 213, 299
Hellens, Franz, 265
Henderson, Archibald, 286
Henderson, T. F., 176
Henderson, W. A., 109, 174, 267, 305
Henley, William Ernest, 27
Henner, 43
Henri (in *The Green Cockatoo*), 206
Henry V, 108
Henry VIII, King, 3, family-tree, 88
Hermanus Blacker Hall, Albany, 310
Hermetic Society, Dublin, 134
Hibbert Journal, 239, 281
Hibernian Nights' Entertainment, 300
Hibernian types, 73
Higgins, Patrick, 102
Hindle Wakes, 245
Hindoo lore, 134
His Majesty's Theatre, London, 177, 309
His Majesty's Theatre, Montreal, 307, 313
Historical drama, 88
History of Ireland, 264
History of the Church of Ireland, 3
Hoare, John Edward, 288, 294
Hodgson, Dr. Geraldine, 275
Holberg, Ludvig, 123
Holborn Review (London), 281
Holland, 169
Holloway, Joseph, C.E., 127, 174, 262, 265
" The Holy Wells," 184
Holz, 17
Home Life in Ireland, 109, 268
Homer, 120
Home Rule, 86, 87, 114, 118, 199, 204
" The Homes of the Harvestmen," 256
Hone, J. M., 282, 296
On Hoop van Zegen: see *Good Hope*.
Le Horla, 27
Horniman, Miss A. E. F., 126, 132
In Hospital, 27
Hotel Cecil, London, 295
Hotel Corneille, Paris, 37
Hotel de Saint-Malo, Paris, 42
Houghton, Stanley, 245
" The House of the Dwarfs," 304
The House of Usna, 303
Howe, P. P., ix, 120, 126, 267, 273, 276, 278, 281, 285, 288, 289, 291, 293, 297
Hübnerová, Marie, 306
Hueffer, Ford Madox, 268
Hughes, Herbert, 287
Hugo, Victor, 54, 55, 165
Hugues, Clovis, 22
" Clovis Hugues on Ireland," 294
Hull, Miss Eleanor, 98, 300, 301, 302
Hume, A., 223
Humour, 92, 101, 107, 138, 180-1, 204, 217-18, 243
Huneker, James, 240, 268
Hunt, Miss B., 241
" Hurling," 193
Hurrish : A Study, 75
Hutchinson, H. E., 307
Hutchinson, Rt. Rev. Bp. Samuel, family-tree.
Hutchinson, Sophia, family-tree.
Hutton, Mrs. Mary A., 100

323

INDEX

324

INDEX

INDEX

INDEX

INDEX

INDEX

Morrow, Harry ("MacNamara, Gerald"), 146
Morvran-Goblett, Yann, 98
Mosada, xiii
Moses, Montrose J., 274, 286
Mossop, 102
Mount Jerome General Cemetery, Harold's Cross, Dublin, 235
Mount Street, Dublin, 212
Mourteen (in *The Aran Islands*), 81, 95, 184, 185
Le Mouvement Intellectuel Irlandais, 263
"Movements," 88, 142
Muldoon, J. Malachi, 213
Mullamphy, Cathleen, 311
Multitude and Solitude, 244
Munich, 16, 182, 183, 260, 310
Municipal Art Gallery, Harcourt Street, Dublin, 297
Munsey's Magazine (N.Y.), 102
Munster, 151
Murray, T. C., 72, 242
Mušek, Pan Karel, xiii, 17, 146, 259, 264, 277, 285, 306
Muset, Colin, 53
Music, 10, 139, 153–4, 166
Musical comedy, 138
"Music and Drama. The Irish Players," 278
Music Hall, Reading, 312
Music-halls, 108, 111
Mystery plays, 105
Mysticism, 45, 74, 101, 104, 134, 140
Mythology, 135, 137, 214
The Mythology of the British Isles, 301
Myths and Legends of the Celtic Race, 302

Nairn, Mary, 312
Naisi (in *Deirdre of the Sorrows*), 213, 223, 226, 313
Nashe, 53
Nation (Dublin), 294
Nation (London), 43, 47, 54, 224, 286
Nation (N.Y.), 57, 109, 309
"National Drama in Ireland," 284
"A National Dramatist," 220, 291
Nationalism, 21, 22, 86–7, 113 *et seq.*, 119, 125, 131, 139, 158, 193, 194, 202, 241
"Nationality and Literature," 294
National Library of Ireland, 26
National Literary Society, Dublin, 18, 102, 119, 280, 282, 283, 294, 295
National Players, 127
National Review (London), 287
Naturalists' Field Club, Dublin, 8
Neil, J. Crawford, 213, 286
Neilson, G. R., 109
Neilson, William Allen, 180
"Neo-Paganism and the Stage," 287
Nesbitt, Cathleen, 310, 312
Neue Freie Presse, 296
Neue Wiener Bühne, Vienna, 260
Nevinson, H. W., 269
New Age (London), 253, 287, 296
New Comedies, 243, 296
New Drama (Boston), 287
New Inn, 108
The New Ireland, 116
New Ireland Review, 42, 76, 107, 109, 119, 254, 287

Newport Literary Society, Monmouthshire, 296
New Quarterly, 242, 287
"News of the Theatre. The Irish Players make their first appearance in New York," 279
"The New Speranza," 21, 294
"The New Spirit in the Drama," 239, 281
The New Spirit in Drama and Art, 265
New Statesman, 193
New Theatre, Cambridge, 306, 308, 311
New Theatre, Oxford, 306, 308, 310, 311
"A New Thing in the Theatre. Some Impressions of the much-discussed Irish players," 281
Newtown Little, 1
New Witness (London) (see *Eye-witness*), 287
New York, 46, 119, 124, 152, 254, 258
New York Dramatic Mirror, 287–8
New York Evening Sun, 271
New York financial paper, 46
New York Press, 288
New York Times, 288
"Le Nez," 156
Nietzsche, 52
Nights at the Play, 270, 298
Nixon Theatre, Pittsburg, 307, 313
Les·Noces du Rétameur, 260
Nora Burke (*In the Shadow of the Glen*), 146, 147, 148–9, 150, 153, 156, 198, 221, 222, 305, 306, 307
North American Review (N.Y.), 288
Northern Whig (Belfast), 288
Norway, 149
Norwegian dramatic criticism, 123
Norwegian National Theatre, 123, 124
"A Note on Irish Nationalism," 193
A Note on the Irish Theatre, etc., 270
"Notes on the Celtic Renaissance," 286
"Notes on Ulster English Dialect for comparison with English Dialects," etc., 223
Notre-Dame, Paris, 44
"Le Nouveau Drame en Angleterre : H. Granville Barker," 286
"Le Nouveau Théâtre Irlandais," 267, 290
Nouvelle Revue Française, 267
Nursery, 6, 190
Nutt, Alfred, 304
Nutt, David, 100

To the Oaks of Glencree, 235, 253
Oaths, Gaelic, 110
O'Beirne, Mona, 313
L'Oblat, 55, 264
O'Brien, Edward J., 75, 79, 258
O'Brien, Lord, 120
O'Brien, R. Barry, 47
O'Brien, William, M.P., 119
O'Brien, Mrs. William (Sophie Raffalovich), 73
"Observer," 280
Observer (London), 288
O'Byrne, W. Lorcan, 302
Occultism, 134
O'Connor, Blake, 109
O'Connor, Una, 313
"O'Critical, Colonel," 223
Octave, 156
"O'Cuisin, Seumas" [Cousins, James H.], 124, 125, 159, 280, 291

329

INDEX

O'Curry, Prof. Eugene, 299, 300
O'Delany, Miss Barry M., 20, 21
O'Dempsey, Brigid, 307, 311
Odéon Theatre, Paris, 37, 150
Odessa, Rue d', Paris, 42
O'Dogherty, Barbara Catherine, family-tree.
O'Doherty, Eileen, 308, 310, 311, 313
O'Donnell, Frank Hugh, 120, 262
O'Donoghue, D. J., 37, 56, 59, 156, 168, 185, 202, 269, 280, 282, 283
O'Donovan, Fred., 307, 311, 313
O'Donovan Rossa, 225
O'Farrelly, Miss Agnes, M.A., 75, 262, 283, 295
O'Flanagan, Theophilus, A. B., 299
O'Grady, Standish, 116, 213, 300
O'Grady, Standish Hayes, 121
O'Growney, Fr. Eugene, 75
The O'Growney Memorial Volume, 75, 262
Oireachtas, 83, 261
Oisín and Pádraic, 99
" Oisin in Tir-na-nOg," 99
O'Kelly, Seumas, 150
O'Kelly, Fr. Thos. [An tAthair Tomás O'Ceallaigh], 213
Olcott, Chauncey, 108
Old Celtic Romances, 301
Old Fortunatus, 108
Old French literature, 52
O'Leary, John, 20, 37, 119
O'Leary, Canon P. (an tAthair Peadar), 99, 116
" Oligarchy," 6
Oliver, D. E., 269
Omar Khayyám, 227
One-act play, 172-3, 177-8
O'Neill, Prof. Fr. George, S.J., 119, 272, 280, 282
O'Neill, James, 102
O'Neill, James J., 105
" O'Neill, Maire " (Miss Marie Allgood: Mrs. Geo. H. Mair), 147, 148, 212, 236, 306, 307, 310, 311, 313
O'Neill of Derry, 101
Opera House, Belfast, 306, 308, 310
Opera House, Chicago, 307, 309, 310, 312
Opera House, Cork, 306, 308, 312
Opera House, Indianapolis, 309, 312
Opera House. Providence, 308, 310, 312
Oppression of Ireland by invaders, 86, 101, 104, 112, 202
" The Oppression of the Hills," 92, 155, 254
Oratory, 114
O'Regan, 108
O'Riain, Uilliam P. : *see* Ryan, W. P.
Orient, 122, 156
O'Riordan, Conal O'Connell : *see* " Connell, F. Norreys."
Orléans, Charles d', 53
L'Orme du Mail, 57
O'Rourke, J. A., 306, 310, 311, 313
Orthodoxy, 105
Orwell Park, Rathgar, 6
Ossian, 99
Ossianic Society, Dublin, 99
Ossory, family-tree.
Osthoff, Prof. Hermann, 75
O'Sullivan, Alice, 311
O'Sullivan, Denis, 108
" O'Sullivan, Seumas," 297, 307
O'Sullivan, Sheila, 312, 313

O'Trigger, Sir Lucius (in *The Rivals*), 108
Ouessant : *see* Ushant.
" Ould Knowledge," 90
" Ould sod," 14
Outlook (London), 288
Outlook (N.Y.), 270, 288
Owen (in *Deirdre of the Sorrows*), 215, 313
Owen, Arthur Synge, 3, 264, 295
Oxford, 3, 4, family-tree, 240, 253, 295
Oxford and Cambridge Review, 288-9
Oxford Chronicle, 289

Pablo Pénaguilas (in *Marianela*), 186
Paddy, 109
Paddy-go-Easy, 108
Pádraic : *see* St. Patrick.
The Pagan, 182
Paganism, 90, 96, 163, 182, 201, 218
Painting, 7, 45, 154
" Pale," 6
Pall Mall Gazette (London), 270, 289, 293
Palmer, John (" P. J."), 291
Pamphlets (P.-L. Courier), 181
Papus, 44
Papyrus (N.Y.), 289
Pardons (in Brittany), 46
Paris, 7, 19, 20, 21, 22, 25, 26, 28, 29, 33, 36, 37, 40, 41, 42, 43, 47, 58, 69, 70, 76, 87, 120, 124, 130, 150, 170, 202, 225, 254, 262, 263
Paris Exhibition, 37
Paris-Journal, 267
Parker, John, 102
Parnell, 76, 86
" Parnell Split," 114
Parsons, Chauncey, L., 288
The Passing of the Shee, 135
Passion Play, 105
Passy, Frédéric, 36
Passy, Paul, 36
Pasteur Institute, 42
Pat, 109
Patch Darcy (*In the Shadow of the Glen*), 147, 155
Patch Ruadh (in *The Well of the Saints*), 185, 191
Pater, Walter, 32, 45, 167, 229, 263
Paterson, James, R. S.A,, xiii, 253, 296, 298
Paterson Gallery, Old Bond Street, London, 298
The Pathos of Distance, 268
Patois, 36, 216, 229, 243
Patrick Street, Dublin, 238
Patriots, 242
Patterson, David, 223
Patterson, W H., 223
Paul-Dubois, L., 1, 55, 269
Pauperism, 86
Payne, John, 234
Peace theories, 36
Peadar an tAthair : *see* O'Leary, Canon Peter.
Pearse, P. H. : *see* MacPiarais, Pádraic.
Peasant, 14, 56, 66, 78-9, 86, 89, 90, 97, 115, 121, 125, 135, 137, 191, 195, 199, 202, 214, 219, 222, 228, 229, 238, 243
Peasant (Dublin), 289
Pêcheur d'Islande, 168
Peele, George, 53
" Peelers," 179, 202

330

INDEX

331

INDEX

INDEX

INDEX

INDEX

335

INDEX

INDEX

INDEX